Typeset by Jonathan Downes,
Layout by SPiderKaT for CFZ Communications
Using Microsoft Word 2000, Microsoft Publisher 2000, Adobe Photoshop CS.
Proofed with Louis Rozier
This edition published in Great Britain by Gonzo Multimedia

c/o Brooks City,
6th Floor New Baltic House
65 Fenchurch Street,
London EC3M 4BE
Fax: +44 (0)191 5121104
Tel: +44 (0) 191 5849144
International Numbers:
Germany: Freephone 08000 825 699
USA: Freephone 18666 747 289

© Gonzo Multimedia MMXXII

All rights reserved. Without limiting the rights under copyright reserved above, no part of this publication may be reproduced, stored in or introduced into a retrieval system, or transmitted, in any form of by any means (electronic, mechanical, photocopying, recording or otherwise), without the prior written permission of both the copyright owners and the publishers of this book.

This publication is © and published by Steve Freight, who retains the intellectual property rights of the work. Where an article is credited to another individual in their own right, then the article remains the intellectual property of such person who gave their permission for its use within the Pages of the Voyage35 Fanzine.

First edition published and © 2020.
Cover Illustration by John Chase.

ISBN: 978-1-908728-95-1

Foreword

Who would have thought back in 1991 that Steven Wilson's Porcupine Tree project would become as popular or as well known to fans of progressive rock as it is today, some thirty years later? Back in 1991 a kind of 'stupid dream' became a reality as over the next decade Steven Wilson's oddball solo project became a band and little by little, through perseverance and arduous work on the road and in the studio, Steven Wilson, Colin Edwin, Richard Barbieri and Chris Maitland developed a loyal fan base in Europe and the USA. Eventually a love of Porcupine Tree would spread to other areas of the world but only after a long, and at times difficult slog.

From 1991 through to 2003, with support from the unstoppable booking agent Glenn Povey, I ran the band's first label Delerium Records and managed all aspects of their recording and touring. It was an experience that I will never forget. Hindsight is a wonderful thing, but I can assure the reader that neither I nor the band had any idea as to where Porcupine Tree would lead. What kept everything going was the fan base who, from that very first gig at The Nags Head pub in High Wycombe, demonstrated their loyalty and enthusiasm for the music.

Back in 1993 'progressive rock' meant anything that sounded like Genesis, and it always seemed obvious to me that a band that could be imaginative and experimental - as bands had been in the 1970s – would stand out from the Genesis clones and find a receptive and thankful audience. My hunch was right and despite being terminally unhip Porcupine Tree picked up an audience slowly but surely. Fans of the band proved to be incredibly supportive buying merchandise at an amazing rate, something that was crucial to funding those early tours, where only fifty people might turn up at any one gig. I will always recall the band complaining about a Voyage 34 T-shirt being available in more than one colour, until I told them a fan had bought one of each. That was typical, and sales of T-shirts and CDs frequently turned gigs that had been loss making exercises into break even scenarios and on rare occasions a profit!

One early fan of the band was Steve Freight who was the first person to start a Porcupine Tree fanzine. Delerium had produced Porcupine Tree's *Transmission* newsletter but that was a vehicle to announce tours and new releases. Steve's fanzine, produced from simple photocopies as per fanzines of yore, was a view from the front-row capturing for posterity the band on record and on tour in the 1990s.

Without Steve and the other fans who, in those early years, came to see and support the band, there simply would never have been a Porcupine Tree catalogue as broad as it is today, let alone a re-formed Porcupine Tree in 2021. It is therefore gratifying to know that Steve's 'Voyage 35' fanzine has been preserved in the publication that you now hold in your hands, not least because it represents an important part of the band's history.

**Richard Allen -
Porcupine Tree Manager
and Founder of Delerium Records
4th of December 2021**

Contents

Introduction   3
Contents   5
Dedications   8
Introduction   9

Issue 1   **11**
   Why What and Who Are The Porcupine Tree? (by Steve Freight)   14
   The Old Trout Windsor (by Guy Thomas)   15
   The Radio 1 FM Sessions (Part 1) (transcribed by Steve Freight).   18
   Live at Brixton Academy 21 October 1995 (by Steve Freight)   24

Issue 2   **27**
   Richard Barbieri (by Michael Seabrook)   30
   Views of Wolverhampton 2 December 1995
   (by Steve Best / Gordon Elcock)   31
   Porcupine Tree (by Glenn Povey & Steve Freight)   33
   The Forum – Kentish Town – December 1st 1995 (by Steve Freight)   35
   Love Death & Porcupine Tree (by Phil Harwood)   38

Issue 3   **43**
   Steven Wilson Interview (conducted by Steve Freight)   46
   An Anoracsic Delight (or how to distinguish the fakes
   (Tarquin's Seaweed Farm, The Nostalgia Factory and Love Death And
   Mussolini)) (by Steve Freight)   52
   Porcupine (Family) Tree   53
   Porcupine Tree Spring 1996 Tour   55
   The Forum 12 April 1996 (by Steve Freight)   55
   Leadmill Sheffield 21 May 1996 (by Jill Douglas / Martin Hudson)   58
   The Garage – London 24 May 1996 (By Guy Thomas)   59
   Cambridge Boat Race 26 May 1996 (by Simon Clarke)   65
   Baltimore "Progscape '96" 29 June (by Matthew O'Grady)   66
   Love Death And Porcupine Tree (by Phil Harwood)   67

Issue 4   **69**
   Colin Edwin Interviewed (by Steve Freight)   72
   Porcupine Tree Sounds Old-Fashioned And Modern   74
   The Radio 1 FM Sessions (Part 2) (transcribed by Steve Freight).   75
   Love Death And Porcupine Tree By Phil Harwood   79

Issue 5	**83**
Chris Maitland Interviewed (by Steve Freight)	86
The Early Tapes; A Look At Altamont And Karma (by Phil Harwood)	88
BBC Derby Radio Interview (transcribed by Steve Freight)	91
Issue 6	**95**
Richard Barbieri Interviewed (by Steve Freight)	98
Steven's Early Bands	101
The Promotional Videos (by Phil Harwood)	101
Strawberry Fair, Cambridge (by Steve Freight)	104
Jansen, Barbieri, Karn – London Astoria 2 (by Nigel Beal)	107
Steven Wilson Deliverance	108
Richard Barbieri And Japan (by Michael Seabrook)	110
Issue 7	**113**
The secret diaries of Peter Clemons (Aged 39 - Going On 40)	116
An Anoracsic Delight (by Steve Freight)	119
Union chapel Islington London 14/11/97 (by Steve Freight)	121
The Radio Active Promo CD (By Phil Harwood)	124
Help (By Steve Freight)	126
Every Home Is Wired	128
Issue 8	**131**
Porcupine Tree At The BBC 9/12/94 - The Inside Story (By Mark Robson)	134
Prog or Not Prog?	136
Steven Wilson Interview 2	138
Linton Samuel Dawson	144
Queen Quotes Crowley	146
Every Home Is Wired - Views From The Net	149
Issue 9	**153**
No Man	156
No Man Is An Island	156
Queen Quotes Crowley	170
Tim Bowness On Flowermouth And Flame (Interview by Tony Herrington)	173
Issue 10	**177**
How I Came To The Tree By Andy Davis	180
The Conversion Of St. Paul By Andy Davis	181
Queen Quotes Crowley	183
Issue 11	**187**
Retroactive Ploy	190
Fabrication – a note from Steven and Aural Innovations Interview	190

1999 Spring Tour	195
Colchester Arts Centre April 1999	195
The Foundry Birmingham 9 April 1999 – Philip Odin, W Midlands	197
Pavilion Theatre Brighton 10 April 1999 – Phil Morris, Hereford	198
Southampton University 24 April 2999 – Steve Smith IOW	199
Bloomsbury Theatre, London 10 May 1999 – Dave Sheen	200
A Final Note From Tim Bowness And Steven Wilson (as at 19 July 1999)	201
12th June 1999 – Divan Due Monde, Paris – Chris Everest	202
Issue 12	**205**
Retroactive Ploy The Aural innovations Interview part 2	208
Queen Quotes Crowley	216
Gig reviews—Autumn 1999	219
The Scala, Kings Cross, London 8.11.1999 (by Steve Freight)	220
Issue 13	**227**
A Letter from Tim Bowness	230
Interview with Steven Wilson	231
Issue 14	**245**
Linton Samuel Dawson / Voyage 35 - Publications to Remember?	248
Voyage 35 – The End?	248
A Message from Didier	249
Didier's Final Web Message	250
A Communication From Steven Wilson	250
Retroactive Ploy Steven Wilson Interview by Simon Clarke	252
Porcupine Tree – Athens gigs	257
Wevemovedon – The End?	261

Dedications

Thanks to the following for their help, support and articles and artwork over the years:

Yvonne, Rachel & Cheryl Freight for putting up with my musical obsessions (and especially Yvonne who helped with typing out the original articles for this edition), Richard Allen, Glenn Povey and Ivor Truman (Delerium), Debi (at Medium), Tim Bowness, Guy Thomas, Brian Tawn, Mark Radcliffe, John and Tom (99th floor for the original recommendation of the Tree), Andy G, Samantha Burt, John Chase, Phil Harwood, Didier Withoos, Chris Everest, Graham Canwell, Lee Wainman, Peter Clemons, Michael Seabrook, Jill Strobridge, Mark Henson, Jerry Ferneaux, Mark Robson, Andreas Stuwe, Santuu Laakso, Ville, Kevin Bolton, Kosmik Ken, Steve Kalidoski, Christian Aupetit, Johnnie (at Snapper), Sean (at Org), Graham Canwell, Andy Davis, Jem Cole, Ken Lowe, Teresa (at Voiceprint), Steve (at Third Stone), Dennis Gough, Steven Best, Jonathan Downes (Gonzo) and anyone I've missed who wrote to me and offered support.

And of course, Steven Wilson, Richard Barbieri, Colin Edwin, Chris Maitland and Gavin Harrison.

Introduction.

Porcupine Tree is an enigma. How do you categorise them?

Over 14 issues of *Voyage35*, I tried to seek out and define them. Just as I thought we, the fans, had it nailed, then Steven Wilson promptly changed styles or threw us a curveball.

Unfortunately for some, the changes were too drastic and had moved too far from the origins of the band (or Steven's highly acclaimed bedroom tapes), whilst others, particularly from the US, embraced the new style.

Having seen Voyage35's selling for some quite exorbitant sums on E-bay recently I thought it time to revisit the pages of the Fanzines and consolidate those articles that formed the essence of each issue.

I have decided not to include every word ever printed within those pages, as some are musings, some short stories that give no insight into the band, and reviews of other albums that may or may not have appealed to fans at the time (mostly label mates of the band). I have also left out the reviews of the Band's albums themselves, as these were either my personal views or copied from other publications.

Here then is a selection of articles and interviews that will hopefully give context to the history of the band and supplements Rich Wilson's book, giving a fuller account of the band's past. Where appropriate I have made updated comments on some of these articles (in italics and dated).

All photos © Steve Freight

Steve Freight 2020

Voyage 35

Issue no. 1

The Porcupine Tree

Porcupine Tree are captured and held by anti-prog militants

PORCUPINE TREE want to give prog a good name.

Issue 1

Published November 1995 (revised Special Edition June 2000)

Original Contents
Introduction to the Fanzine
Introduction to Porcupine Tree
Gig reviews
      - The Old Trout Windsor 17 May 1995
      - Brixton Academy 21 October 1995
Discography
Press Cuttings
Transcription of BBC interview (8 December 1993)
The latest news and some bits and pieces

Record Collector said:
Modest but well assembled, the debut issue of this A5 'zine includes news, reviews and a much needed introduction to its subject: a young prog rock band, veterans of several limited edition releases.

Why What and Who Are The Porcupine Tree?
(by Steve Freight)

These are almost as unanswerable as the ultimate question to Life, The Universe and Everything (I know that answer is 42 but The Porcupine Tree!!?)

Well let's start with the easy one. What?

They are a group of musicians who I happen to admire and like. I cannot play any instrument to any great degree but I know what I like to listen to and what gives me a buzz.

I sometimes feel envious of friends who can play but wonder if they actually get enjoyment out of LISTENING to music as they forever seem to be analysing the chord progression and the reasons they see for these changes etc. I know they get enjoyment from playing but I feel I get more out of listening to music as a layman as I can just lay back and enjoy.

As to Who? Well the guiding light is Steven Wilson. The story goes back to 1985 when multi-instrumentalist Steven worked for three years on recordings.

These were released in limited quantities of about 300 under the titles of Tarquin's Seaweed Farm and The Nostalgia Factory. Tarquin's came with a booklet sleeve containing a fictional account of The Porcupine Tree.

Delerium Records got hold of these tapes and signed the band. They reissued the tapes in improved covers and subsequently issued the material on 2 CDs.

Steven collaborated on these tapes with Alan Duffy who wrote a majority of the lyrics at that time.

Steven then felt it time that Porcupine Tree became a live band and recruited Colin Edwin (bass), Chris Maitland (percussion) and ex Japan Richard Barbieri (keyboards) and it is this line up which appeared on the Up the Downstair and The Sky Moves Sideways.

As to Why? – They have taken the tired old concept of Progressive Rock and are turning it into an art form of their own. The Porcupine Tree are truly Progressive where others hark back to the good old days of Yes, Genesis, Rare Bird etc (and yes I still do like this music having grown up with it but times they must change together with concepts).

The first 2 CDs may hark back at times to the 60s and 70s psychedelia as a homage but the use of the instruments and phrasing of the music is all late 1980s/90s feel.

The Old Trout, Windsor (by Guy Thomas)

This was to be my first Porcupine Tree gig, and I was really excited with the anticipation, having heard most of the material currently available. My friend of many years, photographer Adrian Arbib, was persuaded to come along too with his gear and we arrived at The Old Trout at about 6:30 for what was to be one of the last gigs at the venue before it became a Firkin pub and one of the last gigs of the tour.

We got into the hall before the doors opened to the general public and within 25 minutes we were treated to Saddar Bazaar, the support band, also from the Delerium stable. Their style is completely different to PTs but they were definitely worth a listen in their own right consisting of guitar, sitar and bongos. (Since the gig they have added a fourth member on additional guitar, percussion and bass). They played a 45 minute set of enjoyable music.

At about 9:30 the house lights dim again the Arch Lights pick gradually up and the first sounds of rain of the intro to The Sky Moves Sideways – phase 1 gradually fill the room. Steve starts on the vocal, bathed in soft green light, whilst a diffused mass of coloured radial rays rotate outwards from a core of light, reminding me of Moorcock's "Shield of Chaos" – eight arrows radiating from a central hub. Suddenly the first guitar chord hits the senses and the whole show takes on a 3-D feeling as a sea of light fills the room, dancing on the gentle smoke haze. The middle part of the track picks up with Chris's' "One, two, three and four". We are treated to some lovely fretless-Wal bass-work by Colin, accompanied as ever by Chris's immaculate drumming. On top of all this is Richards keyboard solo hauntingly suggests some classic seventies Moog synth work, all accompanied by a pink and blue pulsing aurora of light. Phase 1 climaxes with some really choppy chord-work from Steve and loads of wah-wah, the strobes matching the rhythm, settling back down to the end of the track – what an opener!

Steve: "Straight on now with some music from the new album" – and Phase 2 hits us, finishing off where Phase 1 started. Lots more Moog? And guitar chord crunching, reminiscent (albeit ever so slightly) of Magazine's

"Real Life" LP from 1978. (Sorry for making comparisons, but it's difficult to avoid when you're really enjoying the music). By now, the lights are fanning up and down as Steve takes up the guitar solo. Phase 2 gradually quietens down and without realising, the keyboard intro to Radioactive Toy is all around. Colin's bass builds up and sustains the rhythm, with Chris's quiet cymbal accompaniment. Occasionally Steve uses his plectrum on the strings of his guitar between the "nut" and the "machine heads" of his instrument to generate characteristic high pitched clicking – what a great sound! The stage is very dark and the single rotary light like the main riff of the song, seems to develop from nowhere, gradually joined by drums and lead guitar. The verses haunt the room, followed by sequences of guitar, crashing through all perception barriers, accompanied by shards of white light aimed at the audience. There's a middle couple of minutes of improvisation which gradually reforms into the main riff which climbs towards the crescendo finish of the song.

Steve: "Thank you. This is the title track from our last EP now. This track gives the band the chance to improvise; it's called Moonloop". And so the gentle trance induced by the subtle rhythm and soft blue lights points towards some tasty lead guitar work by Steve, then onto some of Richard's keyboards, which you feel that you might start to slip into blissful unconsciousness, the guitar and rums change gear up towards the distant end. Reality seems nearer to hand as Steve's chord sequence begins, and suddenly the pace has gone into overdrive with a rude awakening, leaving behind any hint of tranquillity at the beginning of the song, as the drive of the final sequence climaxes towards a powerful end. This track really is a mix of states of mind, to say the least.

As soon as the previous feeling of euphoria was gradually suspended towards the end of Moonloop, it is re-found in the tranquillity of The Moon Touches Your Shoulder. Steve is in silhouette with gently pulsing lights behind. Yet again, the senses are gradually re-awakened, as the track ups-tempo. Suddenly, up two notches and Steve is really punishing his axe, with a really heavy chord sequence, the whole effect enhanced by the strobing lights. Without warning the track breaks into the riff of Always Never. Ten powerful chords later and we hear: "I love you sometimes, always never, you say you're here, here with me now". What a combination! Both tracks are good in their own right, but combined in this fashion, the result is amazing. (Steve & Co: if you're reading this, please re-record them like this or release a live version!) – "It's growing cold, I'm growing old, is this the end?" There is a steady build-up of drums, bass and keyboards, with Steve absorbed in his lead guitar, layered over the top, towards the finale of the track.

Onwards Steve: "Dislocated….(11 second gap)…..Day", followed by Colin's fretless build-up. Having been gently lulled into semi oblivion, and driven by pounding rhythms up until now, Dislocated Day is a real test on the nerve endings. It is hard to distinguish between pleasure and anguish as the track develops, but the phrase "chemical imbalance" springs to mind rather appropriately. I find it very hard to quantify this track, but the set would be incomplete without its experimenting on the mind. Some subtlety discordance guitar work really does test the nerves. The track draws to its conclusion, with one's emotions still confused and ends up with a spot of tight drum soloing from Chris. Steve: "Dame Vera Lyn on drums please!"

Steve again: "One more for you tonight, from our last album. This is called Burning Sky". The track opens up with gentle clock ticking (which almost instantaneously re-attaches the semi-coma that was suspended for the duration of the previous track. It's a shame that this track didn't have Small Fish before it (as on the album), but if every favourite was played, then the band would have to do a three and a half hour set! Pulsing white light radiates outwards like ripples on a pond and back inwards simultaneously, accompanied by Richard's tasty sublime work, followed on with Steve's lead guitar. After some slide guitar, the main riff is achieved again, with the stage awash with red and orange lights. Suddenly, the place is halved, as a peaceful end approaches, but that peace is shattered unexpectedly (I ought to know that this track picks up right at the end, but it surprises me every time!) with the strobes bursting into life along with Steve's three final chord crashes. You would think that it's all over, but no, another hammered chord, then another, one more again (hanging onto the sustain of the previous one), but now it is completely silent – it's got to be over, but no, a quick drum roll and THE final chord of the main set blasts out. Steve: "Thank you, goodnight".

Lots of cheering from the crowd brings the band back within 60 seconds of leaving the stage! A feedback filled intro bursts into Not Beautiful Anymore. Huge drums and relentless bass combine with well-distorted lead axe to form the main chunk of the track. Right now, my eyes need a rinse of Valium dissolved in Optrex, but just in time the track relapses into relative calm as Steve builds up the feedback again. Slowly the pace quickens and again the strobes torture (pleasantly) the eyeballs! Steve starts his guitar thrumming with a long sequence on one solitary chord, pounding the rhythm, bursting back into the riff. All too soon it's over. Steve: "That's it – cheers, goodnight", as he puts down his guitar, still sustaining.

The house lights come on and we realise that the end really has arrived, after one and a half hours of musical voyage. Only 10 minutes seem to have gone by, in all that time. Adrian and I are both totally overwhelmed by this, our first Porcupine Tree gig. It really has been an experience, both musically and visually, combining to really satisfy the senses. It is a rare thing to see such brilliant talent so effectively delivered and really feel what is happening. I knew that Porcupine Tree were great on album, but live in concert they enter a different league. Fortunately Adrian took some fantastic pictures of the show, and a video was also shot for the band's archives. Hopefully, some of Adrian's photos might grace the pages of further editions of Voyage35.

The Radio 1 FM Sessions (Part 1) (transcribed by Steve Freight).

Two sessions were broadcast by Radio 1 on the Mark Radcliffe Show.

What follows is a transcript of the interview conducted on the first such show as far as possible. My tape is incomplete in some areas and where something is missing I will show this.

Session 8 December 1993

Mark Radcliffe (MR): Playing live on the programme tonight in our basement studio down the other side of the palace of flittering delights tonight are The Porcupine Tree. Steve are you there?

Steve Wilson (SW): Hello Mark.

MR: Hi how you doing?

SW: Alright mate.

MR: For people who don't know The Porcupine Tree, and God knows there can't be many, but for people who don't ….how….well you know introduce The Porcupine Tree in half a sentence.

SW: What the line up or the principle behind the project?

MR: Go on the principle behind the project.

SW: The principle behind the project is to drag Progressive Rock kicking and screaming in to the 90s.

MR: Right that says it all I think. We'll meet everybody later but what are you going to play for us first.

SW: We're going to start off with Radioactive Toy.

MR: Brilliant! OK take it away.

We then go into a first class version of the song. The guitar work is excellent with its soaring notes and appears to have more reverb than is normal.

MR: Brilliant. Radioactive Toy – the first one performed live in session tonight by The Porcupine Tree but we've got 2 more songs from them to come. I say 2, they're actually doing 3 but one's one in two bits and we'll have a chat sort of half way through it in the middle type thing.

Then later:

MR: (bit missing)… Porcupine Tree who are downstairs in our drama studio and they are back now with Burning Sky Part 1.

It is then straight into the music and for those of you who haven't got a copy of this session this can be found on the Spiral Circus Tape from Delirium which comes free with the Transmission newsletter.

Then as the music fades away to nothing in comes the voice of

MR: Is it OK to talk now!

SW: Sure is

MR: OK. Porcupine Tree playing live The Burning Sky Part 1. And we're actually talking halfway through the song really aren't we Steve?

SW: We are. That's a bit of a monster that one.

MR: Right OK. Are you going to play the second half afterwards?

SW: We are indeed. In just a moment. Yeah (at this point MR & SW talk across one another so all words are not decipherable).

MR: OK so we won't talk for very long though we'll get back to the song. We said that, you know, when you introduced the band before as the acceptable face of Prog Rock dragging it kicking and screaming into the 90s, it can now be revealed who you are because for a long time I've been playing Porcupine Tree records on the radio and I couldn't say who you were 'cause you were in another band but now we can.

SW: Indeed well it's no great secret really but I have been within 50 paces of a drum machine. So it's true yes.

MR: Right so you're in No man

SW: I am in No Man – yes

MR: You still are in No Man?

SW: I still am yeah we've just finished a new album and that'll be out in the Spring so…

MR: So Porcupine Tree sort of run side by side with that. Who's in the band cause this is the first time Porcupine Tree has been a live act isn't it?

SW: That's right yes. I've just put this band together. I'll just give you an introduction to the band members. We've got Chris Maitland on drums who I've stolen from No Mans live band. Colin Edwin on bass and the Liberace of Lewisham himself Richard Barbieri on keyboards.

MR: Right. Ex Japan.

SW: That's right (again cross talking).

MR: You've played a session with No Man on Radio 5 and Richard and the rest of the Japan boys played and I remember that night we had to wait for you to go on because Millwall versus Arsenal went to penalties.

SW: Yeah

MR: Wasn't that right. I think it's the same draw isn't it Richard?

Richard Barbieri: That's right yeah

MR: Same draw in the next round

SW: Has he got his microphone on?

MR: Right yeah no we can hear him. So you played the first time, you played at High Wycombe recently sort of debut gig so how did that go?

SW: Very well yes we rammed it and we played a bit of a stormer by all accounts

MR: and you play in London soon

SW: Yes we're playing at the Borderline tomorrow which is the only London show for the ..... basically until we go out on tour maybe again early next year. People should come to that yeah.

MR: I mean like you play smaller venues in some ways it sounds like kind of music which should fill football stadiums in a way doesn't it really. Would you like to sort of play on a big stage with you know inflatable dinosaurs and pigs and lasers.

SW: Absolutely. Well our ambition is to have Richard in a cloak and have him actually rising out of the stage with lights resolving and you know

MR: Yeah have him rising right out of the arena

SW: Roger Dean backdrops and all that you know

MR: I mean you know there seems to be something of a kind of Prog Rock revival in some quarters but for some people this kind of (music), something that should never be allowed to return I mean that it did become for a long time a discredited thing due to kind of, well certain people in Lurex capes who shall remain nameless but his initials are Rick Wakeman. It's like Journey to the Centre of The Earth on ice, I mean that, is it worth reviving as a concept.

SW: I think so. I think that particularly, I mean, Progressive Rock has always been about absorbing new technology in my opinion anyway and that's the mistake that people have been making over the last ten to fifteen years in they've not been taking the new technology on board, which is what we've been trying to do, to be truly progressive in the true sense of the word.

MR: Right, right. Just before you play the next thing obviously we're going to do a thing in the last half hour, Frank Zappa sadly died at the weekend. I mean, do you regard him as sort of one of the founding fathers of Prog Rock as he was certainly like keen on innovation and technology and all the things you've talked about.

SW: Very much so yes. I think he was a true progressive rocker in the sense that he mixed all sorts of styles of music that, you know, jazz, avant garde, classical. I'm sure you'll be talking about this later but, yes yes, a true, true progressive rocker.

MR: A hero of yours?

SW: I wouldn't go that far, not in the Dave Gilmour league. (cross talk) 2nd division hero maybe

MR: What do you think of the Floyd without Waters?

SW: You don't want me to swear on the radio so I won't tell you – not very good

MR: Right

SW: Not very good

MR: Fine fine said it all. Alright. So do we have to give a sensitive intro, has it got to build back into full flight now

SW: Indeed. We're going to pick up now where we left off

MR: This is on the current album, isn't it, the last album you made on Delerium

SW: That's right yeah

MR: OK then right

SW: Cheers

We then resume with The Burning Sky Part 2 which although is featured as a track on Spiral Circus is not this recording

MR: Porcupine Tree performing live in our studio down the other end of the Palace of Glittering Delights. Burning Sky Parts 1 & 2 as I said that track is available on the current album. On the Sunday of Life, it should be pointed out. They'll be playing one more song between half eleven and midnight.

After more of the show

MR: (bit missing)....Always Never

SW: Yeah Mark before we play this can I in classic chat show style get one more plug in for our Borderline show tomorrow night

MR: I've just done a dead sensitive intro there says like "and there they are coming back now with Always Never". Hey Mark just before we do it you know go on then!

SW: Alright you do it again and we'll do it

MR: No well go on do the plug first

SW: Alright. Borderline show tomorrow, Charing Cross Road Porcupine Tree, get there about eight thirty to avoid disappointment

MR: Right ok

SW: Here's Always Never

MR: Right oh no I was going to do the intro

SW: Go on then

MR: Right here they are back now live, Porcupine Tree with Always Never

The song finally starts and it is this track which has the bum note so often talked about when Steve gives a cry of anguish. Actually had Mark Radcliffe not mentioned it on his next show I'm not sure it would have been that obvious. This recording is featured on the Spiral Circus Cassette

MR: Porcupine Tree playing live with Always Never. See them at the Borderline London tomorrow night and 2 excellent albums with Up The Downstair and On The Sunday of Life available on Delerium Records. Thanks to Paul Smith for the mix there.

Thus the first radio sessions by The Porcupine Tree came to an end.

Nearly fourteen months later on 30 January 1995 they returned to Radio One and the Mark Radcliffe Show to play tracks from The Sky Moves Sideways.

The featured tracks were Moon Touches Your Shoulder, The Sky Moves Sideways in 2 parts, and the track which gave birth to the Sky Moves Sideways and forms part of Part 2 of the track on the album, Is Not.

This session will be covered in a future issue of Voyage 35.

Live at Brixton Academy 21 October 1995 (by Steve Freight)

At last the night had arrived when I was going to see both Hawkwind and Porcupine Tree on the same bill.

This was going to be a night to remember, I thought and so it was.

I drove the forty miles to Brixton on my own as my friend from Hereford who should have been going with me was late back from his holiday in Italy and I passed away the time listening to tapes of Porcupine Tree to get me in the mood.

First on when I arrived were Captain Rizz who are a hard reggae group, not bad but not really to my taste.

A fifteen minute break for change of set readying for Porcupine Tree was whiled away meeting friends and talking to Raymond who was doing the sound from the mixing board. I feel he was to do an excellent job of conveying the sound of Porcupine Tree as it was only with "the sound" that they convey their music. There were no distractions of a light show save for a few bursts of strobe effects and this I believe was to their benefit as it is the music which sells a group – not gimmicks.

Imagine my disappointment when in discussion I found out that the tour management had only allocated 30 minutes to the group. I'm told they had never heard of Porcupine Tree and therefore didn't feel they warranted any more time – shame on you however you are!!

How were they to do themselves justice in just 30 minutes. I was soon to find out!

I wasn't alone in waiting for Porcupine Tree to appear – the hall was filling up substantially for their appearance and at the first sound of rain the audience erupted ....We were off!

The Sky Moves Sideways was the first song played and this seems to get better and better every time I hear it. I know "Prog Rock" receives bad press from some of the media at present but this song (in all its parts) more than any other must surely reverse the trend and bring back respectability to the genre.

After an enthusiastic response from the audience (not always at the right spot unfortunately) Steven announced:-
"Thank you. OK for those of you who don't know we are Porcupine Tree (cheers from the audience) – For those of you who did know you might care to know this is a new song. This is called Waiting".

This new song for those of you who have yet to hear it follows very much in the styles of Always Never and if it is to be their delayed single will be excellent. It includes a beautiful guitar solo, as you would expect, from Steve. With only 30 minutes to shine I thought it brave to include a new song but it worked.

Steven then launched straight into the driving rhythm that is Not Beautiful Anymore*. I feel this has improved since appearing on Up The Downstair and is one which works well and an obvious crowd pleaser. Steve's soaring guitar was brilliant and complemented by the keyboards of Richard and kept together by the drums of Chris and Colin's bass. I feel they have become a very tight unit and work well together bringing the best out of each other.

Then came the moment of great disappointment – Steven announced –

"We've got one more to play for you"
Was the 30 minutes really nearly up!
Unfortunately yes it was but then:-
"For those that know and those that care this is called Radioactive Toy"

The keyboard intro which is so well known started and the crowd were swaying and many singing, or at least mouthing the words.

"Thanks for listening. See you again next time, Goodnight". The band left with the crowd shouting for more.

Then for most unfortunately it was all over. But for me I was in for a treat although at that moment I did not know it. I felt deflated that they had finished but I still had Hawkwind's set to look forward too and it is with their thanks that the next phase of my evening happened.

I had undertaken some promotional work on Hawkwind's behalf and was privileged enough to have a VIP pass for the night.

I met up with a friend (Guy Thomas) who I had raved too so much about Porcupine Tree that he had become converted and had videoed one of their concerts with their permission. He had copies to give to the band and it was with this excuse that we went to their dressing room and passed a good ten minutes talking to them.

Unfortunately most of what was said has now gone but I do remember discussing the gig they had lined up in Cambridge the next night and that they were off to Italy the following week (I believe some radio sessions were also worked upon and broadcast).

I asked Steven if he had gotten over the bum note he played on the Radio One session and his reply was that it was all part of the game and didn't matter and that he would not have released it on the Spiral Circus tape if he had been worried.

I also asked when Waiting was going to be released and if it was the single we could expect in October/November. Steven replied that no single was going to appear until January/February at the earliest as they didn't want to flood the market with discs but to consolidate their positions with good quality. They were due to be going into the studios 2nd week in November to lay down more tracks.

At this stage more guests arrived and I thanked them and took my leave. I had had a fantastic time and it was following this meeting that I had the idea for Voyage 35.

I later realised that this was in fact a new song at the time, Signify.

VOYAGE

ISSUE TWO

THE PORCUPINE TREE

THIRTY FIVE

Issue 2

Published March 1996

Original Contents
The Voyage 35 intro
The Richard Barbieri story
Gig reviews
The Forum, Kentish Town 1 December 1995
Wolverhampton 2 December 1995
The Porcupine Tree story (see below)
Love Death and Porcupine Tree Parts 1 and 2
Gig list (revised from issue 1).
This issue came with an optional A3 colour spread of photos, taken by me at the Forum and limited in number to those who requested it (approx 70).

Record Collector said:
Issue 2 of this tidy A5 'zine includes a gigography of the progressive psychedelic rockers and an account of their rise to indie prominence.

Richard Barbieri
(by Michael Seabrook)

Since 1981 when Japan (David Sylvian, Steve Jasen, Richard Barbieri and Mick Karn) split, Richard Barbieri has been involved in various musical projects. The purpose of this article is not to provide a complete discography but to focus on a selection of his more recent (and easier to obtain) works outside of the Porcupine Tree.

Those of you that have heard Porcupine Tree will notice Barbieri's ability to fix an instant atmosphere. This is evident on anything he has been involved with. To describe his style in words is almost impossible – to me it is like sonic clouds of fog swirling from some other-worldly place. Well how would you describe it?

I first encountered Richard's work on David Sylvian's Albums "Brilliant Trees" (1984) and "Gone to Earth" (1986). It was also in 1986 that the first Jansen/Barbieri album "Worlds in a Small Room" was released. This was an early "ambient" style album rather like Erik Satie's Gymnopedies arranged for synthesizers were simple and laid back except for the typewriter percussion on Mission" and the percussion breaks on "Moving Circles".

In 1987, Jansen and Barbieri called themselves the "Dolphin Brothers" and released a commercial pop-style album called "Catch the Fall". The title track was a complex piece and the highlight of an album largely misunderstood by the music press. It was a shame it didn't succeed commercially in this country but perhaps it was too understated at a time of screaming Brossettes and Kylie-ites!

In 1990 Japan reformed under the title "Rain Tree Crow". Barbieri's keyboards and programming were intricate filigree swirls of notes and noises that were almost notes. Speaking at the time Jansen and Barbieri commented that with that album they began to express stronger emotions of through their music. This complemented the lyrics and vocal parts of David Sylvian. The single and album were well received especially the single "Blackwater" making single of the week in Melody Maker by the ever tasteful Chris Roberts. The percussion was more rock orientated with guitar solos more to the fore. Songs tended to evolve as they progressed rather than parts actually repeating. Improvisation was the method of composition.

David Sylvian went on to do an adventurous rock album with Robert Fripp – of King Crimson. Progressive? A definite maybe!

In 1993 Jansen and Barbieri formed their own recording company Medium Records. The first release was "Beginning To Melt" which featured the Oystercatchers and Robbie Aceto in the rock orientated "Human Age". This was perhaps a pointer to Barbieri's increasing interest in rock music. The track "The Wilderness" featured the sublime vocal talents of Suzanne Barbieri, who also pops up on "The Sky Moves Sideways" Medium 2 was the Mini-CD "Seed", with a modern sounding reworking of "Beginning to Melt" and three very mesmeric instrumentals.

Mick Karn's experimental but approachable album "Bestial Cluster" features wonderful tracks like "Beard in the Letterbox". Barbieri's keyboards were a welcome melodic contribution to this strange but enjoyable album. "Barbieri also collaborated with Ex Level 42 Guitarist Jakko on "Kingdom of Dust" on four commercial, Level 42 influenced tracks.

This demonstrates the different styles Barbieri turns his hands to.

One CD I did not hear was "Door X" with David Torn (anybody know this?). Were there any tunes on it?

The most notable collaboration for Richard and the most enjoyable for me was that with No-Mans Tim Bowness, the excellent "Flame". The title track actually began life on "Stories Across Borders", a Jansen Barbieri album from 1991. "Flame" is Japan-like in places stylistically but updates the sound and brings it into the 90's. It also features Steven Wilson, who is, as we know, the Tree. Flame was released in 1994. It is less guitar-rock orientated than No-Man's "Flowermouth" (Richard Barbieri appeared on that too!) but things could get complicated if I discuss No-Man as well!

Steven Wilson is also featured on the 1995 CD, (Medium 3) by Jansen/Barbieri, "Stone into Flesh". This features 3 songs in a rock style and 3 energetic instrumentals composed by Barbieri alone. Steve appears on 4 of the six tracks and Colin Edwin supplies Acoustic and Electric Bass on one of these tracks making it almost a group effort! The highlight is "Closer than I" which would surely be a single if it wasn't seven minutes plus in length. Steve's vocals elucidate well the bitter subject of the lyrics. "Ringing the Bell Backwards" should be of interest to Tree fans, as the style is in my opinion quite similar. No repetition, just evolution.

To conclude these items reside in my record collection. I'm sure Richard Barbieri has been to many more recording studios than this! Does anyone out there have a full discography? Anyway, as a fan of the Porcupine Tree track "Moonloop". I recommend all the above releases.

Many thanks to Michael for this overview. Michael is a fan of Richard's work and also produces his own tapes of varied music (which he describes as Rock, Dance and Experimental projects) under the guise of Labyrinth.

Views of Wolverhampton 2 December 1995 (by Steve Best / Gordon Elcock)

Steve Best reminisces on the evening as follows:

The time is 7:59, the lights go down, the band enters.

The sound of rain echoes from the speakers and with the notes of the keyboards drifting across the room the voyage begins with The Sky Moves Sideways (phase 1). The first notes Steve's guitar, enter Chris and Colin, the rhythm section, the song continues. Steve moves to the microphone "We lost the skyline...."

After the vocal passage the pace is picked up by Chris on drums and Colin on bass. I look around the stage – there are 2 large canvas circles, one to the left one to the right with images projected upon them. At times the light show is dazzling.

Before I know it the track is coming to an end, the keyboards drift away to be replaced by the appreciation of the 600+ audience who have gathered. Steve Wilson "That was the Sky

Moves Sideways from the current album. This is from the first – Radioactive Roy".

Richard starts the track and Steve comes in on vocals. They all seem to be smiling at this moment – things are going well. Richard looks to Chris as he points to one of the images on the canvas screens. This is possibly the best live version of this track I have heard. They are certainly becoming a more cohesive band the more sets they do. The track ends – more applause.

Nothing is said this time and the first chords are struck and we move into the heavier side of the Tree – Signify, a new track from the forthcoming album full of heavy chords and layered guitar sounds. The track is lifted by the entrance of Richard which his swirling keyboards, and all through this Chris and Colin stay tight and true – not a note or beat out of place.

Now the time has come. The Tour-de-Force, Voyage 34.

Steve stands motionless as the man speaks "This sometimes remarkable man" (never a truer word was said). The crowd greets the LSD references with jeers as Steve picks up the riff. Colin's bass comes dancing in, the lights run in time with the music. The trip has begun.

On the screen appear images of the Voyage 34 sleeve and liquid like images form the backdrop to the stage. I close my eyes and melt into the music. The end guitar solo brings me back to earth as all too soon the trip is over. It is 8:40, 40 minutes after the gig began. I felt shattered by it but an inner glow kept the gig alive for a while longer.

Steve at the end "Thank you. Goodnight. Enjoy the mighty Ozrics"

And we did.

Was it worth the 180 mile round trip? I think it was and it's off to....Manchester next week!

And so onto Gordon Elcock's view:-

Here we are, my wife Tina and I, to see The Porcupine Tree – but the reason is why? Well for me it started with a now, (sadly defunct radio show Out On Blue Six, which I used to record and edit out Mark Radcliffe (Sorry Mark!). Consequently I didn't always know who'd recorded the tracks I liked.

Lets move forward to a review of an amazing sounding track on C4 Teletext. It described a remarkable recording, part Pink Floyd, part ambient dance, which I just had to have. It was Voyage 34 and I wondered what else was available. Lets move to a small independent record store in Dudley, holding a sale, where I found On the Sunday Of Life. (It cost me £1 (lucky fellow – Steve)) and I discovered that two of my favourite tracks from Mark Radcliffe's show were by the Porcupine Tree (Radioactive Toy and Linton Samuel Dawson.

So now I've got everything legally available by the wonderful group and I discover they're supporting the Ozrics at Wolverhampton and we've got to go.

"Have you heard the support band" said one guy to another in front of me. "No" replied the other and they both promptly left for the bar. Their loss.

The audience grew throughout the gig, though why do some people insist on talking while the band is playing? Go somewhere else please and let those who want to enjoy the music – you are just being ignorant. On stage they come and open with The Sky Moves Sideways (Part 1). Now I have to admit I found this an odd choice as it takes time to get going, though it was almost (too) perfect in its execution, with a nice piece of slide guitar, and a little improvisation towards the end. Little applause. "Thank you" says Steve Wilson, "That was from our last album, and now for something from our first, "Radioactive Toy". Two cheers go up – one from me muted and one from the other side of the hall somewhat louder. More of the audience, the majority sitting down, are getting into it.

At the end of the number they go straight into a new instrumental, this is more what this audience like, and this unknown song, which I'm told by one of the guys on the merchandising stand is called Signify, gets as good a response as any all night. To describe it, well it's a lot like The Gospel According to the IEM, but with a quirky time signature, and a really simple, almost boogie, guitar part. Wonderful, and great to see a new song get such a great response. The audience is warming to the group now. Then – no intro but the voice is unmistakable, the band begin to play Voyage 34 (in a version similar to that on Pick 'n' Mix), the crowd, not exactly dancing, but swaying in time to the rhythm, then all too soon, that was it. Four numbers, and gone!!

Outside the Tree's stand is shifting much merchandise. One guy says to me, "I'd never heard of this band but they were wonderful" (a common enough reaction – Steve). He couldn't afford to buy anything but I suggested he start with Up The Downstair. Other people I noticed were buying two or three albums plus Staircase Infinities. 'til the next tour in the New Year, which can't come soon enough. Oh and nice lights by Fruit Salad too. After this we didn't stay for the Ozrics set.

Many thanks for 2 differing views on the same gig. The truth is probably somewhere in the middle.

Porcupine Tree
(by Glenn Povey & Steve Freight)

For those of you who have never heard of Porcupine Tree they are a band of diverse textures and invention, pushing the boundaries of popular rock music by use of the latest technology and producing a unique blend of contemporary rock, psychedelia and ambient mixes. Whether it's in the surreal landscapes they form or the reflective lyrics written, the music as a whole is both moving and inspired enough to thought provoke and open the ears to a new and creative form of rock music. However we're not talking of the elongated self indulgent wank-ramblings that gives prog such a bad name in pop music today but a new, varied and inventive form that combines the best of what was then but what is most definitely now.

Porcupine Tree's humble beginnings lay in the multi-instrumental talents of Steven Wilson, who was first introduced to the guitar at the age of 12 and a copy of Pink Floyd's The Wall. Luckily he didn't slash his wrists and his love affair with music began. But the real story came about in 1985 when Wilson, having mastered the playing of many and varied instruments began experimenting in various styles of music in the seclusion of his home studio. With the help of Alan Duffy, who presented some of his lyrics to Wilson, he compiled two very limited edition tapes of material. The first, "Tarquin's Seaweed Farm" contained the equivalent of two albums; one being a mock live album and the second, "The Nostalgia Factory" was compiled shortly afterwards. Each tape paid great homage to 60's and 70's psychedelia from the madness of "Jupiter Island" to the quirkiness of "Linton Samuel Dawson", it certainly gave you a unique drive through flowerpot land in a space rocket!

Eventually, Porcupine Tree came to the attention of Delerium Records who re-issued the tapes in improved packaging to test the market. So taken back were they by the response that they signed Porcupine Tree to the label. The resultant release was to create a compilation of the best of the live tapes, re-recorded and re-mixed onto a single CD and a double vinyl album under the title of "On The Sunday of Life". The most remarkable track contained within this collection was the haunting "Radioactive Toy". It prompted sufficient interest for Select to describe it as "helium fuelled madness", and Kerrang to comment that it, "so blatantly ignores any known commercial formula as to verge on the insane!" Incidentally a great deal of the unused tracks from this period were again re-mixed to form the retrospective "Yellow Hedgerow Dreamscape" and released much later in 1994.

The success of "On The Sunday of Life" encouraged Wilson to further the project; where once it was nothing more than an experimental project became a matter for serious consideration. Whilst being influenced by the likes of Pink Floyd, the Krautrock genre and ambient experimentation Wilson did not fully manifest this influence until the 1992 release of the stunning 30 minute CD and 12" single "Voyage 34". "Constructed around a sample of a long forgotten sixties LSD documentary, Voyage 34" traced the adventures of space traveller, Brian, as he slowly descended from elation to the depths of what can only be truly described as a serious bummer. A pounding dance beat reminiscent of Floyd's Another Brick flowed throughout and captured enough attention to keep it in the Indie Charts Top Ten for a full six weeks! A total departure from previous recordings, it increased Porcupine Tree's public awareness and demonstrated the differing styles that it was capable of achieving. Later that year Astralasia remixed the track and it was released as a 12" only single.

In June 1993 Porcupine Tree launched its second album, "Up The Downstair" with an enthusiastic Melody Maker proclaiming it to be "a psychedelic masterpiece and, I'd wager, one of the albums of the year! The most outstanding tracks on this album include "Synthesia" and "Not Beautiful Anymore", the former a pulsating blend of psychedelic riffs and the latter, a far more disturbing track highlighting the dangers of making love under the influence of LSD.

By now, Porcupine Tree's popularity had reached the stage where it became obvious that live performances were necessary to reach a wider audience and indeed satisfy eager fans who had been buying their records over the past three years. In November that year Wilson recruited long time friend Colin Edwin on bass guitar, Richard Barbieri on keyboards (of Japan fame) and Chris Maitland on drums. The latter two of which Wilson had previously performed live with as part of his other band, No Man.

An initial three date tour was booked for December 1993 and admirer Mark Radcliffe took them onto his Radio One programme for a live session to coincide with this. Such was their popularity that the first show instantly sold out and people were travelling very long distances to see them perform. Surprisingly, the live band gelled instantly making it hard to believe it was their first live performance together. Porcupine Tree also utilised the expertise of Fruit Salad Lights, renown for lighting the Ozric Tentacles, Eat Static and Senser and who's illuminations are more than reminiscent of those used in the Fillmore or Winterland in its hey-day, but complement Porcupine Tree's music extraordinarily well. Fruit Salad along with An Arc Lights are still Porcupine Tree's lighting crew giving the live performance a powerful visual edge with tailor made slides, projections and effects. A high quality audio tape of these first shows is available to members of Porcupine Tree's newsletter, "Transmission".

After a couple of summer appearances in Holland, Porcupine Tree headed out on the road again with a five date November tour to support the new EP "Moonloop". Along with "Stars Die", the opener and the instrumental "Moonloop", this release again took the band in a different direction and hinted towards a more ambient/trance like form of space-rock based around a spontaneous jam the band had in the recording studio.

This style extended into the next album, "The Sky Moves Sideways", released in February 1995. An epic, sixty-five minute expansive soundscape of melody and ambient progressive rock experimentation that blends each track into each other; it entered the NME and Melody Maker charts immediately without even so much of a hint of interest from any of the music press, but nevertheless has become their biggest selling album to date.

The year progressed with the most touting the band have ever done starting with a tour of Holland, a three week UK tour and a sell out 1,000 capacity show at the Palladium in Rome (at the behest of Radio Rock, strong supporters of the band from very early on). As 1996 looms, the band have just completed another UK tour (with one supporting Hawkind in London), a further tour of Italy and are out on a five date support on the Ozric Tentacles autumn tour.

Currently, the band are recording a fourth album "Signify" to be preceded by another single. "Waiting" in March next year. What has become apparent over the months is that Porcupine Tree are a considerable force in live performance with a harder edge and stronger presence than on record. Much of the album-to-be has been played live in recent months to test its audience reaction and playability within the band as a unit. This will again see the band take a different "progressive" turn which, if the previews suggest, will be a fascinating combination of "Up The Downstair" and "The Sky Moves Sideways" all rolled into one. In Steve Wilson's own words "I would say progressive music means music without any rules or boundaries... I thought that the whole ambient-trance thing was pretty progressive in the true sense of the word which is, trying to find new ways of making popular music..."

The Forum – Kentish Town – December 1st 1995 (by Steve Freight)

The stage is bare, but then he's there
Picked out in white light
The crowd erupts
His band destructs
Your senses give in without a fight.

The above is the opening to a track called Guitar Hero from Charlie's 1976 album No Second Chance. Listening to it recently I was struck by how well these words fitted the opening to the Forum gig and how overwhelmed I felt when the opening to the Sky Moves Sideways began.
This was my second Porcupine Tree gig and I felt better than the one at Brixton just over a month earlier.

Richard Barbieri (background) Steven Wilson (forground)

For one thing I was treated to a light show and the images upon the circular projection screens complimented the music.

For another the music was, as always, excellent.

I arrived at the gig with a friend from work, one of many I'm pleased to say who has shown exemplary taste in giving Porcupine Tree a listen and finding what we all know: that they are a group for the future.

We met up with John Chase (who has provided some photos for this issue) and collected our photo passes.

This meant we could enter the pit and get a very good uninterrupted view (and my apologies to those whose view we may have blocked inadvertently).

Well the band struck up with opening chords to The Sky Moves Sideways and we were off.

A slow moody introduction of swirling noise making your senses reel a kaleidoscope of light and then the ace guitar starts full of feeling and if you're not swaying yet you must be set in concrete. The sound being produced is unbelievable.

Steven moves to the mike and whistles of encouragement from the crowd precede "We lost the Skyline…"

Richard Barbieri Steven Wilson Colin Edwin

Then after the slow passage of "I Find That I'm Not There" we move on apace to "Wire the Drum" another fine piece which is held together by Colin's relentless bass rhythm and Chris' drumming, overlaid with Richard's keyboards. You just had to have been there to fully appreciate all that was going on – the light show, the music, the established fans swaying in time and the look of awe as I turned round to see the people who hadn't previously seen the band becoming converted as the set continued.

John from the office gave me the "thumbs up" as he became more and more impressed.

The Sky Moves Sideways Phase one ends to tumultuous applause.
Steve "Thank you" and with barely a pause the long held note which begins "Signify" a track one could almost class as an out and out rocker except this is Porcupine Tree and the endless changes in pace and guitar style make this a unique experience in assaulting your perceptions. Brilliant and I can't wait for this to appear on a future release.

Louder applause this time.

Steve "Brilliant. Thank you. We are Porcupine Tree. This is Radioactive Toy".

The track begins and to quote from Guitar Hero again:

His fans all cheer
No critics here
He has them in his palm

This track to my mind gets better and better the more I hear it (its not my favourite track though – I'll tell you what that is next issue when I publish the results of the poll). I've heard it plenty of times but the poignancy of the song and the feeling coming over in the guitar playing gets me every time.

There appears to be a slight problem between the end of Radioactive Toy and the start of the next song as there is a gap of about 30 seconds, which seems a lot longer, before Steve announces "we've got time for one more. This is a story of Brian and his trip – Voyage 34".

This was it – the sampling from a little known sixties LSD documentary brings to life Brian's bummer of a trip and we are left feeling totally drained as if Brian had invaded our bodies and we are left feeling totally flat when the band leave the stage.

I then had the opportunity to talk with some of you and my apologies if the chats were all too brief but hopefully we will meet again at the next gig.

I managed to snatch a few words with Chris in the auditorium afterwards and would like to thank him for taking the time out for a chat. I saw Colin also mingling but he had gone before I had a chance to speak to him.

The Ozrics' then struck up and I have been a fan of theirs for years having copies of the original tapes so was looking forward to hearing them. However I was in for a disappointment. I thought musically they were excellent but the volume was far too high and my ears haven't rung for so long since I first saw Motorhead!

Oh – and to the girl I was chatting with at the Delerium Stand, just what do you and your friends really get up to in your conservatory on your Porcupine Club evenings?

You said you'd write and let me know. I know I said I'd only print the details if there was nothing pornographic going on but I can only assume therefore that you have an absolutely riotous time and I'd still be interested in hearing from you (and after these comments most of the readers to!!)

Love Death & Porcupine Tree (by Phil Harwood)

Part 1 – how I discovered Porcupine Tree (and the sky moved sideways)

I first heard of Porcupine Tree back in January 1990 while reading a fanzine called Ptolemaic Terrascope. This dealt with Bevis Frond and related Woronzow record label releases.

For those who don't know Bevis Frond is Guitarist Nick Saloman who started off as a one man band playing virtually all instruments, writing and producing his songs on a series of privately issued LPs – his first was Miasma in 1987 and he now has a record deal with Reckless Records and his own company Woronzow – he has now produced somewhere in the region of 9 CDs.

The style of music is Jimi Hendrix guitar inspired with the elements of the best of the late sixties psychedelia. There was an excellent article covering his early career in Record Collector

116. Ptolemaic also covered other unusual virtually unknown music in their review section and in issue 3 in amongst reviews of records from Dream Synidicate (what a brilliant guitar bend!). Tangle Edge. The Moffs, was, your've guessed it! – a review of Tarquin's Seaweed Farm. This was described as and I quote "arrangements that teeter on the brink of psych meets progressive pomp" and playing "a Maelstrom of snarling psychedelic sequences". The review was by the editor of judgement ("if freedom freakouts are your cup of herbal this one is probably worth investigating!") I wrote off. The tape was £3.75 including postage from an address given as No Mans Land Hemel Hempstead. I received back the tape and 13 page booklet and that started my love of Porcupine Tree's music.

It wasn't long before I was back in touch with Steve, who was then signing letters as Steven, with £3.00 for Love Death and Mussolini and £6.50 for an LP called Double Exposure on No Mans Land Records. This was an LP of progressive music including a track from Steve's previous band No Man Is An Island Except The Isle of Man. Double Exposure was released in October 1987 and there was a predecessor to this called Exposure which had been released in August 1985 and included another No Man Is An Island track. Sadly when I wrote in for this it had been deleted due to lack of interest. The material on these LPs were unique to them and unavailable elsewhere. I thought I'd put that bit in to make the mouths of collectors water. In the letters I received from Steven he revealed that though he had forgotten sending in a tape to Ptolemaic (he got me to send him a copy of the review) it had resulted in at least 4 other people requesting a copy of the tape. He also said and I quote "I'm glad to hear your taste encompasses contemporary music as well as the antique stuff, because really those are the sort of people I do the Porcupine Tree music for".

He goes on "pretending that the drum machines and synthesisers were never invented is not constructive. These machines are incredibly liberating used in the correct way, as I hope I prove. So do the Shaman, Kitchens of Distinction, Happy Mondays, De la Soul, Momus, The Beloved, 905 State, Gabriel etc. an interesting set of comparisons".

Around March 1990 Steve was talking in his letters of "I hope the next Porcupine Tree offering will be an LP, possibly in conjunction with Freakbeat (Linton Samuel Dawson is on their new compilation LP). "This was Delerium Records "Psychedelic Psauna, but there must have been some delay as it wasn't issued until 25/11/91. The LP reference was DELP 00511), now deleted, and the CD DELCD005.

Around the same time Steve says "there's nothing else available yet" (apart from Tarquin's Seaweed Farm and Love Death and Mussolini) "but I expect the band" (Steve was still fostering the belief that Porcupine Tree were a collection of individuals!) "to start on a new album as soon as No Man's Land studio has been upgraded to 16 track. This one may well be a double with the second record being the best moments from Tarquin and Mussolini. "As we know this became "The Nostalgia Factory". It may interest people who have only seen the Delerium reissues of these early tapes that the originals Steve sent out were normal blank tapes. There were no special labels stuck on them, no numbering or anything like that.

The sleeves were black and white thin photocopied sheets with simple drawings (balloons on Tarquin's and a piano on Mussolini).

The accompanying booklets were just photocopied sheets (3 with Mussolini and a flyer on the Exposure LP's). These were definite "bedroom" tapes, so it is amazing and down to the quality of the music, that the Porcupine Tree got to where they are today. Without the vision of Delerium Records, who on hearing the tapes decided to re-release them to a wider audience. Porcupine Tree would probably have faded away and what a loss that would have been!

Part 2 – Words From A Hessian Sack

The booklet that came with the Tarquin's Seaweed Farm original cassette, when mail ordered from No Mans Land, was a 14 page photocopied set of loose papers. This differed from the shorter booklet that came with the Delerium re-release. The purpose of this piece is to give some details of the original booklet.

The first sheet was the introductory page introducing "The Porcupine Tree play Tarquin's Seaweed Farm. Words from A Hessian Sack".

Page 2 listed the tracks and page 3 the musicians, described as "tripping extrordinaire" . The musicians included the unlikely characters as:- The Evaporating Flan plays drums, percussion, drum computer and speaks Timothy Tadpole Jones on acoustic guitar and percussion Sebastian Tweedle Bampton III on delay circuits and mixing desk Linton Samuel Dawson was credited with the light show and Porcupine Tree himself played acoustic and electric guitar, koto, flute and vocals. The 4th page gave recording details. The studio side (Side 1 ending at Music For The Head) had been done at Periscope Studios Devon between 1988/9. The "live" (allegedly) side was done, in track order, at:-

The Elysee Monmatre Paris,
Digwalls London thru the auspices of JC Camillioni (thanked for the ioning (sic) of the No Mans Land Mobile) and the final tracks The Cross, Hole and Yellow Hedgerow Dreamscape had supposedly been recorded at the Greenpeace Fayre.

JD had been in No Man Is An Island Except The Isle of Man, Steve's other band. He was also credited for writing the sleeve (sheet) notes. There is then a list of credits for inspiration to fascinating bands and individuals.

The list bears repeating so here it is:- Soft Machine, Pink Floyd, Hawkwind, Gong, Syd Barratt, Prince, Peter Hammill, Capt Beefheart, Frank Zappa, Nick Drake, Donovan, Yes, Tangerine Dream, Principle Edwards Magic Theatre, Henry Cow, XTC, Jethro Tull, Fred Frith, King Crimson, 3rd Ear Band, Can, Kevin Ayers, Caravan, Eno, Popul Vun, Mike Oldfield, Joni Mitchell, Cocteau Twins, Durruti Column, Fairport Convention, Philip Glass, Keith Jarrett, Buttonhole Surfers, Robert Wyatt and Ben Watt.

Pages 5 to 8 entitled "How Did We Get Here?" (with subtitles "In the beginning…Cream Cakes for everyone!!!" and "Of What relevance To The Music?!.?") and ending with "This Is Only The Beginning!" detailed an unlikely history of the band. Starting with the Incredible Expanding Mindfuck (see Delerium's latest CD "Pick and Mix" for a track by the then fictitious group whose history has now caught up with them called The Gospel According To The IFM) in 1975 and ending with Tarquins, it charted the history of the members. An individual, Porcupine Tree was described as a deranged genius, a genuine child of the new Paris underground of 1981.

It details events such as how Tree met Saloman St Jermain and an undying friendship was established in a second, consummated with the exchange of a few ounces of grass and a handful of multi-coloured pills! The ! here is mine. The end sheet is dated 1.4.89. Sheet 9 continued the theme with a discography of "Objects of Delight". Unfortunately all were fake except Tarquins.

Sheets 10 and 11 were a short humorous story about Jupiter Island and within this is the Hessian Sack and 5000001 uses for it.

Sheets 12 and 11 are Our Glorious Leader Writes where Tree comments, with the assistance of the ghost of Henry Duncanbowel, on each track such as:

Radioactive Toy — Politics has always bored me. This piece could be about peace, love and harmony. Or it could be about genocide. You decide.

And

The Cross — Let it be said Prince is God. When that is said all else follows. The Cross is his song and is based around a 2 chord thrash which reaches a frenzied climax during which it is common for the audience to see celestial beings accompany us on stage.

The final sheet 14 listed details of the 2 tapes available and comments like "one of the most beautiful pieces of modern psychedelia I have ever heard" ISMO. It gave the No Mans Land address saying "The Porcupine Tree are a 5 piece band dedicated to preserving the music of the sixties psychedelia and the progressive music of bands like Pink Floyd and Soft Machine in a more contemporary setting. They work from their Periscope Station studio in Devon and lace their music with a distinctive personality and a sense of humour".

I hope this short piece has been informative and interesting to those who do not have the original booklets. If there is enough interest I'm sure Steve Freight can twist my arm to do another in more detail.

Many thanks Phil

Phil's arm is currently in a painful armlock as I'm sure you would like another article and I have asked him to do one on the Love Death and Mussolini and Nostalgia booklets for a future issue.

Issue 3

Published September 1996

Original Contents:
The Voyage 35 intro
An exclusive Steven Wilson interview (see below)
Review of the new album (Signify)
How to distinguish the fake ones from the original tapes (Tarquin's Seaweed Farm, The Nostalgia Factory and Love Death And Mussolini)
The Porcupine Family Tree
Lots of gig reviews
Love Death and Porcupine Tree Part 3
Readers Poll

Record Collector said:
A "Porcupine Family Tree" is the main course of this proficient A5 browse, with an in depth interview with the guitarist Steven Wilson providing the hors d'oeuvres.

Steven Wilson Interview (conducted by Steve Freight)

SF: Thank you Steven for agreeing to be interviewed for this issue I would like to start at the beginning if I may. You have said that you first got a guitar at the age of 12 along with a copy of the Wall. Did you know at that time that you had a musical leaning, and who or what inspired you at an early age?

SW: My love of music dates from when I was 8 or 9 years old. One Christmas my parents bought LPs for each other - "Dark Side of the Moon" for my father and Donna Summer's "Love to Love You Baby" for my mother. I heard these two albums played in "heavy rotation" and in retrospect I can see how they are almost entirely responsible for the direction that my music has taken ever since. On one hand a love of experimental album based rock music as exemplified by Porcupine Tree and on the other a love of groove/trance music which is more the No-Man approach (that particular Donna Summer album contains just one continuous 17 minute shape shifting groove across the whole of Side One).

I had actually been forced to learn the guitar when I was even younger, but like a lot of kids forced to play an instrument I got no real pleasure out of it and stopped having lessons when my parents realised they were wasting their money. However, round about my 11th birthday I rescued the nylon string classical guitar from the attic and began to experiment not so much with playing, but with pure sound. I recall scraping microphones across the strings, feeding the resulting sound into overloaded reel to reel tape recorders and producing a primitive form of multi track recording by bouncing between two cassette machines.

Eventually I formed bands with friends at school and started playing live - but my main interest is still sonic experimentation and production. I enjoy playing guitar but it has always been a means to an end for me. I never learnt all the requisite guitar licks and would struggle if you asked me to play anything but my own material - I can't even play "Stairway to Heaven"! (Can do "Smoke on the Water" though)

SF: A number of tapes of Altamont and Karma have surfaced. I also understand you had an involvement in a group called Coltsfoot. Could you tell us about these groups and their history and any details of recordings which may have been issued.

SW: Having these tapes in circulation is a bit like a painter having his nursery school paint blots on display, but I guess it's testament to that fact that the Porcupine Tree fan base is growing all the time that these formative demo tapes are in circulation. The Altamont tape was a one-off tape I made in 1983 (I was 15 at the time), half solo and half with a keyboard player called Si Vockings. It makes use of Alan Duffy lyrics later used for the Porcupine Tree tracks "This Long Silence" and "It Will Rain for a Million Years", though in a very different context. About the same time I had a progressive rock band with a few friends from school - this was Karma. We recorded two tapes - "The Joke's On You" (1983) and "The Last Man To Laugh" (1985), which contained the original versions of "Small Fish" and "Nine Cats", though not "The Joke's On You" (played live but not recorded). Coltsfoot were some friends I helped out with some recordings in 1988 - I was never a member of this band, but I did play on their demo tape "Action at a Distance". I believe some of these recordings were included on their recent CD release, but I bet the cover doesn't tell you when they were recorded !

SF: A few of the early Karma tracks were reworked as Porcupine Tree songs. Do you have any more plans to dip into "the archives" as some of these songs sound very good?

SW: I can't think of any other Karma tracks that I would want to resurrect. However, there are other songs I wrote with Alan Duffy during the eighties which were never recorded but have subsequently made good Porcupine Tree tracks. "Jupiter Island" and parts of "Always Never" date from about 1982 and must rate as some of the earliest half-decent songs I wrote. There are a few more from this period that could make it on to a future Porcupine Tree release.

SF: What was the first song you ever wrote a) on your own and b) in collaboration with someone else? How do you feel these stand the test of time?

SW: It's impossible to answer this question as I honestly can't remember. Some of the early songs I wrote have turned out to be favourites of mine even though the original interpretations of them were very primitive - "Nine Cats" and "Small Fish" being good examples.

SF: When you write songs do you write to a formula? Does the music come first or the lyric?

SW: I certainly don't write to a formula. That would be very dangerous! And there is no one way that I approach a new track. Some are written on the piano, some on the guitar, some develop from a drum pattern. Some are written lyric first, some music first and some are constructed from band improvisations.

SF: In an early interview I remember reading you stated you worked for Sky doing link music. Do you still do this and has any of this music formed the basis of any Porcupine Tree music (or No Man)? Do you intend to write more incidental music for instance for a film soundtrack if asked?

SW: I do a lot of music for television. Most of this work is very creative and can be a lot of fun, particularly when the ideas are interesting. You would probably not realise they were my work unless you were told as they are nearly always in a style dictated by the visuals. I think my themes for "MTV Hitlist UK" and "MTV

Weekend News" are still being broadcast for those that are curious. All this of course makes it doubly ironic that we can't get any TV exposure for Porcupine Tree or NO-MAN on MTV or anywhere else.

SF: When it came to choosing the members of the band how long did it take you to get the right blend and what qualities were you looking for?

SW: Actually, I had a very good idea who I wanted to be in the band as soon as playing live became an issue just after "Up the Downstair" was released. Colin and Richard had both appeared as guests on that album and I knew, based on their musical tastes and personalities, that they would be the right people to ask. Chris initially joined in a session capacity, because I wasn't sure how much the music would be to his taste. But as time went on we realised that there were elements in Porcupine Tree music that appealed to him and that there was much more he could contribute if he was a full time member. This is best illustrated by the fact that he has the first solo writing credit on a Porcupine Tree album - other than myself - for the track "Light Mass Prayers" on the new album.

SF: On the latest tour at The Garage you seemed to be apologetic for not having been able to do a full gig in London up to this point due to "fabulously wealthy groups" asking you to support them. Do you find supporting groups a problem or a necessary evil to get noticed?

SW: Playing as support to more well-known bands has both advantages and disadvantages. The advantages are the opportunity to play in a big venue with a big audience, most of whom are potential new fans. The disadvantages are not being able to use your own lights and equipment and the shortness of the set. Some support gigs are amazing (e.g. - Ozric Tentacles in Antwerp), some are horrendous (e.g. - Gong in Manchester), but then that's no different to doing gigs on our own which are similarly variable in terms of enjoyment. It's certainly not a "necessary evil" - in fact it's been great to have played with so many bands that we admire.

SF: How do you view the music on the new album? Do you feel the fans now expect a certain something from your music (i.e. a static feel immediately identifiable) or do you believe they will progress along with you?

SW: Well, I hope you will agree with me when I say that each Porcupine Tree album has been very different and distinct from any other and that continues to be the case with the new album "Signify". I personally felt that the last album was a little too ponderous and didn't have enough good songs on it. This album is much more "in your face" and has more songs and weird shit on it designed to keep your attention - I don't think anybody can describe this album as ambient! It's also the first album to feature the whole band on every track, so by definition it has more of a rock ensemble feel.
Of course, every time we change our sound, or fail to make exactly the same

album that we made last time, we run the risk that the new material will not appeal to some existing fans. But I hope and trust that most Porcupine Tree fans would want us to develop, without completely abandoning our "sound" (that would be as pointless as not progressing at all) . It's certainly what I expect from my favourite artists.

SF: How do you see Porcupine Tree progressing in the future?

SW: I have no long term musical plan, except to keep making good albums.

SF: It's been noted that you still have the writing credits. Do you still consider Porcupine Tree to be a solo project with the group bringing to life your "creations" or do the other members contribute?

SW: I now consider Porcupine Tree to be a band. However, I do believe that most good bands need someone in control of the ideology and direction of the project and that will continue to be me - I could never relinquish that control, particularly as the band basically was me for the first 3 albums. Colin, Richard and Chris all agree that the balance of control will remain with me, but having said that many things to do with the band are and must now be band decisions and I would be very reluctant to do anything unless I felt I had their support. As regards writing, it's very difficult for the others to write a whole piece in a style consistent with my idea of a Porcupine Tree track (diverse though that may be). It's much more likely that the number of collaborations will increase over the next few albums. Of the 12 tracks on the "Signify" album, 4 of them involve contributions from other band members.

SF: If (and hopefully when) Porcupine Tree become universally massive if the future, will you still continue your collaborations in No Man?
And if the reverse happens will you still continue Porcupine Tree?

SW: I would find it almost impossible to concentrate on just one project, simply because I love working in so many different styles. As well as NO-MAN and Porcupine Tree I have an experimental electronic album finished under the name of BASS COMMUNION, my Krautrock alter ego INCREDIBLE EXPANDING Mindf**k and various collaborations with other musicians, such as the album I'm currently working on with FISH.

SF: I've previously asked who originally inspired you. Who do you consider today to be your main influences and who do you regularly listen to. What were the last 3 albums you bought?

SW: This is so difficult to answer because I listen to so many things. I buy about 20 albums every month, so I couldn't really answer you question about the last 3 - it would be very misleading! However, here's a non-exhaustive list of some of my favourite albums of the last few months : PHOTEK "Hidden Camera", NEU

"Neu", KLAUS SCHULZE "Historic Edition", AUTECHRE "Tri Repetae", UNDERWORLD "Second Toughest in Infants", ENNIO MORRICONE "A Western Quintet", SOUNDGARDEN "Down on the Upside", OVAL "Diskont 94", MEAT BEAT MANIFESTO "Subliminal Sandwich", RED HOUSE PAINTERS "Songs for a Blue Guitar", SCORN "Gyral", BILL LASTEVEN WILSON:ELL "Silent Recoil", VARIOUS "Jazz Satellites", KEITH JARRETT "Solo Concerts 1973", ORBITAL "In Sides", SMASHING PUMPKINS "Melon Collie", RAPOON "The Kirghiz Light", ROBERTA FLACK "First Take", THE WHO "Quadrophenia", TORTOISE "Millions Now Living Will Never Die", UI "Sidelong", JOHN WALL "Alterstill", FAUST "Rien", THE BYRDS "Younger than Yesterday", AGITATION FREE "2nd", BABY BIRD "Fatherhood".

SF: It was good to hear "The Nostalgia Factory" and "Linton Samuel Dawson" being brought into the live set on the last tour. I know these went down extremely well. Will we be seeing other songs being performed live which to date you have not done and if so which would you envisage?

SW: As time goes on it would be great to bring in some more tracks from previous albums - the problem is always having to concentrate on learning and playing the new material. I would be keen to try "Footprints" and "Yellow Hedgerow Dreamscape". Any other requests? (Let me know and I'll pass on to Steve - SF)

SF: Why have "Fadeaway" and "Stars Die" not formed part of the live set to date? (At the Garage there were many calls for "Fadeaway") Could these not be adapted for live performances in some way?

SW: "Fadeaway" was performed live twice in December 1993 - it just didn't work as a live number, no matter what we tried - sometimes that happens. "Stars Die" was performed twice in Italy last time we were there (both broadcast on radio I think), but as an acoustic number, which is how it will be done if and when we play it next. The vocals are too subtle (barely above a whisper on the recorded version) to cut through a rock band going at it hammer and tongs - especially one with a drummer as loud as Chris!

SF: A number of gigs are known to have been videoed. Do you have plans to issue any of these as one of the questions I am asked most is "where can I get hold of a live video?"

SW: I expect that eventually we will do an official live performance video - we certainly have plans to do a proper live album so they could tie in together. I'd like it to be a bit different from a standard live album/video by maybe writing and performing some new tracks especially for the project as well as including other documentary style footage.

SF: You were due to play recently on the Internet but this was cancelled at the last moment. Could you explain why? I've not heard of this being done before.

Would this have been the first such performance and would you have been able to monitor in some way the audience who tuned in?

SW: I'm afraid I don't know much about this - as I understand it our New York show was supposed to be simultaneously broadcast over the Internet by a company called Sonicnet, but I gather that the venue would not allow the broadcast to take place. I believe that Sonicnet have successfully broadcast concerts by other bands over the net, although I wouldn't have thought the quality would be that great (??!)

SF: I understand there will be a range of Porcupine Tree related albums being issued on vinyl. Could you give us more details on these and the thinking behind this venture.

SW: I'm setting up a label with Delerium called Chromatic which will concentrate on limited edition (and exclusively vinyl to start with) Porcupine Tree related releases. I wanted to do this because there is always music which "happens" which is not necessarily for mass consumption but which would probably be of interest to the more fanatical fans. I know for example that there are a number of other artists doing special collector or fan club releases which could not be mainstream releases for a number of reasons - too self-indulgent, archive material, bootleg quality or sheer quantity of output. King Crimson's series of archive live recordings, or Baby Bird's series of 4 track demo CDs are two of my fave examples. The first two releases on this new label will be the Incredible Expanding Mindf**k album (500 copies) and a one off vinyl pressing of the now deleted "Spiral Circus" cassette (750 copies), both on coloured vinyl I hope. Future planned releases are a 7" of the "Sky Moves Sideways" out-take "Men of Wood" (left off for reasons of context rather than quality) and a Porcupine Tree LP of improvisations and "cosmic jams".

SF: And finally before we finish I've had a couple of country bumpkins (their words not mine) from sleepy Norfolk asking when you intend to put some life into that part of the country by playing somewhere close to Norwich?

SW: OK - here's my hopefully not too feeble explanation : When the band and record company decide that it's time for Porcupine Tree to go out on tour, our agent begins to contact promoters and venues to see which of them are most enthusiastic about putting a Porcupine Tree show on. For a show to be booked, we need a fee which will cover as much of our loss as possible (we never make money) and we need to know that the show will be advertised well (this bit doesn't always go according to plan!). It also helps if the venue have a good sound system and engineer (e.g. - not like the Garage in London). I can only assume that the reason we have never played in Norfolk, which after all does contain a number of major towns, is that no promoter has ever expressed enough interest. Hopefully that will change and we could be rolling in to Norwich any day now.

SF: Thank you Steven for taking the time to answer the above questions. I'm sure it will be much appreciated by all readers. Thank you.

An Anoracsic Delight (or how to distinguish the fakes (Tarquin's Seaweed Farm, The Nostalgia Factory and Love Death And Mussolini)) (by Steve Freight)

I know a number of you have asked for "original" copies of the Tarquin's Seaweed Farm and the Nostalgia Factory and are worried about being ripped off by unscrupulous people. As I have mentioned elsewhere in this issue ask for any letter Steve may have sent at the time to verify the tapes authenticity.

Failing that the following information (which forms the basis for a possible entry in the next Record Collectors Guide) may be of help but you may also be in for a disappointment as to the number of each run:-

Tarquin's Seaweed Farm

1989   Private pressing
This was issued on standard black studio tape and came with an A4 booklet with red/black text. Approx. 10 copies only.

1991   Delerium DELC 0002
This was issued on black studio tape and came with the same booklet as the private pressing. This run can be distinguished by the silver pen writing on the cases – there is no printed label on the cassette. Approx 200. There may be some of this run with the A5 booklet.

1991   Delerium DELC 0002
This was issued on black studio tape but had printed label on side 1. The booklet differed in that it was A5 photocopied. Approx 200. There may be some of this run with the A4 booklet.

Love Death and Mussolini

1990   Private pressing
This came on black studio tapes with an A4 booklet and features 2 tracks unavailable elsewhere. Approx 10 copies.

The Nostalgia Factory

1990   Private pressing
This was issued on standard/black studio tape and came with an A4 booklet with Red/Black text. Approx 10 copies only

1991   Delerium DELC 0003
This was issued on black studio tape and came with the same booket as the private pressing. This run can be distinguished by the silver pen writing on the cases – there is no

printed label on the cassette. Approx 200. There may be some of this run with the A5 booklet.

1991   Delerium DELC 0003
This was issued on black studio tape but had printed label on side 1. The booklet differed in that it was A5 photocopied. Approx 200. There may be some of this run with the A4 booklet.

I hope you find those elusive copies if you are after them and get true originals!

Porcupine (Family) Tree

The Incredible Expanding Mindf*** 1 1973

Formed to play at The Festival of Expanding Consciousness in Paris. Album "Ectoplasm Spasm" 1975

Solomon St Jemain *Guitar/Vocals*
Montague Spyglass *Drums*

The Incredible Expanding Mindf*** 2 1976-77

Double live album "My Head Has Not Become A Cricket Pitch (But is Flying To Venus As We Speak). 1976. Tour Germany and France.

Solomon St Jemain *Guitar/Vocals*
Montague Spyglass *Drums*
Tommy Hamater *Keyboards/Flute*
Nivag Paules *Bass*

Band breaks up

The Incredible Expanding Mindf*** 3 1981

After travelling in Africa Solomon returns to Paris. The band reform. Album "Music To Blow Your Mind To" 1982 Triple LP. Montague changes his name to Expanding Flan.

Solomon St Jemain *Guitar/Vocals*
Expanding Flan *Drums*
Porcupine Tree *Vocals/Guitar*
Tree deported for use of "dubious substances"

The Incredible Expanding Mindf*** 4 1983

Due to Trees deportation the band have to work together by swapping tapes (Flan and Solomon are broke and have no passports). As The Incredible Expanding Mindf*** they produce an album "To Darling Lizzie A Noble Cardboard Box" and a solo Porcupine Tree LP "I Proclaim Myself God!" 1985. Tree was helped by a bass player who was staying at his house called Mr Jelly.

Solomon St Jemain *Guitar/Vocals*
Expanding Flan *Drums*
Porcupine Tree *Vocals/Guitar*
Mr Jelly *Bass*
Porcupine Tree 1 1986 – March 1987

Flan and Solomon finally get enough money to emigrate to England. This combines with Tree inheriting money from a deceased relative and purchasing an 8 track studio. Unreleased cassette "Cream Cakes For Everyone". They tour the UK and the bootleg LP "Stoned Hedge" probably dates from this period.

Solomon St Jemain *Guitar/Vocals*
Expanding Flan *Drums*
Porcupine Tree *Vocals/Guitar*
Mr Jelly *Bass*
Sir Tarquin Underspoon *Keyboards*

Porcupine Tree 2 April 1987-8

Live performances begin and Sebastian added. The band play Glastonbury. 19.8.87 French radio broadcast. Part of "Love Death and Mussolini" completed. "Tarquin's Seaweed Farm" is completed but then Jemain is traced by the authorities and deported, so it is not released.

Solomon St Jemain *Guitar/Vocals*
Expanding Flan *Drums*
Porcupine Tree *Vocals/Guitar*
Mr Jelly *Bass*
Sir Tarquin Underspoon *Keyboards*

Sebastian Tweetle Blampton – *Engineer/mixer*

Porcupine Tree 3 July 1988 – Summer 1990

Due to Jemain's deportation, band temporarily give up live work and finish work on "Love Death and Mussolini". "Tarquin's Seaweed Farm" is reworked with extra musicians contributing.

Solomon St Jemain *Guitar/Vocals*
Expanding Flan *Drums*
Porcupine Tree *Vocals/Guitar*
Mr Jelly *Bass*
Sir Tarquin Underspoon *Keyboards*

Timothy Tadpole Jones *Acoustic Guitar/Percussion*
Timothy Masters *Oboe/Cor Anglais*

Sebastian Tweetle Blampton – *Engineer/mixer*
Porcupine Tree 4 – Summer 1990 – December 1991

Tree takes over more instrumental duties and guests are called in to begin extra material to add to "Love Death and Mussolini" to produce "The Nostalgia Factory" released in 1991.

Porcupine Tree *Vocals/Guitar*
Solomon St Jemain *Guitar/Vocals*
Expanding Flan *Drums*
Michael France *Piano*
Sebastian Tweetle Blampton – *Engineer/mixer*

Porcupine Tree Spring 1996 Tour

What follows is a progression of the Spring gigs in '96. This is based upon comments received from various sources.

The tour began with support (or Special Guests, which sounds better) to Gong and Marillion. The first of these at Manchester University (April 4) turned into a bit of a disaster. First the equipment was delayed and only turned up minutes before going on stage. Then they were effectively chucked offstage after 30 minutes thinking they had an allotment of 45 minutes and to cap it all Steven broke 2 strings.

Still it was not all bad news as the people who were there, although disappointed at the short set still thought they put on a good show.

Onto Bath (6 April). This open air event went down extremely well and fans travelled from the continent just to see the Tree. The time allocation was increased and I believe they suitably impressed the audience.

The Forum 12 April 1996
(by Steve Freight)

Porcupine Tree continue to grow in stature following this, possibly their best live performance to date, as special guests to Gong.

On top form were Lead Guitarist and Vocals; Steve Wilson, Keyboards; Richard Barbieri, Bass; Colin Edwin, and on Drums giving the best drumming exhibition I have seen since Keith Moon, Chris Maitland. Chris really seemed to be enjoying himself out there and I was asked by one person in the audience if they had got a new drummer! Keep it up Chris and while you are enjoying drumming the rest of us certainly enjoy listening to and watching you.

I am not sure what they played a fortnight later with Marillion but I believe this is the last time this particular set of songs will be played in this manner.

The evening was delayed from the advertised start and I believe this did Porcupine Tree no harm at all as a fairly large crowd had gathered for the start of their set.

I noticed that a number of people in the audience were talking at the start of the gig but by the time they were halfway through they had stopped and were enjoying the Band. Some people I met had never heard them before but were asking me by the end what discs were available – converts all.

Opening up with The Sky Moves Sideways then proceeding onto Radioactive Toy with

Steven Wilson
Colin Edwin

Steve introducing it thus "Thank you very much, good evening. We are Porcupine Tree this is Radioactive Toy."

After another brilliant rendition of this Steve proceeded to ask for a show of hands – "I'm rather curious, how many of you guys were at the show with the Ozric Tentacles just before Christmas? (loud cheers indicating the majority). You'll probably realise we've put the same set together. Actually this is one we didn't do that time. This is going to be the new single. This is about someone who bides their time, and bides their time and bides their time until there is no time left to bide. This is called "Waiting".

After Waiting a very spirited version of Signify follows – I just love this track live and can't wait for the Album. Then no chat but straight into Voyage 34 and despite it's length, it's over far too quickly.

A brilliant gig and I can now look forward to The Garage in May and I'd also like to thank Colin for taking the time to have a chat after the gig.

The following review first appeared in WONDROUS STORIES the Journal of the Classic Rock Society (they are arranging the event on 27 September in Rotherham – Rotherham Rocks '96). The magazine is full of all things progressive (published monthly) and annual subscription is only £13 and for this discounts are available on tickets for concerts they organise. To subscribe write to Terry Craven, 34 Hungerhill Road, Whiston, Rotherham, South Yorks S60 4BB. Cheques should be made payable to Classic Rock Society. I can highly recommend it.

Leadmill Sheffield 21 May 1996
(by Jill Douglas / Martin Hudson)
(Mr Hudson's Birthday)
by Jill Douglas / Martin Hudson

Thought you might like a review of Sheffield on the great occasion of your birthday, Martin, in case you couldn't remember anything about it, not that I'm implying you were pissed you understand! So, the Birthday Bunny brought Porcupine Tree or The Porcs as they are so fondly known! Grey Lady Down were horrified when they found out I called them that, can you believe it, GLD moralistic! So I asked Steve Wilson if he objected and he said that they'd called themselves porkers for years. That aside, they are quite stunning live. Jasper's Fruit Salad lights add just the right atmosphere to what is essentially space rock. Steven Wilson has said that his mission is to drag prog rock into the 90's and in my opinion he has accomplished it. He is aided in his travels by the very talented Richard Barbieri with his textural keyboards. If you listen to the album Rain Tree Crow which were Japan by another name in 1991, you can see the germination of what is now Porcupine Tree despite the fact that Steven was solely Porcupine Tree for the first few recordings. Perhaps that is why they get on so well together, they both appear to be on the same wavelength. I once asked a very famous bass player why he did not play his fretless bass on stage and he told me that it was too difficult. Colin Edwin manages it admirably in the rather challenging lights of Jasper. I think that speaks for itself. I was in the pit at the Marillion gig taking photos and went in before my fellow snappers to take some shots of the Porcs, so I was privileged to have an excellent view of Chris Maitland on the drums. He is awesome, an absolutely stunning drummer, jaws on the floor job.

The title track of the latest album, The Sky Moves Sideways, is the sort of song that combines all that is best from Porcupine Tree, brilliant. Waiting, which they did the tour to promote, is very short by Porcupine Tree standards and should have been on a bigger label. It would have been enormous. They performed The Nostalgia Factory from an earlier album and Moonloop which was brought out on an EP. Very spacey, phew! Dislocated Day is a big crowd pleaser and features to my delight what a friend of mine terms "motorbike guitars". As a Threshold fan that is right up my alley! The Moon Touches Your Shoulder and Always Never are two more atmospheric well rounded tracks and Up The Downstair to me sums up the whole ethos of Porcupine Tree. The encore was of course Voyage 35, an epic of Brian and his rather unfortunate encounter with LSD. This will always be a Porcupine Tree classic, 34 minutes long too! They finished at Sheffield with my, at present all time favourite, Radioactive Toy, from the first CD. I say at present because I heard them play Signify at Leicester, the title track from their new album due for release in the autumn. It is a total stunner, very, very, heavy. Rotherham will not know what has hit them! Well done for getting them. And just to prove Mr Hudson was not pissed (well, not totally, anyway) here is his review of that wonderful night.
What a birthday present, my first sighting of Porcupine Tree live and I wasn't at all disappointed. I think it was Dave Robinson who first pointed me in the direction of this eclectic outfit as he raved about them. Raved as in the enthusiastic sense and certainly not in the ecstatic and sweaty dance circuit sense as the music of Porcupine Tree moves from progressive through dance and on to or into psychedelia. In fact the music can be whatever you want it to be – even 'kosmic'! As colourful and hypnotic patterns travelled around the ear of the stage Steven Wilson began to get that errie Gilmour feel out of his guitar while

almost hiding behind his long hair. The Sky Moves Sideways became an appropriate anthem and was played to perfection. The pace of the music became frenetic and then dies away almost without you noticing as Wilson's sidekick Richard Barbieri on keyboards holds the key to the sound waves. The atmosphere at a Porcupine Tree gig is different to the midstream prog-rock gig as you can almost taste the music before you feel it – not the sort of music to do the hovering to but more like that to which you can close your eyes and drift with the beat. Rotherham Rocks '96 will see Porcupine Tree headline the first evening and after Credo and Landmarq we are certainly in for a wonderful musical journey from about 9:30pm through to the close. Don't miss them!!

The Garage – London 24 May 1996 (By Guy Thomas)

Having only seen Porcupine Tree headline once, (at the Old Trout, last May) and do a couple of support slots, there was no way that I was going to miss this show.

I arrived early at the venue, in time to see the soundcheck, which involved lots of level testing, but I was treated to a great version of Sky Moves Sideways with nobody else on the floor! I met up with Steve Freight (of Voyage 35 fame!) and photographer/artist John Chase who had also arrived early, just after the soundcheck, whilst I was setting up my video gear, and a few important ales were consumed before the gig started! Another photographer friend of mine, Adrian Arbib, also came along to video the show at the front of the venue. Glen Povey, tour manager, introduced me to Jasper from Fruit Salad Lights, and I set up my gear just behind the lighting rig.

Before the doors opened, Richard Barbieri came over for a chat, and we talked about the video that I had filmed at the Old Trout last year, and he kindly offered his encouragement to "Voyage 35". I said hello to Steve Wilson, and he confided the set list and set times

Colin Edwin

with me, so that I could change camera tapes at the right moment etc.

At 7:30pm, the doors opened, and people started to come into the venue, and by 8:00pm

Steven Wilson Colin Edwin

we were treated to support band: Dr Didge. They are a guitar and didgery-doo based band, who produce some excellent rhythmical-trance style music, with huge influences from the Aussie Outback. Lots more beer was consumed in preparation for the main act, and Richard Allen from Delirium came across to say hello. Gradually the audience fills up to a good size.

At last, at 9:30pm, the moment that we had all been waiting for had arrived, the house lights dimmed, and almost unnoticed through the crowd cheering, the first few instrumental bars of Idiot Prayer emerge from the stage, with Chris accompanying gently from his drum kit. Steve's first few chords erupt from the middle of the stage, complimented by a visual bombardment from Jasper. This is a new track that I haven't heard before, and I believe (and hope) that it will be on the forthcoming album – Signify. The song develops into a really good rhythmically driving piece. It is heavily guitar filled, and Steve produced some excellent slide guitar along with, as ever, first class lead guitar. I hate to compare to the Floyd, but Steve's playing has more than a touch of Gilmour influence here, however, I think he gets away with it well, as a guitar genius on his own right.

Idiot Prayer winds down and amidst the crowd cheering, the familiar intro to The Sky Moves Sideways – Phase 1 is all around. Steve starts on the vocal, accompanied by Richard's lingering keyboards and the song builds up that great feeling of well-being, which I always experience when I hear the track. The tempo of the piece picks up with Colin's faultless fretless basswork, Jasper matches the music with equally frenetic strobes. The end of Phase 1 brings huge approval from the audience. Steve: "Thank you. I'd like to thank you all for coming. I can only apologise for us taking this long to getting 'round to doing a proper London show of our own, but these fabulously wealthy rock bands keep ringing us up and inviting us to support them. "Lots of cheering. Steve continues: "I

wouldn't mind doing a quick show of hands. Who found out about Porcupine Tree, when they saw Hawkwind?" One person responds. Steve continues: "Ozric Tentacles?" Long silence. Steve: "Gong…(pause)…and, Steve Hogarth's not allowed to vote for this one, Marillion?" Bigger response. Steve: "Marillion has it then. This is the new single. This is called Waiting". Lots of approval from the crowd, and Chris starts the drum intro to the track. This song seems to have evolved a bit from when I first heard it at Brixton, back in October, and the overall sound seems a bit fuller. Maybe, having played the single a lot and being familiar with it, is the reason why. The light show here reflects the mellow mood of the song. We seem to be bathed in an aura of soft green and blue light, but the projection of a huge pair of eyes above the band is rather striking. Steve's lead guitar work seems to blend with wave upon wave of soothing synth from Richard.

Lots of applause and some shouts "Fade away" from the audience. Steve: "Thank you. Fade away is unfortunately not one we do. I didn't want you to hurt your throats shouting for it all night!" (I detect a touch of Ian Anderson, of Tull, style humour here!). "This is something off the first album. It's called "The Nostalgia Factory." The crowd delivers its huge approval as the track begins. Chris counts in: "One two three four, as the drum accompanied keyboard line starts. Colin is already slapping on some meaty bass, holding up the back bone of the song, as Steve takes up the guitar. When Steve starts on the vocal, it is quite a departure from the original recording. He sings a harmonised line in a different register to the album version, and I personally think that it's a great success. Richard's keyboards really do fill out the sound here to help evolve the track into the powerful version that was delivered. Lots of wah-wah axe work and at times, the synths line is almost sitar influenced. This really is one of the highlights of the gig.

As Nostalgia Factory reaches its climax, Moonloop has already started, over the cheering. This is one of those great progressive tracks, which lulls you into a trance, with a really warm glow, induced by ghostly lead guitar, with Colin's bass and Chris' drumming holding the riff. The feel-good factor is well and truly in place for the duration, and

Steven Wilson_Colin Edwin

gradually, almost imperceptively, consciousness is restored as the tempo and volume are piled on to the huge crescendo finish. That finish must be one of the definitive Porcupine Tree trade marks!

Lots of cheering and requests for all sorts of songs and after the applause dies down a bit; Steve: "Ok, there's something you people here should know; we have a thing called a set list, and we've already written it, so nothing you say, is going to make us change it!" "He laughs with the crowd. (More wit – Steve is enjoying himself tonight!). He continues "And I know from our set list that the next track is Dislocated Day."

When I hear this track, live or on CD, I always get a certain pang of anguish. It's almost masochistic audible pleasure, and tonight's rendition was no exception. Steve's vocals seem to be calling out to the very core of our souls – the way he delivers the song is almost like someone's distant cry of help for salvation from the very stuff of Chaos. Its inclusion in the set list seems to correct the emotional balance back towards normality, (or Cosmic Balance for Moorcock fans – the rest of the set so far being the stuff of Law!) setting us up nicely for the remainder of the set.

Dislocated Day ends with Chris' characteristic drum solo and Steve starts the guitar intro to Moon Touches your Shoulder. This is a welcome touch of tranquillity, after the soul-testing of the previous track. Blending in with the lead guitar line is some rather soothing keyboard work from Richard, and in typical Porcupine Tree fashion, the volume and pace of the track slowly, but surely, begins to escalate and as soon as you expect the song to die down for its original relaxed end, the whole thing bursts into Always Never. I still think (as I said in my review in issue 1) that both these tracks are far superior when run together, than when played separately.

Steve doodles a bit with his guitar between songs. I thought for a moment that he was going to break into Hurry on Sundown, but he announces: "We're going to finish off with a track called Radioactive Toy" to the audiences obvious pleasure. Richard takes up the keyboard intro, with Chris delicately keeping pace on the cymbal. Steve joins in quietly with his guitar as not to drown out the beautiful keyboard line, before starting on the familiar lyrics. The track develops in its usual style, but towards the middle, there is some excellent improvisation, with Colin's fretless bass playing taking the foreground. This is one of those tracks that I hope will remain part of the live set for a very very long time. It is such a blend of different styles of playing to make it timeless. The track reforms around Steve's guitar chords. Steve: "Thanks for coming, see you another time.....cheers". The band leave the stage.

After a few minutes of cheering, they return to the stage and Steve announces: "Ok, we're going to do our extremely radio-friendly single, Voyage 34". Lots of shouting from the floor as Steve follows up with: "That was irony, by the way." He really is on fine form! Anyhow, the backing tape starts for the intro to the encore: "This remarkable, sometimes incoherent transcript, illustrates a phantasmagoria of fear, terror, grief, exaltation and finally, breakdown." The eerie synth instrumental starts the track off as Chris and Steve pick up the main riff. Colin infills with the bass line, and the whole thing develops into a version of the song more similar to Voyage 34 Remodelled than the original vinyl release. Without realising it, the song has reached its end: "This young man, never had a bummer in some 33 LSD trips, everything was a delight, everything under control. He had only to snap his fingers and down he came, but on Voyage 34, he finally met himself, coming down an up-staircase, and the encounter was crushing".

Lots of noise from a really receptive audience and we really think that it is all over when without warning the band reappear on stage and Steve announces: "We are changing the set 'cos we didn't plan to do this. It has gone down rather well when we've played it. Hope it's the same for you its called Lynton Samuel Dawson." Massive crowd approval! With a huge chord crunching Steve gets it rolling and Jasper hs gone completely wild with the lights. Every strobe mimics the furious pace of this rendition of the song and the stage is a sea of light. Steve starts on the vocal, which he sings in his regular voice, unlike the octave-ed album version. I always thought that the album release was just a bit of a pop song, but the way it was delivered tonight blew any thoughts of that away! It was played really very powerfully in overdrive, and all the better for it. A really good way to finish a fantastic evenings performance. Suddenly, without warning, the track hits a chaotic climax and Steve announces: "See you next time, good night". This time it really is the end, as the house lights come on and the house DJ takes over the use of the PA. it's 11:00pm and we've just experienced 90 minutes of brilliant performance, so good that it seems as though only half an hour has gone by – oh well, we'll just have to wait for the next show!

I met up again with Steve (Freight) and John and were all a bit numbed after the performance. Both of them got some great photos. Another beer was consumed, and the only thing left to do, to nicely round off the evening was for Adrian and I to retire to the nearest Indian restaurant for a large vindaloo – and more beer.

And so onto

Cambridge Boat Race 26 May 1996 (by Simon Clarke)

Call us sad, mad or trainspotters, but for my girlfriend and I this was our eighth gig on this mammoth tour and what a gig to end on.

The Boat Race is a small venue and looks as if it has capacity for about 200 – it appeared to be at least three-quarters full. After an interesting intro tape (unique to this gig) of such bizarre music as The Pink Panther and Black Beauty themes! The intro tape to 'Idiot Prayer' started. The band entered and the dry ice enveloped us – instant atmosphere! This track is going to be one of the standout tracks on the 'Signify' album. Something more familiar followed in the form of 'Sky Moves Sideways' which is possibly my favourite live track – it totally eclipses the studio version. During the 'Wire The Drum' section of this track Chris Maitland proves conclusively that he is one of the best drummers on the planet combining the energy of a Keith Moon with the discipline required to play to click tracks. Steven asks us if we enjoyed the intro tape commenting that he thinks the Black Beauty theme is superior to Oasis! Top Man! After the customary airing of the criminally ignored 'Waiting' single we have a change in the set as 'Dislocated Day' is shunted around to make room for some surprises later on. It's during this track that Colin Edwin makes his fretless bass talk to us – strange sounds that I've never heard from any other four stringed instrument – wonderful stuff.

After this white hot burst of energy we have chance to chill out to the trance-like first half of the classic 'Moonloop'. At times like this, engulfed in dry ice being fed with dazzling images to a soundtrack of perfection, Porcupine Tree take you somewhere no other band ever will. Sheer bliss!! Steven comments "Unfortunately during that number Richard

Barbieri did in fact discover the bogus set list that had been planted consisting entirely of Japan numbers, so he doesn't know this is the next track."

'The Moon Touches Your Shoulder' begins and it's so great on this particular night to hear virtually no talking from the attentive audience as the delicate introduction to this track unfolds. The track dovetails perfectly into 'Always Never' – its always amusing to see the reaction of peoples faces when they realise this songs sneaky introduction!

Then came the first surprise of the evening when Steven introduced the next track as "something that started out sounding like some kind of Kraut rock band and ended up sounding like Metallica" – it was of course the pounding 'Signify'. The fax that a group of us sent to the venue earlier in the day seemed to have had the desired effect as it was a "doctored" setlist with a couple of additional tracks – 'Signify' was one of them – thanks guys! Next up was the classic "Radioactive Toy" this performance being notable for Steven forgetting the words and singing "la-di-da" instead.

"We're gonna do something we haven't done for a long, long time" says Steven. Time for the second suggestion on our cheeky fax – 'Not Beautiful Anymore' – what an absolute killer riff and sounding excellent considering zero rehearsal time. It could only be 'Voyage 34' next although some of the audience only realised what was being played when the distinctive guitar intro started. Then it was will they, won't they time. Yes – time for the zany 'Linton Samuel Dawson' to rear his head again – the perfect manic end to one of the best 'Tree gigs we've ever seen.

That's the end of the tour reviews except for another piece taken from Wondrous Stories (August 96 edition which also features an interview with Steve Wilson):-

Baltimore "Progscape '96" 29 June (by Matthew O'Grady)

This, of course, was the band many of us had come to see. Steven Wilson and the band had made their US debut a few days before at a record company showcase in New York, but this was the first chance for any of the real US fans to see Porcupine Tree. Unfortunately the band had been unable to bring this fabled light show with them, and the DAT recording of their sound effects was left behind in the hired tape machine in New York! This meant that the band had only their music and the strength of their own performance with which to win over the audience. To say that they rose to the challenge admirably would be an understatement – most people I spoke to during the festival cited Porcupine Tree as the highlight. There was an enjoyable sprinkling of old and new in the set – 'The Sky Moves Sideways', 'Burning Sky' and 'Dislocated Sky' being highlights. To introduce the new single, Steven told us that "Frank Zappa once asked, "What's new in Baltimore?" – the answer is Porcupine Tree's new single 'Waiting'. Quote of the festival. The encore was the title track of the new album 'Signify' which augurs well for the autumn release we are promised.

Love Death And Porcupine Tree (by Phil Harwood)

Part 3 – Love Death and Mussolini

Love Death and Mussolini was a limited edition cassette only available direct from Steve Wilson at his No Mans Land address. According to him he duplicated only about 10 copies, mainly for magazine reviews (I was lucky in that I obtained mine direct). Like Tarquin's Seaweed Farm it was on a generic blank cassette with a black and white photocopy insert. Below the words "Porcupine Tree play" was a piano and below the piano was "The Love Death and Mussolini EP". The back of the cassette had the No Mans Land address and a musical stave.

As we know the first side became part 1 of "The Nostalgia Factor". Side 2 was "No Luck with Rabbits", "Begonia Seduction Scene", both going to form part of the Nostalgia Factory.

Then comes "Out", an 8.55 piece allegedly recorded live on 14/7/89 in Paris and overdubbed/re-mixed in the studio in October '89. (Please note this track is called Out and not One as shown in the last issue of Voyage 35. I think this mistake is due to a typographical error on my part in a letter I wrote to Steve Freight).

It appears that some of the Delerium copies of Tarquin's Seaweed Farm had part of Out duplicated accidentally on the end of the tape as an unlabelled bonus track that ends in mid flow as the tape runs out. As Steve said in the last Voyage 35 this sounds very "Hawkwindish". I'm not a great Hawkwind collector but to my ears it sounds like the "X In Search of Space"/"Doremi Faso Latido" Hawkwind sound. Tree intones lines like "Darkness! Get out of my head!" over and over, the words slurring into each other with that characteristic Hawkwind style ending the chant with "Darkness!".

The final track was "It Will Rain For A Million Years" but this is a different song from the one that appeared on "The Nostalgia Factory". It runs for 4.08 minutes and is a strange song with muffled lyrics, all of which I can't make out, but there are lines like "Hello dewdrop" and "There's nothing left to take. The telephone carriage has returned to take the words I do, I do, I do love you. It's raining, raining". The drums beat out the hypnotic sound of rain as Tree says "and the rain falls down". The piece builds and builds until the storm breaks with Tree intoning the rhyme "Rain, rain go away come back another day" as the song ends.

The Love Death and Mussolini booklet was 3 x A4 sheets.

Sheet 1 introduced the EP.
"Here then are 3 songs and 2 instrumentals from the Band Porcupine Tree".
This was the material on side 1 of the cassette.

It was pointed out that an EP was and had lots of italicised passages eg: talking of the additional side 2 material, which seems to have been added as an afterthought.

"This (the addition of this material) is known as *Value for Money*" and "In the music industry it is known as *marketing*".

It continued

"Do your accounting to the sound of *Porcupine Tree*"

It appears Steve was making shrewd observations of the music biz!

Sheet 2 was the details of Side 1 The Extended Player. The songs were listed and then the performers as:
Porcupine Tree – Vocal, electric and acoustic guitars, bass.
Sir Tarquin Underspoon – Organ, mellotron, keyboards
Expanding Flan – Drums, Percussion
Solomon St Jemain Glissando – guitar and vocals on Queen Quotes Crowley
JC Camillioni – Programming, Soundscapes
All tracks were recorded at No Mans Land and Periscope Station in spring/summer 1989. It was shown as being produced by JC Camilioni and Porcupine Tree for Hidden Art.

Sheet 3 was info on the "Extra Material". "No Luck With Rabbits" was shown as being recorded in Spring 1989 at the Periscope Station. The entire sound content was a recording of a musical box that had been slowed up, reversed, overdubbed and speeded up a number of times to create the final piece.

On the next song, Underspoon allegedly, cranked up his mellotron, while Tree played guitar. "Begonia" was only a fragment from a 4 track demo at Periscope Station in October 1987. I've already mentioned "Out" and finally "It Will Rain" was a No Mans Land October 1989 production. Production credits were as per Side 1.

Finally there was another sheet giving info on the "Exposure" and "Double Exposure" sampler LP's of progressive music on No Mans Land Records. These were released in August 1985 and October 1987 respectively and retailed for £3.50 and £5.50 (plus postage) respectively.

There were no Porcupine Tree tracks but Steve Wilson did appear on these as part of No Man Is An Island Except The Isle of Man group. All the tracks on these LP's were unavailable elsewhere. I only have Double Exposure which is a double LP in a gatefold sleeve with 16 tracks from progressive groups such as Haze, Abel Ganz, Weirdstone, Anthony Philips (guitarist for Genesis early in their career) amongst the line up and is worth checking out if you can find a copy.

Many thanks again Phil. The Nostaliga piece will appear in a future issue. However for an insight into how the booklets line up progressed see the Phil Harwood Porcupine Family Tree elsewhere in this issue. Its fictitious of course (so don't go looking for any of the material mentioned) but as Phil told me he had always enjoyed Pete Frame's Family Trees' and felt he wanted to have a go.

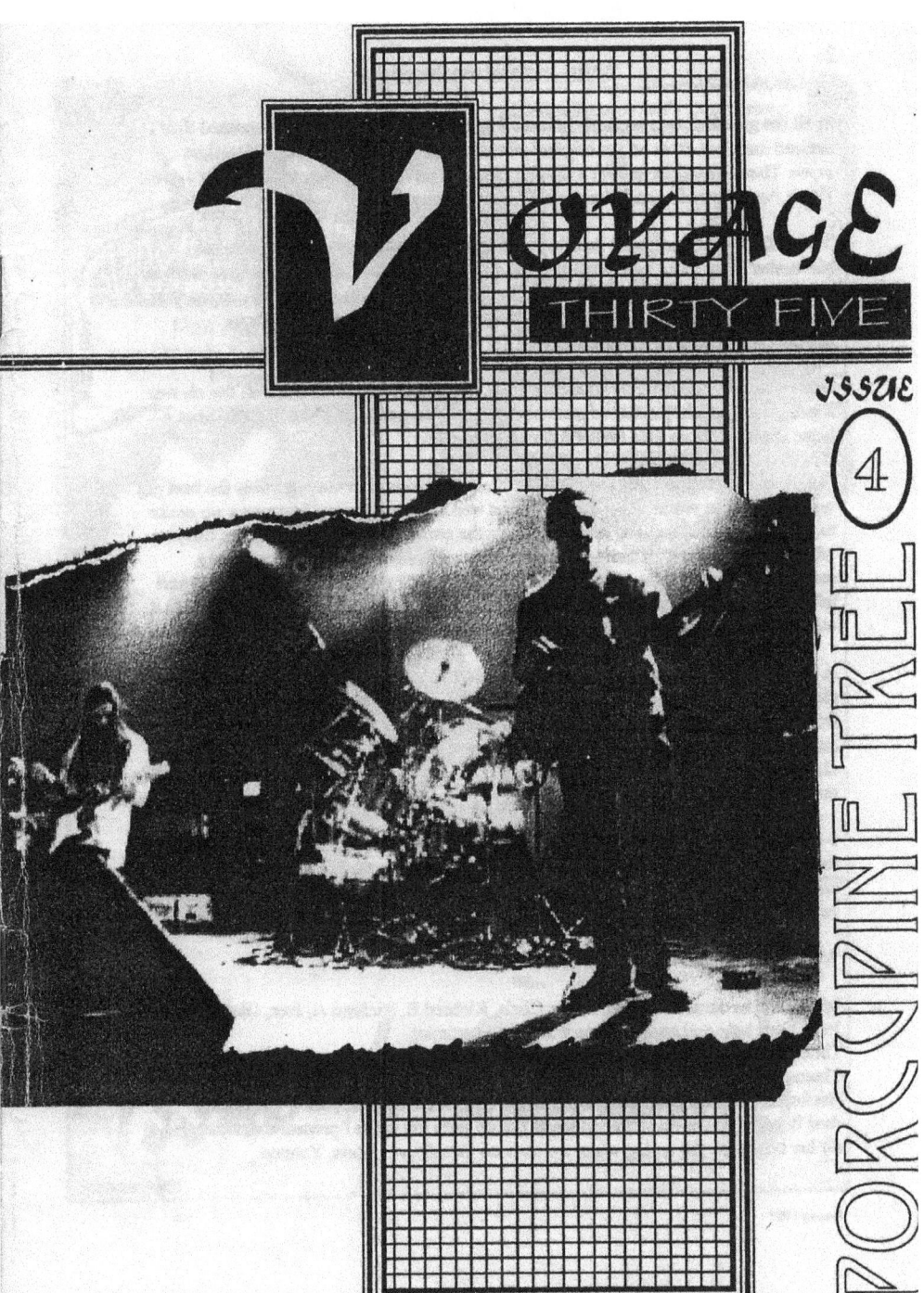

Issue 4

Published January 1997
Original Contents:

The Voyage 35 intro
An exclusive Colin Edwin interview
Love Death And Porcupine Tree part 4 (The Nostalgia Factory)
Information on the Karma Acid Tapes
Gig Review (Zaan Dam Holland 9.2.95)
An Alternative Discography (Porcupine Tree Family Members solo output
      and collaborations)
Radio 1 Session - 30 January 1995
Porcupine Tree Stage Plan

Record Collector said:
The 24 page fourth issue devoted to the psychedelic/progressive gurus, contains the final part of a study of their early tapes and a focus on a Radio 1 session.

Welcome To Issue 4

I'll start this issues reminisces with a couple of extracts from the welcome page.

You will be aware no doubt that Record Collector feature Porcupine Tree in the November issue and a well written piece as well. Now you know exactly what there is out there and what you need to complete your collection (lots of cash!). I suggest you also see Message From a Self Destructing Turnip for appearances on those innumerable magazine mounted CD's.

Due to circumstances I only managed to get to Cambridge this time round, but oh was it good! I was again pleased to meet a number of you and would like to quote from a letter I received from Pete Millar following the gig:-

"My wife and I came away from the gig totally awe-struck. It was probably the best gig we've been to in years! What also struck us was the friendliness of everyone we spoke to, there was a real sense of family amongst the crowd. It is still a feeling I'm carrying with me a week later". This is a common comment I hear and I hope it will long remain. Pete also says he was impressed with Steven's rapport with the audience and felt this added to the evening. I think the fictitious set lists had something to do with it and they will play the Birdie Song on the next tour!!!

6 days after the Cambridge gig I went to see Jethro Tull and my friend and I queued at the merchandise stall. I was wearing my Signify T-shirt and the guy who was serving pointed at it and said "They're a better band than you are going to see tonight". A very perceptive chap indeed.

Well as they say on with the show.

Colin Edwin Interviewed (by Steve Freight)

SF: Thank you Colin for agreeing to answer the following questions. I'd like to start at the beginning so what are your musical roots and influences? Did you at an early age know you had a musical leaning?

CE: Its difficult to pick out influences. I think it's just as possible to be influenced by a good book, film, painting or sculpture as it is by a piece of music. My family were quite musical, my father played jazz guitar, and my brother is a classical guitarist, my sisters were really into 70s stuff (Police, Chic, Strangers, loads of different stuff) so I probably heard an awful lot of diverse music without realising it. If I had to pick out bass players that I like I'd say: Danny Thompson (particularly on the early John Martyn records), Robbie Shakespear, Bill Laswell, Percy Jones, Mike Howlett (from Gong), but really there's loads of people I like to listen to who play all different instruments too.

SF: You are known for playing the bass. Can you play other instruments and if so what?

CE: Yes, I play electric bass (mostly frestless) and double bass (big violin type thing), which can be heard on a few P Tree tracks) I also dabble with keyboards and guitar, but generally I like low notes.

SF: what other groups have you been a member of and are there any recordings available or which were made that we should look out for?

CE: None worth mentioning.

SF: It has been stated that you are a lifelong friend of Steve's. When did you first meet and have you previously played in any band together before?

CE: I met Steve a long time ago through school and I guess both of us have a large appetite for listening to different types of music so we're always had that in common Before Porcupine Tree, we'd never worked on a project together but had jammed a few times with various people, and recorded a few tracks together.

SF: How did you come to be approached to play in Porcupine Tree?

CE: Steve asked me, seemed like a good idea at the time!

SF: How do you see the band progressing? Will you be writing any material for recording?

CE: Hopefully, we'll reach more people, play a lot more countries. As far as the music goes, I'll be just as interested to see what happens. I'd really like the band to develop it's own distinctive sound, which is still flexible, to me all the best bands have this ability, they can change and yet still sound like themselves, Led Zepplin are a really good example, instantly recognisable, yet they didn't just keep making the same record over and over again.

SF: What instruments/equipment do you use in the studio and live environment? If they differ, why?

CE: I use mainly a Wal fretless bass, live I go through a couple of really old bass pedals (an octave and a phaser) and into a Trace Elliott amp. It's best not to get too hung up about equipment really as far as I can tell I've used all kinds of amps and I'll basically use what I can get, once you start paying lots of money for amps, there's little difference.

In the studio I play my bass straight into the desk. Wal basses have great electronics, and you can get all different types of tones from them, so I don't feel I need lots of effects.

If I record the double bass, I use a combination of pick-up (bridge mounted) and microphone to get a decent sound the pick-up on it's own is too buzzy and trebly, but the mike on it's own doesn't give enough punch for me, so it's important to get a good balance.

SF: Not being a musician myself I find any instrument difficult to play. I am told by a number of people who do play that the fretless bass is difficult to play at the best of times and that they are surprised of (and admire) your use of it on stage. How do you feel about this?

CE: Yes, fretless bass can be more difficult to play, purely because if you can't hear yourself or you slip up you run the risk of sounding hideously out of tune. But for me, the extra effort/concentration is worth it, as you can do all kinds of expressive things without frets. Also after playing double bass, electric is slightly easier for me!

SF: Who do you listen to these days for pleasure?

CE: I listen to lots of music, here's a brief selection of fave albums; John Paul Jones & Diamonds Galas 'Sporting Life', Ben Harper 'Fight for your Mind', Ozric Tentacles 'Strangeitude', Faith No More 'King for a Day', Ahrad 'Ahrads Blues'. I also like Material, Killing, Joke, Gong, Tackhead, Magazine and I have lots of obscure eastern music and jazz too. There really is lots of good stuff about if you want to find it.

SF: You've changed your image from the first gig. Why?

CE: The first Porcupine Tree gig was nearly 3 years ago! Lots has happened to me since then, growing a bear is just one!

SF: You appear to be very relaxed on stage and interacting with the audience. Do you get a kick from this? We certainly appreciate it!

CE: I generally enjoy playing live a lot. I think also a lot of the Porcupine Tree material is stronger live, when it can be presented properly in an atmospheric environment. I really like what Jasper does too, he 'jams' along to what we do taking what we do sonically into a visual thing. I often can't really see the audience, but it's good to get a response – no-one wants to do a gig to a waxwork audience.

SF: Are you involved with any collaborations outside of Porcupine Tree and if so what?

CE: Yes I have a couple of things I'm doing outside of Porcupine Tree at the moment, a project with a vocalist friend of mine, and also recording some of my own ideas, which may or may not be suitable for Porcupine Tree.

SF: Well please let us know what the outcome of these ventures are Colin, and thank you for taking the time to answer these questions – it is much appreciated.

Porcupine Tree Sounds Old-Fashioned And Modern

Always one exception to the rule of no reviews from other publications. I was sent one in Dutch luckily with a translation – here is the translation (SF2020).

English guitar/keyboard player and singer Steven Wilson is already a couple of years experimenting. Wilson melts influences from the symphonic seventies pop, the early Pink Floyd and synethesists as Tangerine Dream and Klaus Schulze, with pieces of heavy guitar rock with blues lines and hallucinating dance rhythms. At Drieluik Thursday evening the result sounded live remarkable: both old-fashioned and modern.

Last year the modest songwriter paid only one visit to Holland (Uden) with his band Porcupine Tree. Guest musician then was Richard Barbieri, former keyboard player in once worldwide known pop group Japan (with singer David Sylvian). In the meantime Barbieri has become a regular member of Porcupine Tree and can be heard on the recent, third album The Sky Moves Sideways. The tour to promote the album in Holland (four concerts) by the unknown quartet started in Zaandam. Due to the excellent sound in the venue and a effective lightshow the band also on stage catches your attention. With a stroboscope and liquid projections the music is put into a psychedelic atmosphere. In spite of Wilson's lengthy compositions, they continue to grip the audience by the right turns at the right moments.

Bass player Colin Edwin (barefoot and dressed in a kind of pyjama) and drummer Chris Maitland make up the heavy and sometimes swinging rhythm section. Wilson switches from tuneful screaming playing to cunning rhythms and beautiful wah-wah pedal play. Barbieri produces one soft glossy sound-picture after another and does moreover known how to handle samples, sequencers and more of those tricks to move the listener comfortably to another world.

Porcupine Tree is not particularly the wild raving rock and roll band. Taste, craftsmanship and pure musical talent can do without the hotch-potch. What matters is will there be a breakthrough and will Barbieri stay with the group? He did co-operate with Sylvian on his solo albums and released together with Tim Bownes the hardly known "Flame". The close musical connections with the 'Japan-mates' might tempt Barbieri.

Ton De Lange (Translated by Leendert Flier)

The Radio 1 FM Sessions (Part 2) (transcribed by Steve Freight).

In Issue 1 I covered the first of the Mark Radcliffe session Porcupine Tree recorded. As with that article I present a transcript of the session broadcast on 30 January 1995 as far as is possible.

The session opens with loud reverberations

Mark Radcliffe (MR): Oh my god, flipping 'eck. How are you?

Steven Wilson (SW): I'm fine thanks

MR: You're reverberating everywhere. We nearly came so close to a disaster of stupendous proportions in show business terms didn't we this evening

SW: We did yes

MR: Because you lost the drummer

SW: Well he likes to make a dramatic entrance, so he did leave it 'til the last minute to say the least

MR: (garbled) he spent an hour (looking?) for egg and chips in Notford(?) Circus. Just to put us all on edge. Anyway you have all turned up. The new album is out…is it actually out next week then?

SW: It's out on February 7th that's next Monday

MR: The Sky Moves Sideways – so you're going to play all stuff, all new stuff?

SW: Mostly yes. We're certainly going to start with a track from that album

MR: OK what are you going to play first for us

SW: This is called The Moon Touches Your Shoulder

MR: oh we played this on Thursday from the record. Here we go. The Porcupine Tree

A brilliant version of this song follows full of harmonies and a blistering guitar solo from Steve

MR: Porcupine Tree performing live on tonight's programme music from the new album, The Sky Moves Sideways, which is out on Delerium next week, Moon Touches Your Shoulder. Three more before the end of the programme.

Following a break for the normal show Mark re-introduces the band:

This is the title track of their new album which comes out next week on Delerium, The Sky Moves Sideways. (*cue the rain*).

Another truly cosmic rendition of the track (phase 1) follows which begins with The Colour of Air sequence and breaks after I find That I'm Not There. Mark then proceeds to interview Steve:-

MR: The Sky Moves Sideways Phase 1, Porcupine Tree, Title track from the new album. We shall be continuing with Phase 2 very shortly. Steve?

SW: Yes

MR: How are you?

SW: I'm fine thanks

MR: Good, alright do the honours, do the introductions

SW: We have Chris Maitland on drums/percussion, Colin Edwin on Bass and the Mantovani of Millwall, Richard Barbieri on keyboards

MR: so what have you been doing since last time? Obviously recording the record and everything (?) I mean you do have the dreaded "prog rock" tag hanging over you, does that mean that converts are kind of...er, people are nervous about admitting to a love of prog rock?

SW: Very much so, I mean, if you remember the last time we were on, I did say that our mission was to drag progressive rock kicking and screaming into the '90s.

MR: Yeah...

SW: That's still very much our mission, although I think that even further up the list now is to get a review in "Q" before we get to our 20th album!

MR: Right....Yeah....!(laughs)

SW: It is very difficult....

MR: People are progressively buying the albums in greater numbers I suppose, with each album that comes out, but what about gigs? It is something that works on a relatively large scale – it doesn't have to be Wembley, but it needs to be sort of concert halls and not the "Rat and 'alf a Shandy" in Cleethorpes, doesn't it really...

SW: Absolutely, yeah.... We now have a UK agent, which is the first time we've ever had that, so we're hoping to be able to step up the gigs in the UK...

MR: Right....

SW: But until now, really, most of the interest has come from Europe as far as live performances is concerned.

MR: I mean, they're not so hung up about the tags and things, are they?

SW: No. The British press have got this thing about progressive rock – we found that even when we have had positive press they basically spend 50% of the time apologising for liking the music...

MR: Yeah...

SW: Which becomes, you know, a little tiresome

MR: Another old friend of this programme, Nick Saloman, The Bevis Frond – doesn't sound like you – but he gets branded progressive rock as well and has suffered for years because of it. I suppose so did the Ozric Tentacles and people like that in their early days – they finally broke through, I suppose.

SW: I think it is partly due to the fact that there have been a lot of bands around who have used the "progressive rock" tag purely as a kind of nostalgia trip and I think that has given it a bit of a band name, um, I'm thinking of some of the bands from the early 80s particularly. It's difficult to convince people that you can play progressive rock and still be very contemporary and, if you like, be progressive in the true sense of the word.

MR: The other thing I remember about you being on last time was during one of the numbers you hit an absolutely spectacular bum note!

SW: It's become famous....

MR: it was fantastic! You should release that version because you went into the blistering guitar solo on the wrong note and then there was this agonised howl...!

SW: A lot of people did assume it was you, actually, Mark, but I have to put it on the record now, being on the air, that that was me and I was aware of the "honker" I'd played!

MR: oh no, it was good! In fact there is a little mini CD thing that goes around which is of

Vinnie Riley of the Durutti Column playing with Morrisey, who hits a spectacular bum note and the whole thing just falls apart... it is a much treasured recording! Anyway right it's nice to have you here again. Are you going to continue with The Sky Moves Sideways?

SW: I should just explain that, to your listeners out there that this piece that we're playing, The Sky Moves Sideways is actually very long and we've split it down to two bite sized chunks for your programme so we're going to pick it up basically from exactly where we left off after a count in from Chris.

We then pick up Phase 1 from Wire The Drum but not the Spiral Circus portion

MR: The Sky Moves Sideways Phase 2, Porcupine Tree. Another song live in the last half hour of the programme.

Then

In session from tonight's guests the Porcupine Tree, again another extract from the Sky Moves Sideways – Is...Not

The first recorded version of this song to feature keyboards instead of Suzanne's vocals and a very good version too. And then – the legendary bum note to finish.

SW: you bottled it

MR: (Laughing): What happened there? It's like someone came into the studio on a space hopper and all sorts of things!

Fits of laughter follows

MR: Anyway it was great up to that point. Is this the traditional strange note from the Porcupine Tree during their sessions. Anyway that was Is...Not another extract from The Sky Moves Sideways, new album on Delerium, out next week. And thanks very much to them and to Smithy on the knobs for that.

This concludes the Tree's sojourns at Radio One to date but they did appear live on BBC Radio Newcastle on 14 May 1996 to promote the gig the following day and during which they performed Waiting and Radioactive Toy.

They have also appeared on radio elsewhere most notably Italy and copies of these sessions are still to surface. They played an acoustic set on one of these (possibly both) and included the excellent Stars Die (the only time I've heard this live was standing in the cold outside the Boatrace in Cambridge when it formed part on the sound-check). I know you, like I am, are very keen, if not desperate to hear these – so if anyone has copies please let me know.

How about a limited release for Transmission subscribers of all of the radio performances to date – it would make a terrific CD.

For the record the tracks played on the sessions were:

Mark Radcliffe – 8 December 1993

Radioactive Toy
Burning Sky Parts 1 & 2 (split in the middle for interview)
Always Never

Mark Radcliffe – 30 January 1995

Moon Touches Your Shoulder
The Sky Moves Sideways Parts 1 & 2 (split in the middle for interview)
Is…Not

BBC Radio Newcastle

Waiting
Radioactive Toy

Love Death And Porcupine Tree
By Phil Harwood

Part 4 - The Nostalgia Factory

My "Nostalgia Factory tape (from Delerium, catalogue number DELC003, a black studio tape with no label, but also with no silver writing on the case, which I believe was a first issue) came with an A5 booklet. The booklet was actually two A4 sheets folded to give A5, each A4 sheet was in either red or black ink to give, when assembled, alternating pages of red and black on each side, except for the middle pages in red and the front and back covers in black. The booklet therefore had 6 pages of text inside the covers.

The cover proclaimed Porcupine Tree play and then in a rectangle The Nostalgia Factory … and other amateur tips for golfers. Inside on Page 1 in red ink, under the heading A Diversion was a short story of Lord Percy Blampton (Dad of Sebastian Tweetle Blampton perhaps? See my family tree in Voyage 35 issue 3 for who Sebastian was). The story is quite bizarre involving Sir Percy's suicide, his ghost, Salman Rushdie, Russ Abott, Fred Astaire… you begin to understand my comment about bizarre! I can not even begin to explain it. Towards the end of the story is a section titled The Nostalgia Factory offering Daily excursions to Inner Space (body optional) and suggesting you tie a piece of piano wire to an Apollo 16 space shuttle!! Not a good idea!

Page 2 gives the song info where the tape is split into 4 sides. These are:

1. *Love, Death and Mussolini* with Hymn/Footprints/Linton Samuel Dawson/And Swallows Dance Above The Sun/Queen Quotes Crowley.
2. *The Nostalgia Factory* with No Luck With Rabbits/Begonia Seduction Scene/Colours Dance Angles Kiss/Pray/Nostalgia Factory.
3. *This Long Silence* with This Long Silence/Sinatra Rape Scene/Hokey Cokey/Landscare/Delightful Suicide.
4. *It Will Rain For A Million Years* with Nine Cats/Split Image/It Will Rain For A Million Years.

Page 3 is The Delightful People Party To The Production where Tree has the main share of instruments (acoustic and electric guitar, flute, bass, keyboards, tamboura, vocals, tape processing and programming) and guest contributors are listed as: The Expanding Flan on drums, Solomon St Jemain on vocals and electric guitar, Michael France (who is credited with co-writing Split Image) on piano and prepared tapes, Alix Straighter for laughter, and Alan Imaginary Duffy as verse butcher. (Alan co-wrote Footprints/Linton Samuel Dawson/And The Swallows Dance Above The Sun/This Long Silence/Colours Dance Angles Kiss/Nine Cats and The Nostalgia Factory).

JC Camillioni gets conducting and production credit at the No Man's Land 16 track, and at the Periscope Station 8 track. Mention is made that some of the music (the Love, Death and Mussolini tracks) were from unproduced 4 track demos retouched at No Mans Land. Sebastian gets an engineers credit and recording date is given as between Summer 1989 and Winter 1991.

Page 4 is Time For The Porcupine Tree to Explain Himself which he does by saying I wanted this (the music) to be a whirling light from the other end of the stars. Tree explains "I like instrumentals" and that he "wanted it to be a double album…in loving memory of Ken Dodd and Donovan. People tell me they're not dead but I know differently". He also mentions that "Begonia Seduction Scene was recorded on his front lawn. The piece ends with I think the next one will be a triple album. Don't you just love triple albums?" Yes, please!

Pages 5 and 6 are Chapter 97 - The Plot Thickens (An update to the unlikely history of Porcupine Tree). This was credited to Andrew Paughley and dated 6.1.1991. It gave a resume of the same historical details of the band as recounted in the Words From A Hessian Sack booklet with Tarquin and taking the story up to The Nostalgia Factory. The release was described as a powerful development in the Porcupine Tree's sound with more emphasis on detail and less on rambling solos (inspired though they were). Tree was quoted as saying "Too many so called modern psychedelic bands reject technology in favour (of) recreating yesterday's sounds. To reject the digital sampler or even the drum machine is to deny the spirit that experimental music should always be made in. These musicians become nothing more than a nostalgia factory". Andrew ends his piece with "The title then, is with tongue firmly in cheek".

The back cover gives the No Man's Land Hemel Hempstead address.

This concludes my look at the booklets, and I hope it has been of interest.

ISSUE 5
VOYAGE
35

FADEAWAY By Lee Wainman

Issue 5

Published March 1997
Contents:
The Voyage 35 intro

An exclusive Chris Maitland interview
The Nostalgia Factory (An A-Z of all songs listed, even the unreleased ones, detailing which albums the various tracks have appeared on and the differences between the Remixed versions from the original tapes)
Retroactive Ploy (past Album Reviews from a time before Porcupine Tree were a band (in other words reviews of Steven's "bedroom" tapes))
Phil Harwood's views on The Early Tapes (Karma & Altamont)
BBC Derby Radio Interview transcript.

Record Collector said:
...up together A5 number weighing in with a head-to-head with drummer Chris Maitland, an A-Z of the groups songs and a look at singer Steven Wilson's pre Porcupine Tree recordings.

Chris Maitland Interviewed (by Steve Freight)

SF: Thank you Chris for taking time out to answer the following questions

Could we start at the beginning with when you first became interested in playing music and were drums/percussion always your first interest? Do you play any other instruments?

CM: I first started playing music with my brother and two sisters. We were taught how to read music and play recorders together by our mother. We would swap around playing descant, treble or tenor parts of Elizabethan ensembles. Then at school we moved on to stringed instruments; my brother, the cello; my two sisters and I the violin. Mum would accompany us on the piano during exams and I reached Grade 5 but gave up as I couldn't improvise on the instrument. When I was eight we all went to see the Syd Lawrence Orchestra playing the Glenn Miller repertoire. We had cheaper seats sat behind the band, but this was far better as my brother and I sat right behind the drums and bass which was very exciting and I could see everything that the drummer was doing. We came home with an LP and I learned all the drumming, practising with kitchen roll tubes on waste bins – one of which was a pedal bin which seemed appropriate! I then started lessons and from then on drums were my first instrument.

SF: Who inspired you and why?

CM: First of all Geoff Myers – playing on that Syd Lawrence LP and Fergie Maynard the then current Syd Lawrence Orchestra Drummer, a short chap with a 'crew cut' and a cheeky grin and a blue sparkle drum kit. The first rock drummer that I came across was Roger Taylor. Queens music in 1974 was so exciting and new and different and he had such a big drum sound and really performed when he played. Phil Collins was next. Genesis music was very intricate and Collins would not only play the rhythm on the kit but also be part of the instrumental focus, as interesting as the keyboard lines. Live, he and Chester Thompson would lead the music, providing both 'cake and icing'. Later came Bill Bradford, Neil Peart and also Tommy Aldridge because of his amazing double bass drums approach and visual tricks.

SF: Have you been a member of any other bands and if so for the completists out there what recorded material is available.

CM: I have been a member of about a dozen other bands and though I treasure all my cassette and videos, very little recorded material is available on CD or vinyl.

SF: I understand you have been a session musician. Do you still continue with this and are there any well known numbers you care to admit to playing on?

CM: I do still continue with this though more for the theatre than anything else. I am the first deputy for the West End show 'Grease' which has been running at the Dominion Theatre where the band was on stage as part of the show. It is now at the Cambridge Theatre where we're in the orchestra pit! There are no well known numbers that I care to admit to playing on – though I was a session musician when I played on No Mans Flowermouth Album and Richard Barbieri's and Tim Bowness' album Flame.

SF: Who do you listen to these days?

CM: I you mean drummers: Simon Phillips, Vinnie Colanita, Manu Katche. If you mean music: mainly classical music, a mixture of sacred choral music; Faure, Durufle, Rutter or romantic period; Rachmaninov, Mahler.

SF: When did you first meet the other members of the band? How were you approached to join?

CM: Through working for No Man. I was the live drummer for the Ultravox tour and the TV appearances on The Beat and the Big E. Steve wanted to create a live unit for his solo project: the rest you guys probably know about already.

SF: How do you see the band progressing?

CM: I know how I would like to see the band progressing. I'd like to see more team writing and creating. I'd like us to develop our visual image and be embraced by the wider commercial scene, and play Wembley Stadium!

SF: Your first band song-writing credit is on Signify. Have you written any others which may appear later and how would you describe these.

CM: Most of the musical ideas I have are either bare sketched drum beat frames or arrangement ideas ie. musical form or chord changes so very little gets finished or developed without being used as part of someone else's 'song-writing'. I intend to complete more and hope they appear later.

SF: I also hear you teach drums. Has anyone of any note passed through your classes?

CM: People known certainly in the business are Jody Linscott (percussionist with the Who, Paul McCartney, Elton John, Tom Jones etc). Dave Larcombe from The Bible, Simon Bishop from Banderas and the original editor of Rhythm Magazine though I've not yet made it into its pages!

SF: If someone wanted to learn how could they contact you?

CM: Through Delerium

SF: You seem to enjoy the live environment. Do you prefer this or working in the studio and why?

CM: To me they are two different disciplines both of which I enjoy. The studio is where I concentrate totally on the emotion and the musical language of the drumming coming over aurally. The playing and mixing of the sounds have to be very precise. Live is more exciting because I can perform the drumming; attaching to the sound the visual expression of the emotion and musical language. If and when this is seen people feed off the live energy, and I get the feedback from the audience – I love it!

SF: In the December gigs you double bassed on drums. Why only for these gigs and not anymore?

CM: I always 'double bass'. Its simply a technical change. To take less drums around, to take up less space, and to ensure evenness of Bass Drum sound and also to free another microphone channel – I have recently been using a double bass drum pedal which means I still play with both feet but the beaters hit only the one bass drum.

SF: Do you enjoy going abroad for "one off" gigs? Do you find them worthwhile?

CM: Yes absolutely! The audiences are larger, much more responsive and they don't talk through the quiet sections! Also the bigger venues have more lighting which can bring across visually the individual performances better.

SF: Thank you Chris for answering these questions – it will be appreciated by all readers, and I totally agree with you about people who talk through gigs – it is most annoying to those who want to listen and savour the moment. Perhaps our continental cousins can teach us something here!

The Early Tapes; A Look At Altamont And Karma
(by Phil Harwood)

Pre Porcupine Tree, Steven Wilson was firstly involved with a release credited to Altamont, and then with two releases with Karma. This article peers into the murky depths surrounding these tapes and attempts to describe them.

In 1983, at the tender age of 15, Steven had been in communication with Alan Duffy and they had a shared interest in Syd Barrett (for younger readers Syd was the original vocalist with the Pink Floyd at the time of the "See Emily Play" single and "Piper At The Gates of Dawn", LP, who was sacked from the group due to his mental state and then went on to make 2 solo LPs "The Madcap Laughs" and "Barrett". Syd eventually became a recluse. (Interested readers are referred to the excellent box set "Crazy Diamond"). This friendship had resulted in Alan writing some lyrics for him. Thus "Prayer for the Soul" by Altamont was conceived with half of the tape with Steven going solo and the other half with assistance from a mysterious Si Vockings on keyboards. Does anyone know who Si was?

The tape was released on the Acid Tapes label run by Alan Duffy under catalogue number TAB004. The tape had a white paper sleeve with Altamont at the top above a wizard figure, with a long beard, casting a lightning bolt from his left hand. Under the wizard was "Prayer For The Soul". The sleeve edge proclaimed Altamont and in small case acid. While Acid Tapes in major case was saved for the back. Inside under:

"a" were:
"Altamont" (Wilson, Vocking)
"Watching Statues" (Wilson)
"The Tell Tale Heart" (Wilson)

And the "b" side was:
"Split Image (Wilson)
"Prayer For the Soul" (Wilson)

Wilson was shown as playing "Electric, acoustic and bass guitar, synthesiser, drums, percussion, vocals and vocoder. While Vocking was credited with "Various devices and keyboards". Lyrics were by Ally (sic) Duffy and production to Steven Wilson between July and September 1983. Cover was by Ian Wilmer. To the best of my knowledge the tape itself was originally with red labels with "acid tapes" printed at the top in a "psychedelic" script. The TAB number and band name on side A, and title on side B, were written on in ink. Later issues were in the same format, but with a green label. The tape is no longer available from Acid Tapes as Steven Wilson asked for it to be deleted, as he was a bit embarrassed by it!

For us collectors however, it is a fascinating insight into the roots of Porcupine Tree and has the appearance of the Tree classic "This Long Silence" as "The Tell Tale Heart" with the lyrics spoken and also "It Will Rain For A Million Years" as "Prayer For the Silence" but in totally different forms.

The song "Altamont" is interesting as it has a line "if you met yourself would you understand?" The idea of meeting yourself would later reappear on other songs. "Split Image" is very much in Tangerine Dream style and much longer, 15 minutes plus, than the Nostalgia Factory version.

For completists "Watching Statues" is still available on an Acid Tape Various Artist compilation called "Everyday Heroes" catalogue number TAB 010.

From an interview in the current issue of the Ptolemaic Terrascope fanzine (issue 21), conducted by Richard Allen of Delerium with Steven Wilson asking questions from the Terrascopes' editor Phil McMullen, Steve reveals that there were other pre-Porcupine Tree recordings with local bands, but unfortunately gives no details. He reveals that he has a vast reservoir of songs which he has no intention of releasing and which are under lock and key with him. For those readers interested in the interview, the fanzine has sold out at source but copies were available from Delerium or from Rustic Rods' Mail-order operation at 24 Linden Close, Calne, Wilts SN11 0BB. Best to write with an SAE first to check if it is still available. Rod also was selling the "Succour" various artists CD which has an exclusive Porcupine Tree track on it.

Anyway for Steve's next appearance, we do have tapes. This was in a group called Karma who produced 2 tapes. The first "The Joke's On You" was recorded in October 1983. The cassette has 2 sleeves available. One, I believe the original early version, had a very crudely produced cover of a grotesque hunchback type character with "Karma" in a gothic script above and below him the title. Karma and the title were repeated on the spine.

The cover I have seen was numbered 33, but as to how many were made, I do not know. Inside was the track listing of:

Side 1
"Intruder D 'or"
"Tigers in the Train"
"Small Fish"

Side 2
"Nine Cats"

The only other info was a Hemel Hempstead (Steve's home patch) telephone number for further info.

The second cover is a more impressive, though still a home-made affair. Karma and the title are printed above a map of the Telford area. The band name and title are repeated on the spine above a catalogue number KM01. An address in Swinton Manchester is given for further info and on the inside the tracks are as per the first issue. More info is given on personnel who were:

Tom Dussek on piano/keyboards
Marc Gordon on percussion
Pete Rowe on bass
Steven Wilson guitars/vocals

Production was by Karma with engineering by Steven and Marc At The Close. Songs were credited to Wilson/Duffy and words to Ally Duffy. Thanks went to Solstice/Gothique? Wheatsheaf/RJ (whoever they were). Again "Small Fish" is still available on an Acid Tape called "Advice From A Caterpillar" catalogue number TAB 022.

"Intruder D'Or" is an instrumental piece clocking in around the 4 minute mark while "Tigers In The Rain" tells the tale of Melvyn Mumpkin who climbed upon a pumpkin (Steve's rhyme not mine!) to watch the tigers in the rain. The piece suffers from the vocals being delivered with Steve's voice being treated and below par production, but there are many elements of the Tree style evident, and memorable lines like "solitude and solitaire". This track is approximately 7 minutes.

"Small Fish" is very similar to the track that appeared on "Up The Downstair" but again suffers from lack of dynamics in the production. The tapes tour do force for me is "Nine Cats" a storming nearly 15 minute version. Around 3 minutes the vocals start with a different, though similar in ideas, verse to how the track starts on the "Sunday of Life" LP. It relates that "A cloud appeared outside my door" and Steve goes on to describe how the caterpillar spoke to him and turned into a butterfly. The one that starts off the song on "Sunday"? That is now a pharaoh. There are extra vocals toward the end, and the track ends with the cats crying and howling.

The second Karma cassette dates from 1985 and is in a more rambling prog vein with only 2 long songs. Though long songs, they do have, in typical Prog fashion, different segments. The first song is "Where Is The End If There Is No Beginning?" This starts with "I'm on an island watching statues" around 5 minutes the phone rings and the tempo changes with bass, drums and synth pounding a catchy refrain. There are a number of catchy lines on this tape. I was reminded of Genesis "Lamb Lies Down" period, especially on the second track, and some of the synth lines sounded very ELP to me. It is less Porcupine Tree sounding than their first tape, but no less interesting for that. The track progresses (no pun intended!) with Steve asking "Where is the end if there is no beginning?" And a heavenly choir takes us to the end at around 9 minutes.

The second "Peace on Earth and Goodwill to Pigs" starts with a thunderstorm, footsteps and someone at the door "Let me in I'm drowning!" they proclaim. Unfortunately the vocals are difficult to make out but lines that did come through were "I'll dry our eyes with tear gas". Comments on human suffering and morality were also in there somewhere.

The thunderstorm starts again and with the sound of screaming we are off into the next section. "The judgement has won" we are told and this segment ends with distant voices, synth rumbles, tinkling percussion and electronic effects. A very ELP synth motif starts and an up section starts till at 15 minutes Steve proclaims "I'm sinking". A reprise of some of the earlier themes starts and the track ends with dripping water and the door shutting. I cannot begin to image what it has all been about but it's been fun guessing at all sorts of deep psychological meanings!

I have not got a cover so I'm sorry that I cannot describe it to you and nobody Steve Freight knows has either (Can any readers help?). I therefore do not know if the band members were still the same, so if anyone has information available please let us know.

I hope this has been an informative piece. Any further information would be most welcome and another piece for the jigsaw!

(Note from Steve Freight) I had an interesting discussion with a friend of mine in the music business who recalls Steven Wilson sending him demos. He had the Altamont and Karma tapes but alas cannot find them now. He does however remember Steven sending him other band tapes on which he thinks he performed and even a solo one but can recall no details.

More pieces to the puzzle to find so keep a wary eye open at record fairs and boot sales – you never know when you will find that long lost gem!

Of course my friend may well be mistaken but the fun is in looking!!

After this issue was published Steven wrote to me with the following comments

Phil Harwood seems to have got the two sides of the Altamont tape mixed up (maybe his copy is labelled incorrectly?)*. The original appearance of "This Long Silence" was as part of the 20 minute track "Prayer for the Soul" (not "Tell Tale Heart" which is an instrumental). The lyrics to "It Will Rain For A Million Years" originally appeared in the track "Split Image" (not Prayer for the Soul"). The 15 minute synth track he refers to as Split Image" is actually "Altamont" …etc…etc…oops

"I have 2 copies of the tape myself, an original and a copy someone taped for me. Both of mine are the wrong way round so I think there must be a batch labelled back to front out there. (Steve)

These comments were incorporated in issue 6 but felt for this publication's purposes they fitted better here. (SF 2020).

BBC Derby Radio Interview (transcribed by Steve Freight)

I believe in May 1996, Steve Wilson appeared on BBC Derby Radio on the Ashley Franklin show (I have chosen this date as Signify and Waiting are not mentioned). I also believe this to have been broadcast on Sunday at 3:00pm on a show called Soundscapes. I cannot however confirm this but I'm sure I will soon hear from someone if my assumptions are incorrect.

However before starting on a transcript of the interview (part of which I think is missing from my tape). I will transcribe the beginning of another of Ashley's shows where he is very enthusiastic regarding the band (this was broadcast 3 November 1996 prior to the Rock city gig in Nottingham).

"Along with RMI some tremendous new music from acts who in a true and parallel universe would be enormous I'm sure – Porcupine Tree…(and others) but a British act to start with. They are in the East Midlands next week – (over the top of Sever) Porcupine Tree".

After Sever – "Mmm wonderful musicianship and very clever and effective and economical use of samples. Being labelled Neo Prog Rock, Porcupine Tree, and I suppose there is that sort of prog rock sensibility but a very modern sounding band as well and I think if we suddenly had a world without Pink Floyd we wouldn't feel the loss because Porcupine Tree would be there to rightfully take their place, and in many ways their music is a good deal more interesting, certainly on the two albums I've heard from the Porcupine Tree, than Pink Floyd have produced in recent years".

It sounds to me as if the people in the Derby area have a good show to listen to on Sunday afternoons.

And now for the interview:

Ashley Franklin:
Steven, I know you believe that this band should appeal to a wide range of people, and I would agree, but you also believe you have to quash the notion that you're a drug crazed hippie with a teapot on his head.

Steven Wilson: Yeah well that really comes from, I think the tradition, where psychedelic or progressive music is associated with, the birth of progressive music in the late '60's early '70's, which very much sprang out of the drug culture; and I've found in doing interviews with journalists, and generally just speaking to fans of music, that there seems to be a general assumption that the music is written, recorded, composed, whatever, under the influence of some kind of artificial stimulant; and I've developed a bit of a chip on my shoulder because of this, because I personally take it as a slight insult in the sense that people don't seem to believe that you can have the power of imagination to produce extraordinary music without having to use some kind of artificial stimulant to achieve that.

Up The Downstair is then played from the album.

Ashley: There's also the problem that you have in that some of Porcupine Tree's music is reminiscent of late '60's/'70's progressive rock, which I love, but the music media doesn't. I was reading a review recently of the new King Crimson album for example, by Charles Murray who is an excellent rock journalist but he spoilt it for me by referring to the virus of prog rock. There is this terrible stigma attached to rock that evolved in the late '60's early '70's which I find bewildering because that period was so wonderfully creative.

Steven: Yes. I think unfortunately with the music press, and I have to say this only applies to the UK, because I've done many interviews for many European, American, Japanese magazines and there isn't this stigma that we have in the UK. I think the reason we have this stigma within the UK is that a lot of the journalists that are writing now, actually, at one time in their life really loved Progressive Rock and they've almost been made to feel like they should be ashamed of it; almost like the Emperors New Clothes Syndrome. There is an incredible double standard going on here, where they will condemn Progressive Rock for being out of date and nostalgic and then they will champion a band like Elastica who basically peddle the Punk clichés, and that seems to be acceptable but if you actually take your influences from progressive music, which in my opinion is a much more rich and creative basic blueprint for music anyway, you do tend to be ridiculed and that as I say is a very peculiarly English thing.

Ashley: I do believe late '60's Early '70's prog rock, which is recalled with uniform distaste by the media doesn't really get the credit it deserves for the creativity that was going on.

Steven: Absolutely. I mean King Crimson are a classic example of a band who are still drawing on that original burst of creativity that came in the late '60's early '70's and are still producing music which I think is at the cutting edge, and progressive music is in many ways, the first and the last style of music that had no boundaries, in the sense that it could draw from any other music and combine it and bring it into the overall cocktail of music and produce something new. All other forms of music, and I do love a lot of other forms of music, I'm not condemning them for this, but all other forms of music are by their very nature restricted to a certain blueprint. Progressive rock never was and you only have to look at the original wave of progressive bands to see how different they all were. I mean Jethro Tull were very influenced by Jazz and Folk, Pink Floyd they were very much influenced by the west coast American bands like Love and Velvet Underground, Genesis very influenced by the more Classical tradition as were ELP, an incredible range of influences all under one umbrella if you like.

Ashley: You mention music journalists and their distance for prog rock. I think it could also apply to radio and there is this problem of course for the Porcupine Tree, a major problem really is that 52 minutes of your 65 minute album is made up of 3 epic tracks.

Steven: Sure

Ashley: Doesn't make you very radio friendly and to be honest if I hadn't tuned in just by chance to Mark Radcliffe's radio one show one Monday night a few months ago I still might not have heard of Porcupine Tree.

Steven: Yes. I mean obviously the worst thing I could possibly do when I'm making an album is to be thinking about things like that – no disrespect to the media, but when I'm making a record I'm obviously not thinking about, and I'm sure you wouldn't want me to be thinking about those kind of things. But it's like the kind of conversation I get into with the record company once the album is finished, is along the lines of, well have we got anything here we can push to radio, have we got anything here we can put out as a single, and in fact I don't know if you came across it, we actually did put out a single around the same time as the album which contained a 5 minute track which was not on the album, Mark Radcliffe for example played that to death on his show, and it was actually written and recorded long after the album was finished almost because of this problem that you've highlighted. We didn't anticipate getting any radio play at all.

Stars Die is then played

It is here that my tape ends so whether any more was said I do not know. If there is anyone with a fuller version I'm sure we would be interested in finding out.

Following this issues release I received a letter from Steven with the following comment:

The Ashley Franklin interview must date from about a year earlier than you say because it was just after "The Sky Moves Sideway" came out and was recorded at the GLR studio in London. The broadcast before the Nottingham show must have been a repeat of this interview. The original interview was certainly much longer. (Does anyone have the full version – if so please let me know, Thanks – Steve)

This was originally included in Issue 6 (SF2020)

VOYAGE · 35

ISSUE **6**

Idiot Prayer – LEE WAINMAN 1997©

Issue 6

The Richard Barbieri Special
Published October 1997

Contents:
The Voyage 35 intro
An exclusive **Richard Barbieri** interview
Richard Barbieri discography
News, including feedback from Steven on Issue 5
The Promotional Videos
Strawberry Fair Review
Jansen, **Barbieri** and Karn Review
Steven Wilson Interview (reprinted from Deliverance magazine)
Richard **Barbieri** and **Japan** - a personal view by Michael Seabrook
A free tape offer from Michael Seabrook

Richard Barbieri Interviewed (by Steve Freight)

The following interview was conducted by correspondence and the questions originally set last year. Richard completed this on a long train journey from Tokyo to Osaka where JBK (including Steven Wilson) were on tour, so I guess this was possibly 17th or 18th July 1997 (Tokyo gig was 16th, Osaka 19th).

SF: Thank you Richard for agreeing to be interviewed. We are all aware of your involvement with Japan and I shan't dwell on this too much. Could you however give us a brief resume of your career to date including those "formative years".

RB: Hopefully, Debi at Medium will have sent you a detailed discography by now which should cover all recorded works and collaborations from 1977 to present date. I don't really want to 'ramble on' about the formative years with the group as it would be a bit long and drawn out, however if there are any specific questions about this then I'll be happy to answer them (at a later date).

SF: Who were your influences in the early days? Did you know at an early age that you had a musical leaning or were you originally forced into playing?

RB: I did have a few piano lessons at school but it soon became apparent that I neither had the technique or the talent to play the required pieces. As for influences discovering the first two Roxy Music albums was an important moment for me. I had previously been heavily into the major progressive bands of that time, Genesis, ELP, Yes etc, but when I heard the kind of approach Brian Eno was using with synthesisers I knew that that was what I wanted to do. He was using these synths to introduce abstract sounds and textures into the context of a pop song and the level of experimentation was far more impressive to me than listening to a three minute mini moog solo. Also technique did not come into it and from that moment on programming sounds became more important to me than practising my scales. I would say that Brian Eno and Karlheinz Stockhausen have been my main influences with regards to electronics.

SF: Who do you listen to these days?

RB: I listen to quite a diverse selection of music that ranges from avant garde to simple pop songs. Some of the artists I admire are – Scott Walker, Robert Wyatt, Kate Bush, Talk Talk, Tindersticks, Brian Eno, Arvo Part, Todd Rundgren, Can. Too many to mention really, it could be anything from Sparks to Soundgarden.

SF: How do you feel now that you are cited as being other peoples' influence?

RB: I guess that's the nicest compliment you can pay to a fellow musician. A long way back (whether by luck, hard work or a musically confused mind) I managed to develop an individual style and approach to playing keyboards that gave me a more recognisable sound than most other keyboardists. Mick Karn and Steve Jansen did the same with bass and drums respectively. If a few people out there can use your work as a catalyst to inspire their own, then that's very satisfying.

SF: How did you come to know of Steven Wilson and subsequently join Porcupine Tree?

RB: I met Steven through working with No Man, his other project with Tim Bowness, Myself, Mick Karn and Steve Jansen were invited to attend a showcase gig they were doing at Ronnie Scotts. I thought they were the best new band I'd heard in a while and their enthusiasm for music in general was rather infectious and I became involved. Studio recording sessions followed along with a disappointingly low key tour of the UK. Soon after Steven asked if I would play some synthesisers on a track on the 'Up The Downstair' album. He wanted it "spacey and electronic" and I found I enjoyed getting back to using more electronics than I had been doing for a while. I was more involved in the 'Sky Moves Sideways' albums and things progressed naturally from there.

SF: How does playing smaller venues to those played with Japan compare? Do you find the Porcupine Tree audiences to be appreciative?

RB: I've played both large and small venues and from my point of view there isn't that much difference. It's possible to come off stage at a 10,000 seater feeling non pulsed and yet be totally into a performance at a small club and vice versa. It's more to do with your state of mind at the time and whether the adrenalin is flowing or not as to how much you enjoy the experience of a live concert. Many factors come in to play, the general group vibe, how much time you spend in the dressing room before the gig, whether Chris performs a 'floor show' before you go on etc.

(See the Insignificance tape sleeve for possible clue! – Steve)

As for the audiences, I think they have been really appreciative and supportive of the group. London audiences are always a bit too 'cool' and 'laid back' though. The one gripe I have is that I hate it when the crowd starts talking during the quieter moments in the set. I don't understand this at all.

(This is something which appears to be mentioned all too often. I for one do not understand this either).

SF: Are your collaborations with Steve Jansen going to continue and are there any more releases in the pipeline? (If so please let me know of any collaborations and I will give them a mention in future issues).

RB: I'm very busy at the moment and there are quite a few projects in progress. Steve Jansen and I will continue to make albums together although the next major release will be a Jansen/Barbieri/Karn album. I'm nearing completion of a mini CD with Suzanne Barbieri which will be released on Medium in the autumn under the name 'Indigo Falls'. An album called 'Changing Hands' has just been released in Japan as I write. It's a collaboration between Jansen/Barbieri and a Japanese DJ, remix artist called Takemura.

The music is quite varied but the direction is a little bit new for us in that it has more of a 'club vibe' than our usual material. Some tracks are more 'groove, drum and bass' inspired and others tend towards 'ambient trance'. It should be released on Medium soon. At this moment the JBK tour of Japan is keeping me busy and hopefully we will perform further concerts with new material next February or March.

SF: Do you find that the Porcupine Tree music is having an effect on your other music projects? If so in what way?

RB: I don't think so. My other projects usually involve me composing the material so there's a bit of a different approach there.

SF: I am often asked what equipment is used by the group a) on stage and b) in the studio if different. Could you tell us what you use and reasons for the differences (if any) between the live and studio environments.

RB: On stage I use a Prophet 5 synthesiser which goes through a selection of guitar pedals and then into a multi FX unit. I use this keyboard for the more interesting sounds and for electronics. I also use a Roland D50 and Ensoniq VFX which provide the sound backdrops while the other musicians are more to the fore. In the studio I additionally use a Roland System 700 Lab series modular synth. This module allows for complex patching and is the main source of the electronics on the albums. I also have a couple of vintage mono synths, a micro moog and a Yamaha CS2.

SF: How do you see the band progressing and do you see yourself increasing your involvement in sharing the songwriting duties?

RB: I think that the band members will become more involved in writing with Steven in the future. However, it has been clear from the word go that Steven has directional and production control over the output of the group.

Its not a problem for me personally as I have so many of my own projects underway on my own label and I have enough opportunities to express myself compositionally on my own albums. Chris, Colin and myself play a large part in arranging the music and as I said earlier you will probably see more writing input in the future.

SF: I recently saw a photo of you with Japan (in Q Magazine) where you appeared to be in full makeup. Do you feel you are now more yourself in style and do you prefer not having an image to live up to?

RB: Most young kids go through a phase where they are searching for an identity and tend to experiment with different images. I suppose the idea was to look different from the norm. The more outrageous the image the more you felt ostracised from society, which was the desired result. The thing about wearing make up is that you've got to have conviction and attitude with it. People then accept it as a natural part of your image. I would feel totally uncomfortable wearing it now, but don't in any way think that there's anything wrong with guys wearing make up. I've just grown out of needing to project any particular image of myself.

SF: You always appear to be in the shadows at gigs (it's difficult to get a good photo). Is this deliberate on your part and if so why?

RB: It's not deliberate on my part, but I'm quite happy to lurk in the shadows. Whether a lights guy decides to feature me or not is not really a concern for me. It has occurred to me though that I may have the ability to absorb all light sources directed at me. (Steven Wilson concurs with this theory as well, I believe).

SF: Thank you very much Richard for taking the time out to answer these questions.

RB: Sorry it's taken so long to get round to it.

Steven's Early Bands

What follows is an extract from this issue's Message From A Self Destructing Turnip (Readers letters page) (SF 2020)

Sorry Steven but it is now skeletons out of the closet time. Following my comments about a friend of mine recalling having been sent demo tapes I have received the following information from a reader (who wished to stay anonymous) as follows:-

From the demise of Karma in 1985, Steve joined a band from the Aylesbury/Hemel Hempstead area, called Pride of Passion. This band existed from Jan '85 'til Dec '87 approx. The line up consisted of a few local celebrities from their early Marillion days, Brian Jellyma (keyboards), who later left in Sept '85, Diz Minit (bass), both ex Marillion, Deborah Hopper (Vocals), Grant Gilmour (drums), ex End, Nigel Child (guitar) and Steven Wilson on (keyboards). Steven was with the band for approx. 6 months from early to mid-1987.

It is believed only 2 items were produced for public consumption. The first was a four track cassette sometime in '85/'86 simply entitled Pride of Passion. The four tracks were called: *Steven, Somewhere Else (Flying High), Ageless Minds, All the Walls Are Falling Down*. The second item was a 7" single, which my informant can't remember the title of or year but remembers it came in a white sleeve and "may" have had some kind of wrap around sleeve or even a fold out sleeve. The sleeve was mainly white with typical low budget 2 or 3 colour printed sleeve, in typical prog fashion from that era (maybe a chess board or trees?). Whilst Steven didn't play on any studio recordings, I thought this information would still be of interest.

Pride of Passion also performed a few supports at the Marquee to such bands as Solstice and Liaison. Anyone with more information please let me know and I'll pass it on.

Steven has agreed to an interview about his early career and Phil and I are currently working on questions to form the basis of this. If you have any comments or want to know anything specific now's your opportunity to ask. Please therefore let me know any questions you want to raise as soon as possible. Working parameters of the interview are, and I quote "I'm not going to volunteer information so if you don't ask I'm not telling!". Phil and I want to probe as much as possible so if you have any info, suspected or otherwise please let me know.

The Promotional Videos (by Phil Harwood)

In Issue 4 of Voyage 35, there was mention of 2 videos, issued by Delerium, for promotional purposes, this article is a look at those.

Live at Nieuwe Pul-Uden 7.1.94

The video cover was in fluorescent green and had the words "Porcupine Tree Live at Club Nieuwe Pul" above a picture of Steve holding a dolls head and continued to the left was "Friday 7th Jan 1994" while on the other side was "Uden Netherlands" and below that some backwards writing which when viewed in a mirror still doesn't make sense (maybe Dutch?) reading "wkgby lkg.foi yrgf!" At the bottom of the picture is a sloping rectangle with "For Promotional Purposes Only Not For Re-Sale". And Delec Promo Vid 4. The spine reads "Porcupine Tree – Live at Nieuwe Pul-Uden, 7/1/94" and on the back cover are pictures of the "On The Sunday of Life" LP, "Up The Downstair" LP, the "Radio Active CD EP and "Voyage 34" 12 inch mentioning both the original and also the Astralasia remix. The Delerium address is given and a 1993 copyright. There were approx. 100 copies made, most of which were distributed through a University gig booking organisation, (Leeds?) with the purpose of getting the group gigs.

This concert was the first appearance outside the UK for the band, following on from the 4/12/93 Nags Head, High Wycombe gig, the first Mark Radcliffe show appearance of 6/12/93 and the 2 other UK appearances of 7/12 and 11/12 at The Borderline London and Antics Coventry. The video does not show the band come on stage and does not open with any intro titles. The video just starts with a slight touch of dry ice and gentle radiating lights at the back of the band. Richard on keyboards is over on the left of the stage as you face it, with Steve in the middle, with Colin to his left and slightly behind him and Chris over to the right. A bank of spotlights are positioned behind Steve and Colin on the floor and facing the band are 4 small monitors. A stack of speakers are behind Steve. The video is shot throughout, from an elevated position either in the middle or maybe at the back of the room, perhaps from a balcony, slightly skew right of centre. There are some people standing at the front, but it is in no way crowded in the club. Annoyingly there does seem to be a lot of talking, and general noise going on behind the camera, probably at the bar, I suspect, which is perhaps upstairs.

Slowly, without any introduction from the band "Burning Sky" starts and builds. White clouds appear on the back screens and are replaced by flowing patterns as the song progresses. At 9.50 minutes in Steve says "Good evening, this is Radioactive Toy" which then eventually goes back to "Burning Sky" at the 19.24 mark, as the crowd whistle and shout, via some instrumental work that I unfortunately don't recognise. Throughout the spotlights have been lighting up the stage and at one stage strobe lights stab the darkness. The band are fairly motionless with Steve hunched over his guitar. A guy at the front starts taking photos around the 25 minute point. The song ends at the 31 minute point and then my favourite "I feel no pain" sings Steve and the poignant "Always Never" starts, unfortunately slightly spoilt by the talking at the back. Some one else is taking photos as the dry ice billows.

The song ends at 39.00 and Steve says "Last year, er, in England we put out, possibly the most un-commercial single ever made. It was 30 minutes long, continuous unbroken music it was all about LSD (roar of approval from the crowd). The radio stations didn't play it, we are going to play it for you now in it's entirety, its called Voyage 34". The crowd claps and the spoken intro begins a big circle appears on the back projector, while Steve drinks from a bottle of mineral water, then off we go. The band are fairly motionless as the music flows. Unfortunately the background talking intrudes at the point where Brian meets himself, when the band go into a quiet effects passage, Steve turning his back on the audience to face Colin at this point. The video ends just as the song does the same, abruptly stopping at the 62 minute mark.

The second video was a much more limited affair (exact number unknown but believed to be less than twenty) with a black and white label. This was only distributed to the band and record company. The cover shows what appears to be a giant snail rearing up from a sea, with perhaps icebergs, floating in it! Above, and below, is written in large letters "Porcupine Tree" while at the bottom is the additional "Live In Den Bosch 10th Feb. 1995

Nederland. This is repeated on the spine and on the back is a discography. There is also a picture of the band around a table (see Voyage 35, issue 1, page 18 where the same picture is reproduced). The catalogue number is Delec Promo Vid 6 and the production date is 1995.

This was recorded on the 2nd of 4 dates in Holland on 10.2.95 at Willem II (I assume a club?) at Den Bosch. This short tour followed on from the Mark Radcliffe Show on BBC Radio 1 of 30.1.95 and before the band commenced their UK tour of that year. The video starts with the camera fighting for a view of the stage from behind a sea of bodies. The band are playing "The Sky Moves Sideways Part 1" as the cameraman moves through the bodies to get an unobstructed view from his left across the stage, Steve is wearing his stripy sweatshirt, with the drums behind him, bass to his left keyboards to his right. Once at his new position the cameraman remains where he is though he does zoom in and out as required, and focus on other members of the band beside Mr Wilson. There are a few special effects on the video at one stage a shrinking box effect is utilised on Steve's head.

From "The Sky", we go into "Is...Not" with shots of Richard, some nifty guitar from Steve. Someone else is videoing the performance from Steve's left. Then it's time for "Radioactive Toy". There are flashes from photographers during this track. We're 25 minutes into the show now and Steve is applying heavy whammy bar to his guitar. Blue lighting plays on the band as they go into the effects section of the song. Towards the end Steve is playing low on the neck of his guitar. The song ends and the crowd whoop their approval. "Thanks a lot. We're going to try and improvise a bit for you now. This is called Moonloop" says Steve. The screen above the band is showing a stylised sun with a face, as Steve applies whammy bar and his hands shoot up and down the neck of his guitar. High floating notes are elicited. The camera man then moves onto Chris then back to Steve who is taking a drink. There is the usual problem of the crowd talking a zodiac ring has now appeared on the overhead screen as the familiar lopping bass lines of Moonloop are played. The tempo picks up as Steve hunches over his guitar. There are whoops and a cry of "Alright!" from the crowd. The show seems to be going down extremely well with our Dutch friends.

"Okay, this is the point in the set where we try out some new tunes. The first one is called Moon Touches Your Shoulder". The tune starts and Steve brushes his long hair back behind his ears as he solos. The song seems to go down well with the crowd, Steve has another drink and makes some comment about a short one? We're 46 minutes into the set. Next it's "Dislocated Day", there's a haze of smoke behind Steve, through which Chris is drumming furiously. The song ends with a small drum solo. The crowd are shouting "Rolling Stone" (I think) but the metronome is starting, heralding "Burning Sky". Steve gesticulates, his palm pointing up, up, at Colin. More bass volume? At 61 minutes as the feedback drains away Steve announces "That's all. Goodnight!". The crowd roars, it's all over, or is it?

There is a slight break in the video. Suddenly they're back! "Was anybody here last night?... not here, (it's a bit garbled next but Steve must be referring to Drieluik, at Zaandam Holland that they played the night before). Well this is especially for you as we didn't play this last night, this is Always Never".

This leads unannounced (a lot of the songs in the set were not introduced so if I got any titles wrong, sorry!) into "Up The Downstair". The band go off stage again and return for a second encore of "Not Beautiful Anymore".

Then Steve says above the final feedback chord "That really is it. Goodnight!" and it's all over.

Strawberry Fair, Cambridge (by Steve Freight)

"Traitor!"

This is what I was called by a person I like to consider a friend (hi John) when I said I was going to Cambridge to see Porcupine Tree, instead of Blackheath to see Hawkwind on 7 July 1997. My response was that it has taken 25 years but I have finally found a group who have knocked Hawkwind out of the number one spot *(albeit Hawkwind are now back in their rightful place SF 2020)*. Sorry lads, but there it is.

The Fair was not what I had expected and I was also surprised to note that this was the 24th year it had been on. Someone remarked to me that it reminded them of the old Stonehenge Gigs with all the side stalls promoting all manner of charitable causes and selling of wares.

With 5 music stages to choose from the time passed very quickly. Other than Porcupine Tree the other act to catch the eye was John "my CD contains 21 songs and one hit" Ottway who was in one of the minor tents and should have been on the main stage. The crowd was at least 5 deep outside where he performed, and I had previously heard how good a showman he was and feel he would have been more at home on the main stage.

A few of us had been lucky enough to have a chat with Steven before the gig and most of the talk centred around the Album he had produced for Fish.

Still come 6:40 and Porcupine Tree took the stage (we had seen them setting up for 20

minutes). This was what we had been Waiting (!) for. No tantrums from our favourite group we hoped, (the previous band's female singer had stormed off in a huff because the audience wouldn't applause!).

Opening with Up The Downstair to tumultuous cheers from us die hard supporters at the

front of the stage (including one who had travelled from Holland (hi Didier)) despite the sound system and lack of preparation the performance was very good.

Richard was playing with 2 fingers strapped together but this did not deteriorate from his playing at all. In fact it was only after the gig when I managed to have a few words with him that this was at all evident.

They then continued with Waiting Phases 1 & 2 which again was well received and then upped the tempo with Dislocated Day.

Rob (another of the over faithful) was then beside himself with joy at the first strains of Moonloop, and I have to agree with him that this song has improved with "age" and matured beyond recognition. For the definitive version of this check out the new album.

Closing with Radioactive Toy the set was over far too soon, but from the applause I believe they won a new audience. With the sun continuing to beat down we were still shouting for more but with the tight schedule knew it to be fruitless. Still it had been a good set and I for one can't wait for the full Autumn tour.

Jansen, Barbieri, Karn – London Astoria 2 (by Nigel Beal)

The very unglamorous, seedy night-club setting of the Astoria 2 played host, on 12 April 1997, to three quarters of the ex new romantics group Japan. The band, playing together in London for the first time in over 2 years, played a varied selection from their collective solo and collaborative works.

The packed crowd were treated to some excellent tracks, kicking off with "Sleepers Awake", from the Jansen/Barbieri album "Stone to Flesh", followed by Mick Karn's popular track "Bestial Cluster". I was lucky enough to speak to Mick before the show and his modesty about his vocal performance was very "unpopstar" like. In fact the banter between the band and crowd was very enjoyable.

In all my years of seeing this band perform I have never known them seem so relaxed. Richard Barbieri chatted and introduced more songs than I have ever known. This relaxed atmosphere seeped through to the music and with the brilliant performance of Steven Wilson of No Man and Porcupine Tree fame on guitar and the gorgeous Suzanne Barbieri on backing vocals, it made the long journey down to London worthwhile.

More solo tracks from Mick's catalogue continued the show "Plaster the Magic Tongue", "Saday Maday" and then back to Rich and Steve's material with a great intro from Rich. Again for the track "Lumen", from the "Stories Across Borders" album. "After this album we got dropped by our record label!" what a mistake by Virgin/Mr Branson!

The next treat for the crowd was the vocal talents of Natacha Atlas who sang "Feta Funk" and "Lodge of Skins". I was disappointed that Suzanne didn't take centre stage like Natacha for the hauntingly beautiful Oystercatchers track "The Wilderness", but you can't have everything. The crowd also wanted an all time first of Steve (Jansen that is) singing live on stage, but alas this didn't happen – Steve looked the most uncomfortable before and during the show. Will we ever hear a Dolphin Brothers' track live, guys?

The set came to a close with "Long Tales, Tall Shadows", "Little Less Hope", and the awesome dance track "Beginning to Melt", which got everyone begging for more. The encore didn't disappoint in any way, with the old Japan classic "Life without Buildings" with the David Sylvia vocals being performed by all of the crowd!

The band then finished off a wonderful night with the brilliant Rain Tree Crow (Japan 1990 style) track "Big Wheels in Shanty Town".

To sum up a great night, with some very talented, unpretentious "Popstars". I only wish they'd do it more often, even if we can't persuade Steve to sing.

Steven Wilson Deliverance

The following interview, recorded 20th January 1995, was on behalf of a midlands entertainment magazine called DELIVERENCE – now sadly defunct.

I had been into Porcupine Tree for several years prior to this interview and considered it quite a coup for them (Deliverence). It had been apparent to me, even from his early tapes, just what a rare and gifted musician / writer Steven is, totally dedicated to experimentation and progression.

What I didn't realise at that time was the warmth of the man, who always seems to have the time to say hello regardless of how busy he might seem. This is coupled with an enviable knowledge and appreciation for a wide range of musical styles from the '60's to present. I personally have been a record buyer for 30 odd years and can quite honestly say that it has been a long time since I last got this excited about a band.

Credit and appreciation to Richard and Ivor at Delerium and to a host of other bands they have introduced to me.

Anyway the interview ...

PC: How did you team up with Alan Duffy and why is Porcupine Tree not on Imaginary Records?

SW: Actually, all of Alan's lyrics for Porcupine Tree date from the period 1983-85, long before I started recording Porcupine Tree music. We wrote the songs for an entirely different project that never came to much – I was very young – about 16 years old. Then in the late eighties when I started recording Porcupine Tree music, I had little confidence in my own lyrics, so I went back to Alan's and found that they fitted very well. In one or two instances ("Jupiter Island" and "Nine Cats" spring to mind) I even used the original music that I had written for the words many years earlier.

When I started recording the cassettes I wasn't really looking for a record deal at all. It was purely to satisfy my own musical whims. Porcupine Tree began entirely as a studio project without any CD/vinyl release in mind I was not particularly interested in a record deal at that point and it was only after Delerium approached me and offered me the opportunity to record for them, that I began to see the possibilities of reaching a wider audience, with CD releases. Although I briefly communicated with Alan to sort out the publishing rights for his lyrics, I still don't really know what he thinks of Porcupine Tree or if he likes what I've done with his work. Having heard some of the material that he signed to imaginary, I don't think we would have fitted in anyway.

PC: Why do Porcupine Tree find it so hard to get gigs?

SW: Ridiculous though it may seem, we have had to prove ourselves to promoters and agents, much more than any boring guitar indie band would have had to, simply because what we are doing is so different. We had to prove that we could attract good audiences and get good press playing the music that we do, which we have now done. It has been an uphill struggle, but now we have an agent in the UK who is booking our first full blown UK tour for the Spring.

PC: Do you enjoy playing live and how did the recent gigs go?

SW: Funnily enough, although I have played live with many band, Porcupine Tree are the first band that I really enjoy playing with in a live context. I think this is for a number of reasons. The material lends itself well to live performance, my fellow band members are incredibly gifted and pleasant people to work with and the audiences have been so appreciative. Also we do a fair amount of improvisation in each show, which keeps it fresh regardless of how many times we have played the material.

PC: Presumably the new album (The Sky Moves Sideways) had major surgery before you were happy with it?

SW: I'm not completely happy with it. Although I think production wise it is the best album yet, I think there are many areas for improvement. I wish I had used real drums all the way through the album and secondly, I wish I'd written a couple more good songs to balance out the long instrumental sequences.

In answer to your question – the 35 minute title track was a lot of work and could have ended up being anything from 20 to 50 minutes in length, depending on how I edited it together. A piece as long and complex as that one had to be recorded in about 6 separate sections and then edited together for the album. The final edit you hear on the album was about the tenth attempt to cut things to the right length and in the right order and it's still not perfect!

PC: Do you prefer to record musically more consistent records as opposed to "On The Sunday..." etc?

SW: I enjoy doing both. I love the idea of making a sprawling mess of an album and this is my favourite aspect of "On The Sunday of Life...", it covers a very wide range of moods and ideas. It is not always successful musically, or a consistent listen, but it will always be one of my favourites. In making that album I discovered the direction I wanted to take, at least for a few years. If I was to make another album like "On The Sunday...", it would be because I was closing a musical chapter and searching for some new paths to take. I'm sure I will do this again at some point, though for now I'm still happy with the current direction and sound.

PC: What Porcupine Tree track has given you the greatest satisfaction.

SW: "Fadeway" – such a shame it doesn't work live. I'm really satisfied with the "Moonloop" EP too.

PC: Do you have any more production plans?

SW: I would like to produce some other artists, but it would have to be something really special for me to divert time from my own projects. I enjoyed doing Dean's album because it followed no rules at all – I think I'd find it pretty boring doing a "rock" band.

PC: What's the next project for Steven Wilson?

SW: I'm currently working on the next No Man album "Wild Opera". It should be finished by the end of March.

PC: What plans for the future of Porcupine Tree?

SW: In the immediate future, the new album "The Sky Moves Sideways" is released on January 30th and we want to play as many concerts as possible to promote the album. It will also be the first of our albums to be given a release in the USA, so it will be interesting to see how it is received there. There will probably be another single next summer and we would like to release a live album sometime in the next two years. We also want to continue to develop the live show by using more lights and projections and creating a whole "environment" for a live performance to take place in. This hopefully will also extend to video and film. I'm also looking forward to working on the next LP (to be released in 1996), which I already have some rough ideas for. I want the next album to be the first in which the whole band are involved from beginning to end in both writing and performance.

PC: How many more unreleased tunes yet to see the light of day?

SW: Hardly any – "Yellow Hedgerow Dreamscape" and "Staircase Infinities" mopped up nearly all of the leftovers. Of course there are loads of alternative mixes and versions of released tracks, but hardly any actual unreleased tracks.

My thanks to Peter Clemons for supplying this interview. I enjoy looking back over old reviews and interviews and seeing how things change, I hope you do too!

Richard Barbieri And Japan (by Michael Seabrook)

Following on from my last article, I thought I'd pen an article about Richard Barbieri's involvement in Japan. Well it follows, but first I must mention Jansen & Barbieri's latest release, "Other Worlds in a Small Room".

This excellent CD represents three earlier tracks from 1984's "Worlds in A Small Room", with three longer, new pieces. If you like Richard Barbieri's work on "Signfy" you should enjoy this. The shifting moods and textures of the pieces make it a constantly absorbing CD, which bears repeated listens. I've heard many ambient CD's where one idea has been stretched to breaking point – not so on this. There are even a few unexpected musical twists and turns, so those of us familiar with their music will find something new and different even to their previous releases.

"Write from the heart", said my Editor (does he mean me? – Steve) "about Richard Barbieri's involvement with Japan". After pages of crossing out I started thinking about my favourite music, LP's especially, trying to work out what made me like certain things.

Removing Dead Can Dance, John Foxx, Sisters of Mercy and a few others left me with my favourites. "Signfy" by Porcupine Tree is one of them. Two David Sylvia albums, two Japan albums and the Japan "reformation" known as Rain Tree Crow continued the list.

A common factor in all these releases is the keyboard work of Richard Barbieri and its strong identity and personality. Wherever it appears, it seems to have its own presence. But I think it was the combination of four very different musicians that made Japans music so successful.

David Sylvian's vocals ("crushed velvet" I read somewhere) were unlike any other. Basically he could have sung the telephone directory and made it sound interesting! Steve Jansen's drumming was a combination of solid, rock orientated fill ins and unexpected patterns (Steve used programmed and live drumming). Mick Karn's bass would either play oblique melodies or produce a wide range of squeals and grunts which, curiously enough, fitted in perfectly with the rest of the music. This basis was augmented with guitars, saxophones and other instruments. Lyrics were complex or dramatic, worldly or personal, and fitted the music perfectly.

The immense spectrum of sound that can be produced by synthesisers was really tested by Japan. But rather than sounding like synthesised noise, the effects could have been acoustic instruments caught up in the tunnels of space and time. To my ears Richard's sounds appear to be a result of combinations of different timbres and instruments put together, much as in the way you combine say strings and an electric organ, you get a combination of two acoustic sounds which makes a new one. The sounds were so unique in the way they combined that now Japan's music does not sound dated at all, listen to "Gentlemen take Polaroids", "Ghosts" (their biggest hit) or "Alien". It's not music that sounds like 1981.

(In a similar way, I would image that "Signify" will also sound fresh and inspired in seventeen years time).

The album "Quiet Life", with excellent pieces such as "Halloween", showed the group really gelling together. Whilst there were albums before, the group tend to think of this as their first "proper" album. Two epic pieces on this, "The Other Side of Life" and "In Vogue" typify the compelling style and arrangements. Strings, saxophones, fretless bass, guitars, keyboards, drums and vocals.

"Gentlemen Take Polaroids" was an even better album. Richard's keyboards were more in evidence. All Japans music is powerful stuff, tracks like "Despair" and "Burning Bridges" had a brooding melancholy whereas the title track and "Swing" were percussively driven songs with prominent synthesised melodies, effects and all kinds of noises. I have a particular liking for the percussive fill ins on the title track.

"Tin Drum", Japan's final studio album features tracks like "Sons of Pioneers" (which still crop up on TV "Holiday" programmes from time to time as does "Canton") and saw them become more eastern in style, but this was not just a musical affectation, the music itself was very popular in the East, and it was music that almost defined elements of Eastern music for Western people. But for some it was too different, too hard to get used to.

I myself didn't like Japan's music at the time of its release. (I was too young to appreciate it!). It took a few listens quite a few years later to get into it but since then I've been totally hooked. Maybe that is a definition of good music. This listener hears songs played on the radio which sound good on the first couple of listens, but often tire or even annoy by the 20th hearing. I of course would never tire of hearing Porcupine Tree or Japan on the radio!!

1982 was Japans most commercially successful year, they had more weeks on the album chart than any other group. But at the height of their fame they split after "Tin Drum", only to reform and split again in 1991.

This information, under the name "Rain Tree Crow" has some small points of comparison to Porcupine Tree. Methods of composition in Japan are reported as more rigid, whereas improvisation is used in Porcupine Tree and in Rain Tree Crow.

The pieces tended to evolve, growing in dynamics and then fading away. Richard's parts were intricate swirls of high tones on tracks like "Blackwater". On others dramatic bass tones emerged. Speaking at the time, the protagonists recognised that there was more of a rock influence there. Richard mentioned he used to like Led Zeppelin. I thought Barbieri's keyboards on this were again, appertaining to his style, but quite unique approaches which I haven't heard elsewhere.

"Rain Tree Crow" was mostly a melancholic, slow album but it also showed signs of the anger and intensity which occurs on "Signify". Some tracks could at a considerable stretch be described as progressive, there are certainly some complex arrangements and swift changes of mood and timbre.

All the ex-members have new releases currently out except David Sylvia, who has been quiet since his live album with Robert Fripp several years ago now. All the releases mentioned above are well worth seeking out.

Issue 7

Published February 1998

Contents:
The Voyage 35 intro
Readers remarks and letters
The secret diaries of Peter Clemons (gig reviews and memories)
The Remasters and how to tell them from the original CD issues

Mojo Rising
The Italian TV appearance
Full Colour Centre spread
News
Gig reviews
Coma Divine and remaster reviews
The Radioactive Promo.

Record Collector said:
Issue 7 has gig reviews and the tour diary of a truly devoted fan.

The secret diaries of Peter Clemons (Aged 39 (Going On 40))

Peter has kept a diary of all the gigs he has been to. The following are extracts from this diary and feature the Porcupine Tree gigs (naturally). Read on!

Nags Head - High Wycombe 4.12.93.

Voyage 34 / Always Never / Nostalgia Factory / Burning Sky / Radioactive Toy / Fadeaway / Up The Downstair.
Encore : Not Beautiful Anymore

Memories

1 First ever show
2 Packed Audience
3 Buying the new Bevis Frond album off Delerium Stall
4 Colin Edwin not wearing cap
5 Knowing that I'd just witnessed something special.
6 No support!
7 Mark Radcliffe show next evening

Old Trout - Windsor 9.11.94

Up The Downstair / The Sky Moves Sideways / Radioactive Toy / Moonloop / Always Never / Burning Sky.
Encore : Not Beautiful Anymore

Memories

1 Great venue in a great setting. River just across the road.
2 Good support band - Kava Kava.
3 Hearing for the first time the Dead Flowers album "Altered State Circus" from the D.J. desk.
4 Hearing Moonloop live for the first time
5 Finding out that both Kava Kava & Dead Flowers were support bands next evening in Bradford. *(Did he go though as not in his diaries - Steve)*

Roadmenders - Northampton 27.4.95
General Wolfe - Coventry 29.4.95

The Sky Moves Sideways 1 / Is...Not / Radioactive Toy / Moonloop / The

Moon Touches Your Shoulder / Always Never / Dislocated Day / Burning Sky
Encore : Not Beautiful Anymore
(same set list for both shows)

Memories

1 Fantastic support band at Northampton - "Moom", who then went on to release impressive "Toot" album.
2 Being very pleased that PT were playing my home town again. Disappointing P.A. though according to band - I thought gig was terrific.
3 Taking my 2 children to watch sound check / band rehearsing during afternoon prior to gig.
4 Driving the band into Coventry City Centre for a walk prior to gig. My children had to sit on bands lap as I drove.
5 Hearing The Sky Moves Sideways for the first time.

Roadmenders - Northampton 11.10.95

Signify / The Sky Moves Sideways 1 / Radioactive Toy / Cryogenics / The Moon Touches Your Shoulder / Always Never / Moonloop / Dislocated Day / Up The Downstair
Encore : Not Beautiful Anymore

Memories

1 Again "Moom" support. Totally brilliant set, playing music (4 long numbers) from a second album still yet to see day of light.
2 Only a small stage at Roadmender. "Mooms" keyboard player could not get his Hammond on stage so he had to play on floor just in front of stage.
3 "Moom" would have played all night if not threatened with plug being pulled.
4 Another excellent PT gig, with new music Signify, Cryogenics.

KING TUTS - GLASGOW 1.5.96

Idiot Prayer / The Sky Moves Sideways / Waiting / The Nostalgia Factory / Moonloop / Sever / The Moon Touches Your Shoulder / Always Never / Radioactive Toy / Burning Sky
Encore : Voyage 34

Memories

1 Good venue. Super audience.
2 Yet more new music live.
3 Richard Allen turning up.
4 Excellent show.

ROADMENDER - NORTHAMPTON 5.5.96
Idiot Prayer / The Sky Moves Sideways / Waiting / The Nostalgia Factory / Moonloop / The Moon Touches Your Shoulder / Always Never / Signify / Radioactive Toy
Encore : Up The Downstair / Linton Samuel Dawson

PRINCESS CHARLOTTE - LEICESTER 22.5.96
Idiot Prayer / The Sky Moves Sideways / Waiting / The Nostalgia Factory / Dislocated Day / Moonloop / The Moon Touches Your Shoulder / Always Never / Up The Downstair
Encore : Voyage 34 / Linton Samuel Dawson

Memories

Probably because I saw PT three times this month, the memories drift into each other. I did get quite drunk at Leicester as I went there with a crowd of friends.

ROADMENDER - NORTHAMPTON 7.11.96

Signify / Waiting (1) / Waiting (2) / Sky Moves Sideways / Sleep of No dreaming / Idiot Prayer / Dark Matter / Dislocated Day / Moonloop / Radioactive Toy
Encore : Voyage 34 / Not Beautiful Anymore

Memories

1 Fourth time of seeing PT at this venue.
2 Richard at Delerium brought me my copies of "Gorkys Zygotic Minci" and "Ptolemaic Terrascope" CD's thereby saving me postage - thanks Richard.
3 Another excellent gig.

FOUNDRY - BIRMINGHAM 29.10.97

Even Less / Signify / Waiting (Parts 1 & 2) / Sleep of No dreaming / Up

The Downstair / This is no Rehearsal / Moon Touches Your Shoulder / Ambulance Chasing / Moonloop / Voyage 34
Encore : Radioactive Toy / Not Beautiful Anymore

Memories

1 Again, went with some friends. Due to drinking round Birmingham missed support.
2 New music, particularly "Even Less" - what a tune.
3 Disappointing crowd size-wise.

KING TUTS - GLASGOW 6.11.97

Even Less / Signify / Waiting (Part 1) / This Is No Rehearsal / Moon Touches Your Shoulder / Always Never / Moonloop (Part 1) / Idiot Prayer / Ambulance Chasing / Sleep of No Dreaming / Voyage 34
Encore : Dislocated Day / Radioactive Toy

Memories

1 This is a super venue with very appreciative crowd.
2 "Even Less" - a favourite of mine already.

Thanks Peter and sorry for giving away your age (your still younger than me though).

I hope this was of interest and also helps to fill in the gaps on some of the set lists.

An Anoracsic Delight
(by Steve Freight)
As you will be aware the first 3 albums have been reissued.
On the Sunday of Life and Up the Downstair boast better sound quality and all three have improved packaging.
For your edification the following is a brief description on each, so you can tell the original from the reissue.
All 3 discs confusingly retained the original catalogue numbers and it is only by examining the discs and covers that they can be told apart.

On The Sunday Of Life

Original	Reissue
CD has purple label	CD is picture disc
No see through inlay tray	Clear inlay - picture is same as on CD Trees with yellow/orange tint
PORCUPINE TREE in caps	Porcupine Tree in "wavy" font.
8 page booklet	12 page booklet
Centre pages only illustrated	full booklet illustrated
track listing on rear left justified	track listing centred on insert
© date 1992 Delerium Records	© date 1997 Delerium/S Wilson

Up The Downstair

Original	Reissue
CD has black label	CD is picture disc - grey "ghost" on black
PORCUPINE TREE in outline	porcupine tree in lower case
"boxed" front picture	full page front picture
fold out sleeve 6 pages	8 page booklet
no clear inlay cover	clear inlay giving Delerium & copyright information.
plain black cover with track listing and copyright information	back cover has red version of the CD picture
© date 1993 Delerium Records	© date 1997 Delerium/S Wilson

The following is by far the hardest to detect change to. There are only subtle differences and without having both to hand would be difficult to tell which you have. However look for the following:

The Sky Moves Sideways

Original	Reissue
Front cover has small text	front cover has expanded text which nearly touches the rock outcrop.
rock outcrop not detailed	rock outcrop clearly defined - picture is much sharper
"chess" photo is dark - you cannot make out Richards features	"chess" photo clearly defined.
Centre spread "murky"	Centre spread clearly defined
inside back page has discography of 1992 / 1993 / 1994 releases	No discography.
© date 1995 Delerium Records on page 7 of booklet and on reverse	© date 1997 Delerium/S Wilson on page 7 of booklet and on reverse
Vital distribution logo on rear	no logo
Back of jewel case carries blue tinged photograph	Grey tinged photograph
CD - Version 1 - no picture disc Version 2 - Limited edition picture disc which has "Phone Box" picture, and should also have sticker on from stating Limited Edition DELEC CD 028L	Picture disc CD featuring same picture as page 8 of booklet on it is a mirror image.
Picture Disc has no writing on it	Copyright info runs round edge of disc.

Union Chapel, Islington, London 14/11/97 (by Steve Freight)

The only way to survive is on your knees! Not really but bearing in mind the venue one almost felt encouraged to offer up a prayer (for the soul?).

This must be the most unusual venue I have been in for a concert and the architecture still in tact from when it was a church added to the atmosphere. You almost felt sacrilegious placing your pints on the prayer book shelf of the pew in front.

But oh the acoustics. The old nature of the building really added a certain something and the 500 plus audience were so appreciative there was actually no talking during the performance (at last!).

The only thing that detracted from the performance was that the PA System had an annoying buzz coming from it when Steven was introducing the songs.

This time I managed to persuade Yvonne to come along and while liking some songs was not a convert to the cause (another religious sounding term). However she did enjoy the evening and agreed that the gig was a great success.

Apart from Yvonne, I understand there were a number of celebrities in the audience who paid their own way. Amongst them Steve Hogarth, Jools Holland's Manager (hopefully checking them out for Later, but I don't know that so don't go starting any rumours) and Miles Copeland. Mojo were also in evidence reviewing the gig, with John Chase and Rob Crossland taking pictures for them.

Opening up with Even Less, a new song performed in Italy for the first time, this bodes well for the new album to be recorded in early '98. This near 16 minute epic is one to treasure with it's many faceted approach you are reminded of the Sky Moves Sideways but this is superior in every way, musically, vocally and structurally.

Then onto one of the crowds live favourites, Up The Downstair. I never tire of hearing this and with the performance on this day being possibly their best ever (a view shared by many I spoke to after the gig) this performance was just - well awesome.

Waiting followed (part 1 only) and again a perfect rendition of the song.

Steven then introduced another new song This Is No Rehearsal, and fairly rocks along. By this time I was really enjoying the gig and savouring the thought of the new album to come. All around me people were getting into the music and Alexis and ?? as usual were dancing in the Aisles.

Then Guy suddenly goes mad! His favourite coupling (!) starts with the strains of Moon Touches Your Shoulder. I'm still disappointed that Moon Touches You....Never was not on Coma Divine. One day I'm sure we'll see this on CD but again we had to make do with the best live version of this I've heard yet. Sometimes the join between the 2 songs jars but tonight it was perfect.

I don't know if it was familiarity with the music and each other, or the relaxed nature of the gig, playing to an appreciative audience but the crowd loved the band tonight and I think Steven loved playing in front of an English audience who at last were prepared to listen. Indeed Steven came across as relaxed and having a banter with the audience.

After Moon Touches You...Never, Steven introduces Theo Travis on stage, who has appeared with Jansen, Barbieri, Karn on stage before, and off we go into another new song, the last of the evening Ambulance Chasing. This is another cracker destined for the new album (possibly the title track), it starts strongly with Chris's pounding drums and then builds with Theo's Sax very much in evidence, I'm a sucker for Sax (even when played badly (intentionally) ala Nik Turner of Hawkwind) and Theo's playing over this song added to the overall effect. I think this is probably my favourite of the 3 new songs.

Moonloop followed, and you will recall I thought the definitive version appears on Coma Divine, well I think this performance surpassed that. Theo took up the flute on this and it seemed to add a certain "Moody Blues" feel to it. My only disappointment was the Coda was missing.

Driving guitar chords slow at first fill the air, and suddenly we are into Signify. What can I say about this I haven't said already. It was again brilliant.

Do you get the impression I enjoyed the evening? You are right. I can't recall the last time I enjoyed a concert as much as this. More was to come.

The 60's feeling of Richard's Keyboard introduced The Sleep Of No Dreaming. This was my favourite track from Signify on the first few listens, and I still feel this would make an excellent choice as a single. And my favourite track from Signify - it's now Dark Matter.

Next was a real surprise for me as I'd been under the impression that this was not going to be performed live again. Voyage 34 is pure genius and gives the impression of drugging the audience with the rhythmic beats, something Hawkwind were adept at in the early '70's. I had tried to stay away from seeing any set lists that were sent to me so while it was performed on the tour I was unaware of it until this point.

The band then leave the stage to thunderous applause (as much as 500 people can muster) and screams of more an pounding feet on the floor follows for a good 2 minutes.

Chris and Colin come back on stage on their own and Colin's "dipping" bass playing is joined by Chris pounding the drums and they both get quieter as Steven and Richard return and we are into Dislocated Day. Chris, as usual, gets a standing ovation at the end following his drum solo.

Steve then apologises " We're going to end on our usual downer. This is Radioactive Toy".

The shortened 5 minute version follows as it's now close to 11 o'clock, and suddenly its all over.

The audience rise as one as the band stay on stage waving and soaking up the applause.

Kosmic Ken then becomes the most unpopular person in the hall - It's his job to tell us that it's the end and that T-shirts and CD's are on sale at the back.

The lights come up and that's it. 101 minutes of sheer and utter brilliance.

And Yvonne - she say's she'll be at the next gig I go to so from the both of us to all the people we met and chatted to:-

See you next time!!

The Radio Active Promo CD (By Phil Harwood)

This was a 500 CD issue, originally intended for UK radio broadcast use only, that Delirium sold a few copies of, at £5.00 each, including postage, in early 1993 to defray the cost of production. It promoted the then current album "On the Sunday of Life" with a "Short Version" of "Radioactive Toy", clocking in at 4.11, and a 4.09 "Edit" of "Synesthesia" from the forthcoming, at the time, "Up The Downstair" album. As the Radio Derby interview in issue 4 of Voyage 35 revealed the record company needed shorter tracks to get the all important Radio play needed to increase awareness of the band. They felt that shorter versions would stand more chance of being played, hence these edits, which were achieved by purely fading the originals, rather than cutting and pasting them. To my mind the Short Radioactive Toy version (which does include an alternative guitar solo) works best from this method of editing, coming as the track fades into the ambient mid section.

These were joined by 2 tracks at the time "exclusive to this release" which were "The Jokes On You" clocking in at 4.00 and "Cloud Zero" a 4.20 instrumental (Times taken from the CD player). These were tracks destined for "Up The Downstair", but which did not make the album when the decision to downscale it from a double to a single album was taken. Subsequently these exclusive tracks lost their exclusivity by being released on "Staircase Infinities," initially a 10" vinyl limited edition of 2000 copies (I know Record Collector said it was only 1500 copies but it does say 2000 on the sleeve!!) a Delirium Netherlands only release (Lazy Eye 3094). On this they were timed as 4.05 for "Joke" and 4.39 for "Cloud Zero". In Steve Freights' recent A to Z article, "Cloud Zero" is listed as a separate mix. I have compared the 2 side by side and to my ear the differences are only slight, a few seconds here and there, though there appears to be a different tonal balance between the two. Later "Staircase Infinities" was re-released as a CD. For completists "The Joke's On You" also appeared on Audio magazine CD from Greece in August 1996.

The "Radio Active" CD has a black cover with "Porcupine Tree" at the top and "Radio Active" at the bottom with "(Delec-Promo-CD1) For Radio Broadcast Only" below. In the middle of the front cover are bare artwork shots (i.e. With no titles on them) LP cover shots of "On The Sunday of Life", "Voyage 34" and "Up the Downstair". On the back is the Delirium address and the titles, plus the statement that it is one of 500 CD's for radio broadcast only and not for resale. The copyright and production date is 1993. Wilson is given credit for all titles except "The Jokes On You" which is from the Duffy/Wilson period. The sleeve tells us that the tracks were "programmed, produced and performed by Porcupine Tree at No Man's Land 1990-93." However, the lyrics of the song predate this. Most readers will know that "The Jokes On You" was the title of Karma's first tape, though the song did not actually appear on the tape. The song was, I believe, originally performed by The Jabberwockies, on their self titled Acid Tape (Tab 043), dating from February 1986 to November 1987, where the lyrics are credited to Alan Duffy, and Limo (of Fit and Limo). See Voyage 35, issue 4, page 10, for more information. Publishing credits on the CD go to Hit and Run Music (Publishing) Ltd.

In the recent Record Collector discography this CD promo was priced at £25 reflecting its limited numbers, although it is known copies have sold for more..

Help
(By Steve Freight)

On 27 March 1997 Porcupine Tree appeared on the Italian TV show Help, presented by Red Ronnie who, it is said, is to the Italians what John Peel is to us.

What follows is a review of this show.

Whilst being presented, naturally, in Italian, Red Ronnie speaks to the band in English and then translates the answers and comments given.

He begins the show with his introduction and introduces the band who are positioned at the back of the studio initially. He moves on to talk to a member of the audience who it later transpires is Foxy Gardelli (who runs a fanzine in Italy). I'm afraid her words of wisdom will remain a secret until someone can translate them.

Unfortunately for Richard Barbieri, Red Ronnie plays on the fact that he used to be in Japan the whole time that band were there. It begins in the 5th minute when Richard is invited to step forward and is asked if he knows this video. Richard comments "Thank you" with a slightly uncomfortable quality to his voice. Asked what song it is Richard comments it is from the first album and when the video begins, comments that he hasn't changed much.

After Red Ronnie has shown various newspaper stories on his overhead projector and commented on various pages from the internet, he invite the band to go to the stage at the front of the studio to perform, but before they can begin he begins to chat to the band. He asks who writes the material and begins to read the lyrics from Waiting. "Waiting for the day. Which day?" he queries of Steven. Steven tells that the lyrics are about people who wait for life to come to them instead of making their own lives. Colin looks on in amused silence.

We then move into the song live in the studio. No miming for our lads; the artificial nature of the studio does not stop them from giving a very good account of themselves with this song which features a few minor changes in style and chords so that we know it's live.

After the song Ronnie is back to his overheads with reviews of Porcupine Tree from various papers.

A discussion then ensues on the Tree's popularity in Italy as opposed to England and Steven again gives his views on the acceptance of the band by the English press and Progressive Rock.

He moves onto Chris (figuratively speaking!) and asks why was he asked about the length of the songs to play. Chris's response "Because some of the songs we do are very long!" Asked about the longest song they do Steven talks about Voyage 34 at 30 minutes and Ronnie remarks that that is an album!

Ronnie seems bemused at the fact that fans of the band have all the albums by the band and that is why they are doing a cross selection of tracks from various albums. Dipping into the last but one album they introduce Dislocated Day.

Internet messages are coming in now and one person thinks the band have been influenced by Depeche Mode. Steven refutes this and says they are low on any list of influences, but that when you like a group you hear their influences everywhere.

Unfortunately it's now time for Richard to be made to feel uncomfortable again. Ronnie begins by asking about his equipment and lets his fingers do the walking across the keyboards of his favourite organ.

He then asks about the fans who have followed him from his Japan days and Richard diplomatically says that before he joined the band, Porcupine Tree already had their own following. He concedes that people have followed him as a natural progression from Japan.

He then proceeds to quiz Richard over the demise of Japan and he states it was pressures of friendships from early days and they just had to have a break. "Are you still friends?" "Three of us are" replies Richard. "I can imagine which one isn't a friend" responds Ronnie "I'm sure you know" Richard re-joins. Richard clarifies this by saying they are not enemies but haven't seen each other for a few years. It becomes increasingly obvious that Ronnie wants to know more on the break up but won't get anything else. He then introduces another Japan video, Life In Tokyo, this time.

After this it's straight into Signify – scorching stuff!

It's then back to the net messages which sounded like congratulations to the band and comparisons to Floyd (again). Radioactive Toy is next and Ronnie asks why Radioactive Toy. Steven refers him to the lyrics which he reads and then asks "Why do you want to destroy?". "It's ironic" replies Steven "written from the point of view of politicians".

The band then play. Unfortunately there appeared to be an echo on Steven's voice for this song, but a couple of times it made it sound very eerie and atmospheric.

At the end of this Ronnie asks them to think of 2 other songs to do – a bonus it would appear that was not planned for.

It's then back to Richard again regarding the concerts for Jansen Barbieri Karn, and asked what music they will play. Richard states they will be concentrating on the music from 1990 to the present day – not the past, and finally gets to say that he is not interested in the past and therefore is not keen on seeing the videos for that reason. A discussion then ensues on the merits of Japan's music and Richard admits he is happy with what was done but there was better music produced towards the end and again says it's in the past.

Ronnie then goes on to play a video of a performance filmed on one of his shows featuring Steve Jansen and Mick Karn.

Asked which song the band will now play live Steven says they only have one more song under 10 minutes and they will play that. He announces it as The Moon Touches Your Shoulder and Ronnie is in raptures as there is a video playing on the back screen of a moon landing. I don't know why they think of Ronnie as their John Peel. I can't understand Ronnie but I'm getting a bit tired of him now. Just let the band play!

The Moon Touches Your Shoulder is performed – again very atmospheric. Pity it wasn't coupled with Always Never, but there you go, can't have everything.

It's then back to the net and a question for Richard again. He confirms they will play Beginning To Melt at their shows. He asks the band to play another song and Steven tells him they have run out of short songs. At last he finally realises for 2 minutes there are other members in the band except Richard and Steven, and Colin and Chris actually get to say "My name is…".

For those old enough to remember, Ronnie sees Steven's Sandie Shaws. He asks why he doesn't wear anything on his feet, Steven says it is because he can't operate the pedals with shoes and demonstrates their various uses including his Sly and Family Stone and Stone Roses impressions.

There are freebies then given out by Red Ronnie of some Italian Crackers (by this time I'm getting worried by Ronnie). After more comments from the net on various points, including their 3 nights in Rome, Ronnie invites them back at a later date (he's not that bad then) to play a 20 minute song (Steven says 30 but Ronnie draws the line at 20).

Foxy is then invited forward to show her fanzine on his overhead and it appears it is all over. But no, he has to get his final Japan fix in and yes, it's another video, this time Visions of China. Richard's reaction is not recorded.

Well that's it and a very enjoyable hour and a half it is too. I've probably been a bit harsh in my view of Ronnie because I couldn't understand all that was said and have to say that if a show like this was on UK terrestrial TV it would be a hit – come back Bob Harris and the Old Grey Whistle Test!

Every Home Is Wired
Oh how times change! How did we ever manage without the internet?

I'm not wired but am sent the occasional article which appears on the net. I know a number of you are on the 'net but probably the majority are not. If you find anything while surfing that you think would interest others please send me a copy and I'll consider including. My thanks to Jill Strobridge for sending me the following and to Hans Van de Pavert who is the author.

ATHENS GIG REVIEW (by Hans Van de Pavert)

Hello mates

Here's a short review of the PT concert at the Rodon Club last night (22/11/97), their third and definitely most stunning gig in Athens yet.

The club was jam-packed, proving that it had been a good idea to show up one full hour before the hall opened to the public, so that we had front row on the balcony, from which we had a perfect view on stage.

The band was in fabulous shape and looking very relaxed. For the first time (out of the three gigs I've seen) Steven seemed really comfortable, being at home on the stage, looking almost continuously at the audience, thanking for the applause in Greek and even walking up to the edge of the stage a few times to have front row chicks try to touch his (bare) feet and hair.

Chris was giving drumming lessons to all who have ears, Colin's playing was better than ever before and Richard, as usual, very humbly playing at the left side of the stage.

The sound quality was much better than last year, especially towards the end of the show, and the light show was a treat for the eyes.

Set List

Even Less (great new song, wonderful vocals, can't wait to hear this on the album)
Up The Downstair (all time favourite)
Waiting (both parts)
Moon Touches Your Shoulder / Always Never (merged as they should be)
This Is No Rehearsal (about which Steven didn't feel quite satisfied, but we did)
Moonloop (first part only)
Signify (8 Richter scale)
The Sleep Of No Dreaming (now here's where the singing lessons really show off)
Ambulance Chasing (announced as "what might be the title track of the new album")
Voyage 34 (didn't mind at all hearing this one again, it's still sounding fresh)

Encore 1
Dislocated Day (with the jokey start and break)
Radioactive Toy (getting better all the time and with audience input on vocals)

Encore 2
Not Beautiful Anymore (just to be sure it would remain an unforgettable gig)

All in all, the Tree were more perfect than ever, giving a performance that could easily match with the Coma Divine recordings. And, as far as we could tell from the new songs, the next album is going to have some very interesting ("more contemporary" as Steven put it) material.

VOYAGE 35 ISSUE 8

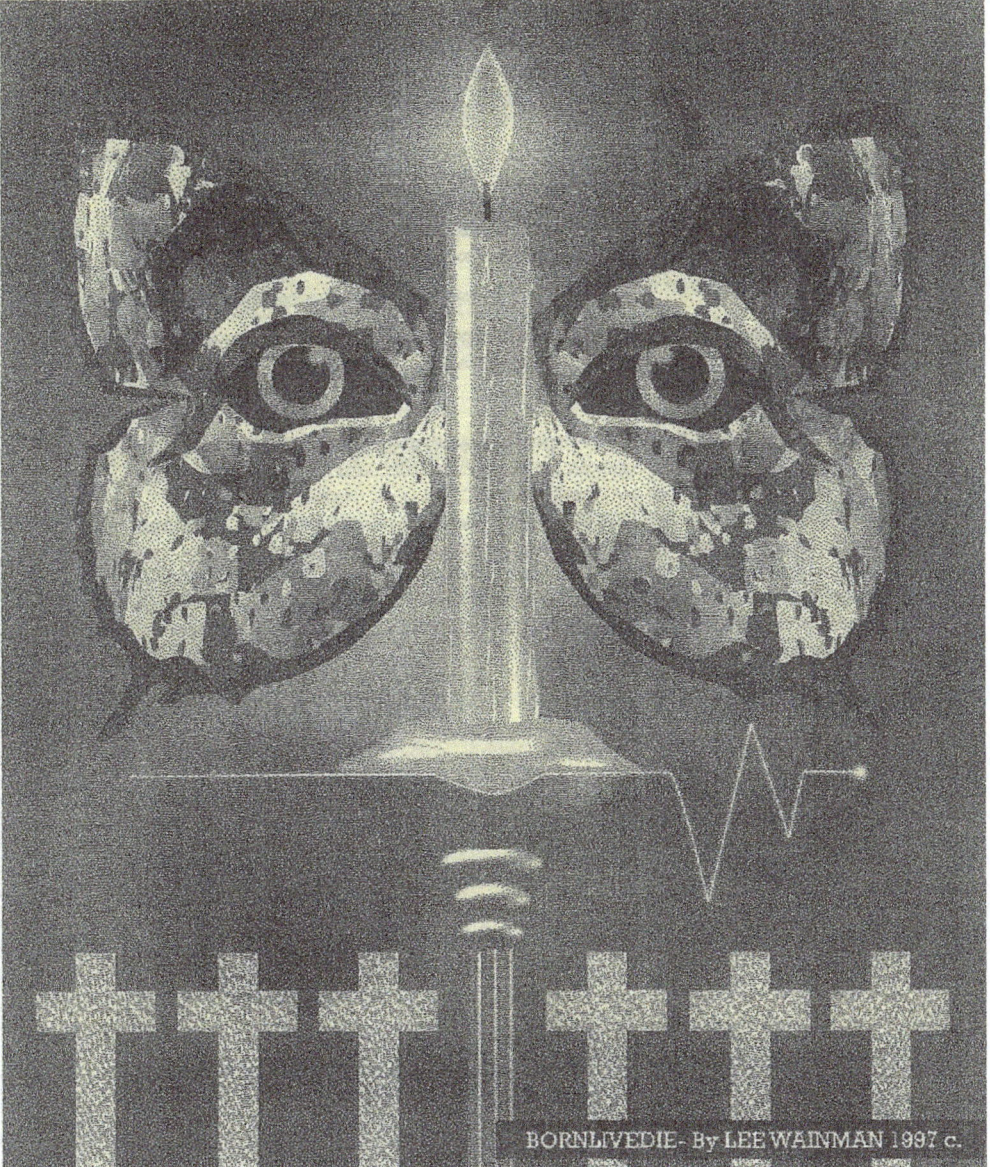

BORNLIVEDIE- By LEE WAINMAN 1997 c.

Issue 8

Published June 1998

Contents:
Welcome to Voyage 35
An EXCLUSIVE Steven Wilson interview for SF
Porcupine Tree at the BBC 9/12/1994 (the inside story)
Prog or no Prog (a discussion topic)
LSD, An introduction, by Didier Withoos, to a web site now sadly no longer with us
Views from the net
The latest news
Results of the readers poll
Gig reviews
Readers mail
Full Colour Centre spread (pictures taken at Strawberry Fair, Cambridge)

Record Collector said:
The 8th issue of Steve Freight's A5 b&w periodical dedicated to the progressive psychedelic noodlers features an interview with Steven Wilson, although Wilson being such a mysterious and reclusive chap, the questions were answered by post. Features include a discussion on whether Porcupine Tree are "prog" or not, an insider's view of a BBC radio session, the results of a reader's poll and various observations and letters.

Porcupine Tree At The BBC 9/12/94 - The Inside Story
(By Mark Robson)

I will always remember my friend Andrew's phone call that night. You could tell by his voice something special was afoot. "What are you doing on 9th December ?" he gasped, "Cancel everything because I have just been talking to Steven Wilson and he says we can go to Manchester and watch Porcupine Tree record a session for Mark Radcliffe, as long as we will act as their road crew". That sounded a fair deal so naturally I was up for it, also it would be a chance to hear the band live for the first time.

The arrangement on the day was we had to arrive at the Oxford Road Studios around 6pm. Right on time we marched up to the front door, pushing through the surprisingly large crowd only to find the doors locked. "Fire alert mate, they are not letting anyone in or out" was the explanation. Could the day be over before it had started ?.

While pondering this and the logic of locking the doors during a fire alert we walked around the massive building to what seemed the tradesmen's entrance, controlled by one very harassed security guard. Why harassed?, because there were queues of cars wanting to get out and in but his orders were to keep the gates locked. This was a no win situation for the old boy, and he knew it. Some tact was required, and a polite enquiry if this was the correct entrance for the band in session tonight. Checking his clip board, he confirmed Porcupine Tree were indeed expected, and we were first to arrive. Thinking we were the band he invited us into his cabin to wait. Being civil worked wonders.

About 6.30pm the alert was lifted and the traffic started to clear. First to arrive was Chris in a car that had seen better days. We had not seen any pictures of the band we were not 100% sure what anyone looked like. Still feeling like intruders about to be discovered and ejected any minute we went over to Chris and introduced ourselves. Thankfully he was a very approachable and started talking like long lost cousins.

Not long after the rest of the band arrived all in cars with their gear in the boot and on the seats. More introductions followed but these were cut short as the Engineers Assistant came down to get us organised. A very pleasant young lady (who caught the eye of more than one of our party) gave us all passes, so we had the freedom of the studios.

The band were required to move their own equipment, thankfully close by was a small lift so only a couple of trips were needed to get it all up to the correct floor, from where we took it into the studio. I was very surprised how large this was compared to the other studios I had been in. They were about a 10th of the size of this room.

The band started to set up various people drifted in and out. Richard wanted to use headphones, but it took the Engineer three pairs before they could find a pair that worked properly. Most of the conversation centred around what songs they were going to play. The BBC wanted four, but the band pointed out that due to the length of their songs three would be more practical. At last a compromise was agreed and "Burning Sky" would be played in two parts with the interview in-between.

Hospitality arrived on a trolley Richard grabbed a bottle and stashed it behind his keyboards. Alas for those hoping for debauchery this was only mineral water. Alcohol was not on the menu just yet.

Round about now I realized it was not only the band who were strangers to me. A small shabby slob slouched into the studio, who looked like the cleaner but turned out to be our host Mr. Radcliffe. He seemed to know Richard very well, but spotting us he pointed a grubby finger and inquired "Who's these two then".

"Road crew" replied Steven. We smiled and gave him a wave.

Doing his best to grease Radcliffe's palm Richard gave him some CDs which soon disappeared into his deep pockets. With that he left never to be seen again as his studio was on a different floor.

During planning of a radio show timing is important. The whole show was totally scripted, and the band had been allocated a certain time slot. A first run through the set was required, and the news was not good as they had over run. A quick discussion followed as to what would have to be shaved. "Radioactive Toy" was rejigged, and the set replayed. The Assistant was pleased they were well under, but did not tell them only saying that would be fine. Things were now ready for showtime. It was suggested we should adjourn to the BBC bar which seemed a sensible idea, even more attractive when we discovered the price of Boddingtons. Chris saw they were also serving chips and ordered two portions. A couple of drinks later and it was fast approaching 10pm so we had to dash back to the studio just before they were about to send the search parties out.

We settled back down into the control room as Radcliffe starts his patter "Tonight Porcupine Tree Prog Rock, Ambient, Dance, Bossonova overlords live in session". The band took their positions looking tense but confident, arranged in a loose circle of Steve, Colin, Chris, and Richard.

"Radioactive Toy" was the first song which passed uneventfully. After we returned into the studio to chat, everyone seemed very happy with the way things had gone. I remember commenting to Colin how unreal all this felt with us here and the unseen millions out there. He said he had never thought about it until now. So if there were any shaky bass notes during the next number "Burning Sky" then I accept full responsibility.

Whatever happens to Porcupine Tree history will remember tonight for the "Always Never Bum Note Incident". If you are going to do it, so they say do it in style. Your debut Radio One Session being as good a place and time as any. The pained cry of Steven said everything. The Engineer and his Assistant exchanged shocked glances wondering if the thing was going to fall apart. As the song built up again there was real tension in the control room, would he be able to manage the second solo. Being a true professional Steven pulled it off, but after they had finished he was gutted shaking his head and saying to anyone who would listen he did not know how it happened.

Before returning to the hotel booked by Steven (sleeping arrangements separate rooms for the interested) they got the Assistant to make reservations at a famous curry house. We were offered the chance to join them but we still had a two hours plus drive home, and work next morning which for Andrew was a 6am start so we just had to go.

A classic moment in Prog Rock history, and we were proud to have been there.

Prog or Not Prog?
Are Porcupine Tree progressive?

This time old question still haunts the band and cannot be easily settled. The band certainly do not consider themselves to be a progressive rock band if by this you mean Pendragon, IQ et al.

Labels are all well and good when something fits easily into a mould, but to have to find a place for a band's music can be derogatory to the band in question.
I personally have never liked labels but always (if you look back on previous issues) fall into the trap of trying to categorise music for the

benefit of trying to DESCRIBE the music, not to label it.

Hawkwind are Space Rock, not due to the style necessarily but the concepts explored. However they spawned a whole subculture of bands who try to emulate their style of playing and it has become a sub genre.

What should matter is the MUSIC ITSELF. Do you enjoy listening to a band? If so that should be all that matters.

Many people say they only like Progressive rock. What do they listen to?

In their day Pink Floyd, Genesis, Yes and even Led Zeppelin were considered progressive, and yet how many of these would be said to be today?

Progressive rock has become a style of music not a progression as it was in the 70's. in those days (and I'm old enough to remember the delights of the new Yes or Floyd album being released and finding it fresh) each album built upon the previous one, not sounding stale and "samey" as many of the prog bands today do. I'm not slagging them off, some are very good musically and do sound good, but the music itself is derivative and you know what to expect before you put it on the turntable (I still like the thought even if now it's the CD player, but it doesn't have the same ring to it).

Not so Porcupine Tree – they evolve from album to album and you know you are going to get something fresh and interesting with each new release. They explore new musical styles and are not afraid to experiment.

Look at the diverse nature of Steven's talent: No Man, IEM, Bass Communion and tell me this all fits into one genre. It doesn't and it does not give full credit to Steven's and the rest of the Band's talents.

Richard also has his own style when away from Porcupine Tree and very refreshing it can be to listen to diverse music from musicians we listen to in the group. Chris likes the classics and has introduced us to this in the group context with his composition Light Mass Prayers. This was what progressive music was in the 70's.

The band first used the Progressive Rock tag on the Mark Radcliffe show to describe how they fitted new and different styles together and used the newer instruments available. This seemed at the time like a good way to describe their music, however subsequently when trying to describe this journalists have only heard what they want to hear and unfortunately have stuck with the "Prog rock" tag.

Red Ronnie on his TV show in Italy again brought this to the fore. The band did not mention it, Ronnie did and Steven had to explain his thoughts again. It was from one stating of progressive rock on the radio that everyone has assumed they are in this bracket. Ronnie made a comment about ELP and prog rock – just how far removed are Porcupine Tree from ELP. Make your own mind up but they certainly can't even begin to be compared.

Let's just say they are a rock band which we like and are the best thing since --- (but that would be another cliché!)

As I said they are evolving with every album so perhaps we should coin a new genre for Porcupine Tree – Evolving Rock – but that would be back to putting a label on them again and we could start this article all over again. However this is a "label" which would suit better than Progressive.

I'm sure you're reading this and there are some of you nodding your head in agreement and others thinking what a load of old…

Let me know what you think and I'll print your comments in the next issue. I know this could keep us arguing for issues to come but I'd like to get some idea of what you think so I'll try and keep this to one issue only.

Steven Wilson Interview 2

Steven has again agreed to an interview and this was conducted by post in February 1998.

V35: Many thanks Steven for agreeing to undertake another interview.

Firstly I'd like to ask how Karma was formed and if there are any other recordings you know of which are around, other than The Last Man Too Laugh, The Joke's On You and the live Chesham Underground tapes.

SW: Karma was formed in 1982 and comprised myself and 3 friends from school. I think we were very much inspired by the success of bands like Marillion to play in that particular style. We only ever made 2 demo tapes, the two that you mention. I have in my possession several tapes of live performances, although I was not aware that a cassette of a Chesham gig was in circulation (or even remember doing the gig!)

V35: Did Karma do many live gigs and can you remember how you felt performing live in those days?

SW: We must have played between 30-40 gigs in our 3 year existence. Since all us us were still at school and none of us were old enough to drive, it was very difficult to perform outside of our local area. So nearly all of these gigs were in Hertfordshire. I never really enjoyed playing live until Porcupine Tree. I was very shy and hated being the one who had to stand at the front and sing. Also our equipment was very basic as we had to rely on our parents to buy it for us. I remember having to complete a gig in Luton with only 4 strings on my guitar because I didn't have any spares!

V35: Do you have any contact with or know what the other members of the group are doing now?

SW: Mark Gordon (the drummer) is still a good friend of mine. He works for a company called Natural Audio who are specialists in digital recording technology. He has just helped me to upgrade my studio to a computer based recording system called Pro Tools 24, which I will be using to record the new Porcupine Tree album. I don't really have any contact with the other ex-members.

V35: You said when I mentioned Pride of Passion that there was worse to come. If you don't want to divulge who or what these groups were could you fill in the time scales illustrating by way of group 1, group 2 etc. interspersed with Karma, Altamont so that we know just how many different groups we need to look out for.

SW: There weren't really any other "groups" as such – at least none that played concerts or made recordings. However there were lots of one off tapes made by various combinations of friends from school. At least one of these was quite extensively copied and distributed – in fact I recall it made No. 4 in the Sounds "DIY chart". I'm not about to tell you what this tape was though – it's bloody awful! *(start searching those old issues, if you have them – Steve).* There were also several cassette compilations that I contributed tracks to, at least once under my own name. These kind of things were very popular in the early eighties in the wake of the "industrial" ethic.

V35: Are there any tapes to look out for by these groups?

SW: I never recorded with Pride of Passion, the Karma and Altamont tapes you know about, so I think it's just the above I think.

V35: As previously mentioned in V35 it was rumoured that you had sent out tapes in your own name for promotional purposes. Can you confirm this and tell us if any of the tapes you have mentioned have any songs on that we know from either Porcupine Tree or No Man.

SW: No – I don't think I ever would have sent out tapes under my own name. Tapes of No Man and Porcupine Tree (and probably Karma, Altamont etc) would have gone off to all the usual suspects in the vague hope of obtaining lucrative record contracts, radio sessions and gigs – and some of these would almost certainly have included tracks that have been subsequently released or subsequently consigned to the dustbin.

(As an aside my friend when going through his loft full of tapes found some tapes by another person with the surname Wilson and had confused the two. He says they are nothing like each other and it was his mind playing tricks – Steve)

V35: How did you get the ideas for the booklets which accompanied the Tarquin's and Nostalgia Tapes?

SW: That was purely for fun – and maybe slightly because I didn't want people to treat the tapes like they were just another guy making tapes in his bedroom.

V35: On a recent Dave Allen show one of his stories featured Porcupine and Trees. Is this by any stretch of the imagination where you got the inspiration for the name from?

SW: No

V35: Are you still remaining coy on this?

SW: Yes

V35: I have been asked why No Man releases are so low key. Could you let us know how we can find out about these when they are issued.

SW: The reason they are so difficult to find is because we record for quite a small label and the distribution of small labels tends to be quite erratic. The best way to find out about No Man plans is simply to get on our free mailing list – simply us us a line and you will always be informed of forthcoming releases and details of how to obtain them via mail order

V35: What is the story about the non-appearance of No Man's "Strip Wild EP"?

SW: I don't even remember what that was supposed to be. There are countless projected No Man and PT releases that got cancelled or replaced by something else (eg the "lost" second single from "Signify")

V35: And the 7" single of Men of Wood?

SW: May still come out one day. This was originally recorded for "Up the Downstair" and then re-recorded with live drums for "The Sky Moves Sideways". It was very much in the "Jupiter Island" / "Linton Samuel Dawson" vein and really didn't fit into what I was doing by that time.

V35: How do you feel about the move to Ark 21 for future releases? Will this affect the way you approach Porcupine Tree music in the future?

SW: No – it certainly won't affect the music at all. It just means that we will have a lot more money and clout behind us than we did while we were on Delerium. Basically Art 21 are part of EMI, but we would never consider doing a deal with a company who were going to try and change the way we made music. Porcupine Tree are developing anyway and I've no doubt that some people will view the changes in the next album as being down to label influence – but all of the tracks were written long before we agreed a deal and I hope our albums will always show a development from the ones that preceded it.

V35: Will this affect the future release of "collectors" items such as the tapes with Transmission and the LP's? The view is that these cater for the true fans desire for alternative and collectable items and are always welcome.

SW: No – I definitely want to continue to cater for the collectors and loyal fans. It's good for us too, because there is always music that isn't necessarily right for a major release. As with the "Insignificance" tape, there will almost certainly be a whole load of demos, fragments of songs and improvisations left over from the current recording sessions and I would like to put together another collection to cover these.

V35: Whilst some of these items, like the IEM album was said to be Vinyl only there are now plans we hear of this appearing on CD. There are rumblings from some quarters that this is taking advantage of the fans, likewise the re-issues without bonus cuts. What would you say to these comments?

SW: I do understand this but it does put me in a very awkward position. I really was very unhappy with the sound quality and packaging of the first three albums, particularly in the wake of the high standards set by the "Signify" album. I had been hassling Delerium for a couple of years to replace the old versions so that at least the people discovering the band from now on would be buying superior editions.

We made the decision not to put extra tracks on the new editions for two reasons, firstly because it spoilt the continuity and completeness of the original albums (I do put a lot of thought into this) and secondly because it would have meant that fans not so concerned with the mastering/packaging issue would not feel cheated at having to buy the re-masters just for the extra music. However I know that there are always fans who will re-buy CDs if they feel that there is any improvement at all, even if it's just cosmetic. I myself am the same, having bought for a second time all of the Marvin Gaye, Talk Talk, Tangerine Dream, Pink Floyd and Miles Davis catalogues for the improved quality and packaging. But I have to say that I was happy to do this even though I might have moaned about the expense at the time!

With the Chromatic releases, I did say at the time that the "Spiral Circus" album would NEVER again be reissued in any format, but that the IEM album would be issued on CD at some point. When it does come out it won't have any extra material (there really isn't any to include), but I am hoping to persuade Delerium that it should be sold at mid price.

V35: In issue 7, I mentioned the rumours that there was going to be a "Delerium Years" best of. Is this likely to happen and if so what is intended to be on this?

SW: Yes – I think both I and Delerium would like to do this at some time in the not too distant future. I haven't really thought that hard about what format it should take or what should be on it (maybe your poll will help us there!), but we would certainly try and make it appeal to both the newcomer to Porcupine Tree as well as the established fans who have the albums already, by including rare EP and compilation tracks.

V35: Did you play as a 3 piece in Coventry and did the set as rumoured consist entirely of Voyage 34? How long was it and who was missing?

SW: Yes – Richard Barbieri had to fly to Japan to fulfil a prior commitment, so we did the whole of Voyage 34 with the keyboards on tape.

V35: Regarding the new album, how is this progressing and what plans are there for releases from these sessions?

SW: It should be finished by mid June. I think everybody involved feels it is by far the strongest album yet. There should be a single from the album out in the Summer (probably "Stranger by the Minute" or "This is No Rehearsal"), with plenty of non-album material also included. The album should follow in September – October. (I have recently heard from Steven and the album is still not quite finished). In Steven's words "the track listing seems to be changing by the day, so unfortunately that means that it will probably not emerge in September as we hoped. The best way for people to keep up to date on the albums progress is to check my own personal website. This includes bang up to date news and plans for all of my projects as well as very thorough discographics and my own playlist (people are always asking what I listen to)". Steven's website address is:- http://www.nomansland.demon.co.uk

V35: While you have gained a following in the UK, do you feel you have suffered from a lack of press and/or poor reviews?

SW: When the reviews have come they have been pretty much 50/50 for/against. However the reputation we had as a "progressive" rock band did us no favours at all and set us back at least a couple of years. Incidentally it was a deliberate policy not to send out review copies of the live album except to MOJO and one or two others – that one was for the fans

V35: What is the press like in countries such as Italy and Greece where you have a larger following?

SW: Obviously much better – national newspapers review our gigs and the style of music is not used as an excuse to prejudge the band.

V35: Chris's antics in the studio and backstage have been mentioned a couple of times, but without any real specifics. What type of things does he get up to and do they help the band relax before a gig?

SW: No comment – *(shame – Steve)*

V35: How would you ideally like to prepare for a gig, and does it get easier as time goes on?

SW: It certainly doesn't get any less scary, especially as the audiences get bigger and more expectant. These days a couple of glasses of wine and a floor show from Chris help to relax me.

V35: Well, I look forward to the new album and concerts this year. Thank you Steven for your time.

SW: Always a pleasure.

My thanks again to Steven for his time and continued support for Voyage 35.

As you know I would like to arrange interviews with the other band members in the future so if there are any burning issues you'd like to know the answers to please let me have your questions and I'll do my best to get you the answers.

Linton Samuel Dawson

Didier is the name, 29 years old, I live in the Netherlands and work as a scan operator/DTP-er in a printing office for some years now. That's more than enough about me so now a bit about the Tree.

The first time that I saw Porcupine Tree they were playing at the "Planet Pul Festival" in Uden, The Netherlands. They were not headlining although they were a lot better than the rest. I guess the audience was quite impressed because the PT stand was well visited.

They sold a lot of CDs as I recall. Anyway, I bought the CDs and like them very much and haven't missed one Dutch gig since. The best gig I attended was in Antwerp, Belgium. Scanner, Porcupine Tree and Ozric Tentacles gave acte de presence in the Belgian amphitheatre I really loved the atmosphere and I hope they will do it again sometime

I saw the guys strut their stuff in the UK 2 times now. The first time at Hawkwind's 25th anniversary in Brixton Academy, London. Going to England for only one night is quite a trip when you live on the mainland of Europe and it was quite a bummer when I realised that they only played for half an hour. Oh well, that's life.

The second time I saw a Porcupine Tree gig over there was just plain luck really. We had planned to go to London for a few days and after we had set the date for our few days off in England. I heard that they would play at Strawberry Fair in Cambridge. By train it takes only one hour to go from London to Cambridge so that was a done deal. The nicest thing about going to Cambridge was that I finally met Steve Freight (Editor of "Voyage 35" the Porcupine Tree fanzine) and some people who I knew via the PT-Trans mailing list.

The above story you can find on my homepage as a sort of introduction. So why the Porcupine Tree Fan Page you might ask? After the first time I saw them in Uden I listened a lot to the albums and asked Delerium for more info. in about a year I had basically all PT Items available. The only problem was that there was no fan club/fanzine who could provide you with news about the band.

At that time I was involved with the Dutch Pink Floyd magazine called "Echoes" so I knew that running a fanzine is an awful lot of work. I was thinking about starting a PT fanzine but because a) I knew it was a lot of work and b) I didn't have enough material like interviews, articles and such, it held me back. In the meantime the fanzine "Voyage 35" saw the light of day and since PT isn't the largest band in the world (yet) I thought that it was a bit overdone to start a Dutch fanzine for Porcupine Tree because most Dutch people can read English, so ... internet! Internet was the solution for me because one fanzine (international) is enough, in my humble opinion.

Since I like to muck around with computers and because there was almost nothing to find on the net concerning Porcupine Tree I thought…that's it. The only thing there was in the time I started in August 1996 was the Delerium homepage which was made by Ivor and there was a page with a Bio including the discography on the net. That was all so since August 8, 1996 you can find "Linton Samuel Dawson" on the internet. What's in it? Articles from magazines, interviews, reviews, giglist, setlists etc.

The purpose of the page is to provide information about Porcupine Tree and hopefully this way they will get the credit they deserve.

You can find it at http://www.tip.nl/user/didier

(Sadly no more. I don't think that Didier really got the appreciation that he deserved for being the first to really promote the band on the web. SF2020)

Queen Quotes Crowley

First an extract from a letter from Rodney Kidd which throws up some interesting arguments for reissues, but at the same time only goes to reinforce the marketing aspect for Record Companies.

The last time I talked to Freakbeat the IEM album was due to be released on CD. This is something I am looking forward to as I didn't buy it on Vinyl. I don't actually like buying things on vinyl, mainly due to the fact that I have yet to upgrade the record deck in line with the rest of the hi-fi, also CDs are far more convenient, especially as I tend to listen to about 3 hours of CDs on my Discman going to and from work every day! And I also disagree with albums only being released on one format (this goes both ways – if there is a market for vinyl still – which there is – albums should still be pressed on vinyl).

This also brings me to the point about what should and shouldn't be re-issued. Music is a strange phenomena, it is essentially a produce (or at least that's what the record companies want you to believe), but it also has an intangible element, ie the listening to and enjoyment of the music. Also you get fans (I am one – you are one), and when you become a fan a strange thing happens – you want everything by that artist. You will, for some strange reason, quite happily go out and buy what is essentially the same thing over and over again. I have both the limited edition vinyl of "Sky Moves" and the CD. The record isn't there to be played, it's part of the collection. I think this is something that is overlooked by certain people. Also we will travel miles to see the band play, and sometimes go and see them more than once on a single tour – I saw Marillion three times in the space of ten days last year!

And so this brings me onto the subject of "Yellow Hedgerow". Now Steven Wilson has been quoted as saying he doesn't like this, and that's why it isn't currently available. Fair enough, if it had never been released, but it was. Therefore there are copies out there (obvious I know but...), and therefore we all want to own it. Problem is you can only buy it from collectors and other fans, or possibly as a bootleg. I noticed someone had written in to Issue 7 saying they had bought "Yellow Hedgerow" through an advert at a highly exaggerated price. Isn't this self-defeating? Surely it goes against Steven's idea. He's saying that the product is below par, but by it being deleted it is selling far and above it's true value. A contradiction in terms, I think!

It would be far better to just release it, at a cheap price, with a minimum of profit, stating that it isn't that good, but if you really must buy it – here it is! It could then be controlled, and people wouldn't need to spend an exorbitant amount for it! Or is this too simple an idea?

I should add that I am all for limited editions, of picture discs and special packaging, but don't limit the availability of the music, that's what makes us fans in the first place, the special packaging is just an added bonus…

Robert Fripp is/was considering doing something similar with "Earthbound". A truly badly recorded live album, but people want it, so it would be better to re-release properly and have control over it, than let the bootleggers get in on the act, and of course people don't have to pay huge sums of money for it.

As for why prog rock doesn't get it's just desserts here in Britain, I'm not really that concerned by it. We could have the situation like in America – niche radio stations who only play one type of music. Ok, so Radio One is based on a play list, but then again the current top 10 (20?) is pretty dismal anyway. I, for one, have a range of musical tastes, classical, rock, pop, blues (jazz is proving to be a bit elusive!) etc. OK so we are stuck with Radio One and Virgin, but can you really see a radio station playing a 10 minute plus track during the day? It's also still got the stigma of the 70's rock dinosaurs attached to it! True it would be nice if more people could listen to it, but then again, the people I have got to listen to Porcupine Tree, and 90's King Crimson etc. either a) hate it or b) like and don't listen to any of the general outlets of music ie don't listen to Radio One – so they won't have heard it either…I only got to see/hear Porcupine Tree from via the Marillion gig at the Forum a couple of years ago…and from there got in touch with Freakbeat and I bought the Delerium sampler and discovered a whole new set of bands! So we get there eventually!

Thanks for your thoughts. I know there are lots of people who collect every version of the same record. I used to with Hawkwind until they lost control of some recordings via poor licence deals and those tracks have been reissued under so many different titles you just can't keep up. Providing reissues are kept to a minimum fans can't accuse bands of ripping them off (see Steven's comments in his interview). I think Floyd's Dark Side of the Moon must take the biscuit for the most times it's been re-mastered, 5 times at the last count I believe, and just how different can these be, and can anyone actually tell the difference? Anyone have any further thoughts on this?

Please find enclosed, for the Gig List / Review book you mentioned at the end of my diaries, some reviews I wrote myself for Deliverence, a magazine I am proud to say gave Porcupine Tree a lot of exposure early on. Also enclosed is a flyer for Porcupine Tree's second gig in Coventry, put on in conjunction with Deliverence which I omitted from my diaries and was probably about the most significant and unusual one they did. It was part of an ambient night and they played as a 3 piece (Richard being unavailable) and to my memory they played just one long tune all evening – Voyage 34. If possible could you ask Steven on my behalf if my memory is accurate? Peter Clemons *(consider it done Peter – See Steven's interview)*.

I've been to a Porcupine Tree gig recently (Uden 18 April 1998), and what can I say, it was just brilliant, the best one I've seen so far by them! And it was the first time for me to hear those 3 new songs. The Venue is a rather small one and there were about 400 people there. I just can't understand why they have to talk all the time during the performance, it's so annoying. Anyway my wife and I really enjoyed the show though the light show was a bit disappointing – no slides this time. I also enclose some tickets I picked up for you (thanks – Steve). Andreas Stuwe

Didn't get to see this concert as I had a fever, so there is not much to tell but here's the set list:

Biebob Vosselaar, Belgium 16.4.98
Even Less, Waiting Parts 1 & 2, Sleep of No Dreaming, Up The Downstair, Moon Touches You ... Never (my abbreviation – Steve), Moonloop, Signify, This is no Rehearsal, Ambulance Chasing, Voyage 34. *Encore Dislocated Day, Radioactive Toy.*

I almost stayed home (still had fever) but I went to Delft (17.4.98) anyway. Verderop is a very nice venue but not made for rock concerts. There were some technical problems, the band couldn't hear themselves on stage, the sound was OK but could have been better. They skipped 2 new songs (Rehearsal and Ambulance Chasing) because of these problems but at last we got to hear Voyage 34!! Oh and I hardly recognised Steven Wilson as he had had his hair cut. Possibly 300+ in the venue. Set list the same as Biebob except tracks mentioned.

De Pul, Uden 18.4.98 and Tivoli, Utrecht 19.4.98 had the same set list as follows:

Even Less, Waiting Parts 1 and 2, Sleep of No Dreaming, Up the Downtair, This is No Rehearsal, Ambulance Chasing.

Moon Touches You...Never, Signify, Voyage 34. Encore Dislocated Day, Radioactive Toy. Encore 2 Not Beautiful Anymore.

Tivoli can hold 1200 people but about 300 people attended the gig. Porcupine Tree played even better than in Uden but the atmosphere in Uden was better. It was however very funny to see Colin mime the intro from Voyage 34. This concert (Tivoli) was the best of the Dutch tour.

As you can see the set list was almost the same very night. They opened with Even Less every night and I have to say that Even Less is so damn good. I was flabbergasted when I heard it. This is No Rehearsal is very good too but I wasn't that keen on Ambulance Chasing to be honest. Hmmm Music is and always will be a matter of personal taste. At last I heard Voyage 34 live. I heard it on tape many times but that's not quite the same. It was a short (15 minute) version but I'm not complaining. And Dislocated Day, I don't like the album version very much but live it's really something different. In Uden and Utrecht I stood right in front of the stage and this was the first time I took notice of Chris's drumming. I mean you can hear that he's a good drummer and it looks like he's doing it very nonchalantly, but every hit is just right and on the right place. Chris is, in my humble opinion, the best drummer on the planet. It's really a pleasure to see him doing his job. *Didier Withoos*

Every Home Is Wired - Views From The Net
My thanks to Kevin Bolton for sending me the following 2 reviews.

Rock City, Nottingham, 30 October 1997 by Andy Narracott

Hi all

This is my humble review of the gig at Rock City which I feel honour-bound to produce as I used this as an excuse to get hold of a copy of the set list.

The set was as follows:
Even Less, Signify, Waiting, Sleep of No Dreaming, Downstair, No Rehearsal, Moon Touches, Ambulance Chasing, Moonloop (Coda), Voyage 34, The Sky Moves Sideways, Radioactive Toy

I saw the band at Rock City at roughly the same time last year and so this was a bit of a nostalgia trip for me (hence I was the idiot grinning inanely in the middle of the room...).

Even Less was magnificent, heralded as "the long track from the new album that hasn't been recorded yet…" I must admit I normally don't like hearing new songs at gigs but all the new stuff really impressed me.

Signify romped home the way it always does…and with the extended live section from Coma Divine (as much of the album material is treated in this way it always makes the gigs so much more worthwhile).

Waiting was great, although I'm sure we only got Phase 1 (unless the change was so seamless that I missed it…).

Sleep of No Dreaming has grown on me much more since I've heard the live, slightly more beefy version.

Downstair provided a nice break into that style that the Tree do so well (a little bit of feedback but then in venues with small stages it must be hard to keep that much equipment from self destructing. When's the Wembley Stadium gig guys…??? Then another newie…No Rehearsal…which had a bit of a false start…(due to the Dat machine not coming through loud enough on the monitors)…but it was well worth the wait…and well worth the Dat Machine, which allowed an acoustic guitar break in the middle of the song…

We were informed at some point in the evening why Colin Edwin was seated throughout the evening…he has done his back in which is a crying shame as the frontline of the stage just didn't quite look the same…but it didn't seem to affect his bass playing which was as solid as usual.

Moon Touches was graceful and ethereal with the punch at the end that always makes me sit up and pay attention…and then into Ambulance Chasing which is another new track in the style of many of the Tree's instrumental classics. Moonloop was presented tonight in its shortened form and then into Voyage 34.

The encore obviously had to contain at least one of the two songs that we were graced with, and luckily we got both…Radioactive Toy was shortened as well (or maybe it's just that the entire gig seemed to be over far too soon).

Anyway that was it, I left wanting to hear Always Never, Dark Matter and the live version of Linton Samuel Dawson, which completely amazed me the first time I heard it…but there's always the Leeds gig I suppose…

What was nice as well was that the band came to chat with everyone at the merchandising stall…which was great fun and something that a lot of bands just don't seem to do nowadays…(well Steven and Chris did and I managed to catch Richard briefly as he was rushing off…)

All in all it was a thoroughly top night…and I liked the way that I turned up on my own and by the end of the night I'd already chatted to several groups of people simply 'cos they were into the band as well (friendly fans…another bonus).

Anyway sorry this mail has been so long (I'll try not to do the same after the Leeds gig).

Yours (a firm Tree fanatic).

And Jill Douglas' view of Leeds, 2 November 1997

Stunning, absolutely stunning.
Sever Tomorrow

(Short but to the point – Steve)

Please remember that when surfing, if you come across anything you think will be of interest to other readers, please take a copy and send by pigeon post to yours truly. I'll do my best to include reviews, gossip etc in the following issue and give you a name-check.

Many thanks

voyage 35

issue nine

dedicated to

porcupine tree

this issue **No-Man** special

Issue 9

Published October 1998

Contents:
The BIG No Man Special (this contains everything you want/need to know about No Man)
Intro to issue 9
The latest news
Full Colour Centre spread
Readers letters including Feedback from Steven Wilson on the band Karma
Tim Bowness on Flowermouth and Flame
Retroactive Ploy - a reprinted article from ISMO

No Man

The Discography and comments relating thereto, in the following article are by Phil Harwood. The history notes are by Steve Freight and for ease in tracing this narrative are in Italic. This article will give the fullest possible discography on No Man to have appeared anywhere, including Steven's web page, and also a history of this band.

It appeared that this 'zine is dedicated to Porcupine Tree but I will continue to explore the other facets of Steven's (and other band members) musical works. Hopefully by doing so we will be able to build up a unique insight into the individual talents that go to make up Porcupine Tree.

No Man Is An Island

The story begins in 1986, when 2 prolific musicians got together. Like Steven Wilson, Tim Bowness liked experimenting with various musical styles. Steven had already put out a private album, Exposure and was looking for ways to expand his natural talents, both as a musician and a producer.

Date	Album	Format	Tracks
1986	Exposure 700 only, private pressing. Deleted	LP	From a Toyshop Window

Steven was putting together the album Double Exposure and originally contacted Tim for a contribution by his current group, After The Stranger. After many conversations the two found they had touched base on their musical influences and decided to record together. This they did during the period 1987 to 1989 but the fruits of these collaborations did not appear on record...

...until the issue of The Girl From Missouri. This sold in very few numbers and it is understood that the band destroyed all remaining unsold copies a few years ago. This has

1987	Double Exposure 1000 only, private pressing. Deleted	LP	Faith's Last Doubt Also includes track by Plenty (Tim Bowness) Forest Almost Burning / Sacrifice

Date	Title	Format	Tracks
6.1989	Expose It. Run unknown, private pressing. Deleted	LP	Screaming Head Eternal. Fresh Tree Terror Suspect

therefore made this a very collectable item. In addition to Steven and Tim, Ben Coleman contributed violin and Stuart Blagden, guitar, during this period and had already performed together in early 1989 in the Hemel Hempstead area.

Date	Title	Format	Tracks
6.1989	The Girl From Missouri EP (PLASS012) Deleted	12"	The Girl From Missouri Forest Almost Burning Night Sky Sweet Earth The Ballet Beast

(Whatever happened to this? – Steve)

The Girl from Missouri *(A review from a source unknown)*
"Vocals swoop, violins soar, pianos twinkle and the whole world dreams of teacakes". It's a long way from those progy Exposure compilation albums to Missouri, I never expected No Man Is An Island to sound like this (with) elements of Dead Can Dance, Hugo, Largo, Steve Reich and All About Eve. This is a three track 12", No Man are now a five piece and feature an electric violin that's very soothing, in fact the whole sound is soothing. This is Hypnotic (an over used word). This is sensuous, it's like a feather but it's not lightweight. It's like a calm deserted beach at night, only the slight sound of the sea. The violin takes it into classical territory, real Prog, not prog but progressive, another link has been formed, - Mekong Delta brought Metal and Classical music together, Pop has now met Classical music and No Man are unique. Classical Pop. There should be an LP called Prattle on the way.

| 11.1989 | Swagger EP (Sold only at gigs) Deleted | Cass | Flowermouth Life Is Elsewhere Bleed Mouth Was Blue |

No Man

In 1990 Stuart left and with him so did the tag "...Is An Island". A conscious decision was taken by the remaining three members to continue with the style of music they had been playing (no musical tags this time) and to expand this to encompass the current dance scene as well.

The first result was Colours, the old Donovan song.

| 7.1990 | Colours (Hidden Art HA4) Deleted | 7" | Colours Colours (Remodelled) |

This item was never actually available in the shops, but was used as a promotional item and limited to a run of 500 only.

| 11.1990 | Colours (Probe Plus Records) Deleted | 12" | Colours Drink Judas Colours (Remodelled) |

Commercial re-release of the Hidden Art single, including an early mix of "Drink Judas".

Colours made record of the week in Melody Maker and Sounds and from this their potential was spotted by the label One Little Indian.

They didn't exactly rush things and it was 7 months into 1991 before their first release on the new label came about.

7.1991	Days In The Trees EP (One Little Indian 57TP7CD) Deleted	12"	Mahler Ives Bartock Reich

All tracks are different versions / mixes of "Days in the Trees". There was a Japanese edition of this on Columbia which contained 2 additional remixes, one of which was by The Shamen.

This was a "nearly hit" and again made record of the week in Melody Maker.

4.1992	Lovesighs – An Entertainment (One Little Indian TPLP47MCD) Deleted	CD Cass LP	Heartcheat Pop Days in the Tree (Mahler) Drink Judas Heartcheat Motel Kiss Me Stupid Colours Irish Murdoch Cut Me Up Days in The Tree (Reich)

This 35 minute mini album contained material from the first 2 singles, plus tracks recorded for what was to be the third single, "Heartcheat Pop" but never released.

Following the release of this album, Steven and Tim wished to take No Man out on the road. This they did later in the year employing the talents of Steve Jansen, Mike Karn and what was to be the beginning of the relationship with Porcupine Tree member, Richard Barbieri.

> **Lovesighs: An Entertainment** *(A review from RCD issue 1)*
> No Man are an Island, refusing to slump into the grey waters of indie mumbling. Their colossal ambition welds together great operatic swoops of emotion and clipped staccato street rhythms. Superficially their approach may recall that of The Beloved but this visionary trio aim higher, displaying inventive devotion to Roxy Music, Mahler and Joe Tex. Literate and witty, they chase Tim Bowness' magnificently poignant vocals with venomous violins and an erotically ferocious backbeat. Zenith of this stirring debut is *Days In The Trees*, a tearstained ballad to sell your mother for. *Iris Murdoch Cut Me Up* is more garrulous but equally atmospheric. No Man are aeons ahead of their time. Book early to avoid sensory deprivation. ****

| 9.1992 | Ocean Song (One Little Indian 63TP7CD) Deleted | CD 12" | Ocean Song Back to the Burning Shed Swirl |

This relationship continued and produced the next single Sweetheart Raw.

| 1.1993 | Sweetheart Raw EP (One Little Indian 73TP7CD) | CD | Sweetheart Raw Bleed Say Baby Say Goodbye |

A collaboration with Jansen, Barbieri & Karn and available through mail order only.

| 1.1993 | Hit The North Session 3.10.1992 (Hidden Art) Deleted | Cass | Ocean Song Heartcheat Pop Break Heaven Days In The Trees Taking It Like A Man |

A mail order cassette only release of the BBC Radio 5 session, featuring the six piece line up that toured the UK in the Autumn of 1992.

3.1993	Only Baby (One Little Indian 83TP7CD) Deleted	CD 12"	Only Baby (Move For Me) Only Baby (Breathe For Me) Only Baby (Be For Me) Long Day Fall

It was then decided that, for fans only, another mail order cassette should be issued featuring early No Man ambient style experiments.

4.1993	Speak : 1988-89 (Hidden Art) Deleted	Cass	Speak Night Sky Sweet Earth Iris Murdoch Cuts Me Down Riverrun French Tree Terror Suspect Life With Picasso Curtain Dream Forest Almost Burning The Ballet Beast Heaven's Break Desert Heart Death and Dodgson's Dreamchild

Another mail order only cassette, believed to have an original working title of "Death and Dodgson's Dreamchild".

Loveblows and Lovecries – A Confession
A review from Melody Maker)

When I happened to remark to a colleague that the word "pretentious" may feature heavily in this review, he turned round and pleaded "Don't you be too hard on them. "On the contrary," I told him, "I'm *all for* No Man's pretensions. "Were it not for pretension, we would have been without David Bowie, Brian Eno, A Flock of Seagulls' preposterous haircuts and this miraculous LP. Pretension is intrinsic to rock's finer history, and recently there hasn't been nearly enough of it.

Commencing a pop album with a burst of impeccably cultured classical music is fairly pretentious, but it's essential to assume the correct stance (po-faced, brow furrowed, twiddling with imaginary moustache) to listen to the inspired stuff that follows. No-Man's landscape is one of tenderly stroked violins, breathy passions, subdued disco beats, art, death, empty shags, in suburban railway stations, decaying English stately homes and grandiose waltzes accompanied by the lonely ghost of "Stranded" era Roxy Music. And it is very, very wonderful. Take "Only Baby", an erotic pulse-scape to rival "Heart of Glass" shimmering and obsessive. Or "Sweetheart Raw", an impossibly tortuous sculpturing of overwrought pleadings and sinuous Mike Karn bass. Even better, perhaps, is "Tulip", where Tim Bowness' intimate, alienated whisper seems to crawl out of the speakers and physically tug at your ear. Quite where this cornucopia of elegance fits in nowadays is anybody's guess. It's spiritual home is somewhere between "Heroes" and "Gentlemen Take Polaroids": amid grunge, industrial thrash and techno, it simply makes sense. That, of course, is much of the appeal. It's like stepping out of time. And utterly loveable. *Dave Simpson*

5.1993	Loveblows and Lovecries – A Confession (One Little Indian TPLP57CD) Deleted	CD Cass LP	Loveblow Only Baby Housekeeping Sweetheart Raw Lovecry Tulip Break Heaven Beautiful and Cruel Painting Paradise Heaven's Break

The LP version of "Sweetheart Raw" is an edit of the 9 minute CD single version. The version issued in the USA, released on Epic, also contains "Taking It Like A Man" and a remix of "Days in the Trees".

A further collaboration with Jansen, Barbieri and Karn brought forth the track Heaven Taste, for the next single.

6.1993	Painting Paradise (One Little Indian 93YP7CD) Deleted	CD 12"	Painting Heaven

This is a different version to the album and was an attempt to rework the song as a single. It is completely different (and in many ways inferior to the album version).

Painting Paradise *(A review from Melody Maker)*

Great things have been expected of No Man for long enough that you have to wonder why it hasn't happened yet. They have a lot going for them: Tim Bowness is a charismatic singer and the tunes have an appealing pop sheen, in a Pet Shops kinda way. "Painting Paradise" itself brings to mind "Waiting For The Love Boat" era Associates, which is fine as it goes, but somehow less than it should be. Perhaps they're spending too much time in the studio. Perhaps they're taking the wrong vitamins. I don't know, but it's a shame.

Not yet a tragedy, but moving in that direction.

4.1994	Taking It Like A Man (Epic – USA only release) Deleted	CD 12"	Taking It Like A Man (edit) Taking It Like A Man (Buddha Pic Mix) Taking It Like A Man (full version) Taking It Like A Man (Buddha Pic edit) Housekeeping Long Day Fall

The Buddha Pic remixes were undertaken by Pichotti & Bristol in New York and were commissioned by Epic without the approval or input of No Man. The 12" contains further "club" remixes. Taking It Like A Man was originally recorded for Loveblows and Lovecries but not included.

For the next album, Steven and Tim brought in various friends to help out with various tracks. Amongst these were, inevitably, Jansen, Barbieri and Karn, Robert Fripp of King Crimson fame, Lisa Gerrard of Dead Can Dance and Ian Carr who contributed trumpet.

However Flowermouth was the end of Ben Coleman's involvement as a band member, and he appeared purely as a guest musician. That old phrase Musical Differences being cited as the reason.

During this period Steven was also working on Porcupine Tree material and Tim collaborated with Richard Barbieri on their joint album Flame.

6.1994	Flowermouth (One Little Indian TPLP67CD)	CD Cass LP	Angel Gets Caught In The Beauty Trap You Crow More Beautiful Animal Ghost Soft Shoulders Shell of A Fighter Teardrop Fall Watching Over Me Simple Things Change

> **Flowermouth** *(A review from Mojo 8)*
>
> Once touted as the new Smiths, this duo now sound like a collaboration between The Beloved (ambient instrumentation) and James (vocals rippling with emotional sincerity). With touches of tastefully muted trumpet, Flowermouth makes for atmospheric listening. Themes of loss and yearning permeate the lyrics, particularly effective in the arresting You Grow More Beautiful. One to listen to while getting over a doomed relationship this summer.
> *For a review of two tracks in Tim's own words see page 173*

10.1995	Heaven Taste (Hidden Art Hi-Art)	CD	Long Day Fall Babyship Blue Bleed Road Heaven Taste

A collection of rarities and B-sides, including a "Bleed" remix. Babyship Blue is an outtake from *Flowermouth* and "Road" is a Nick Drake song originally included on the compilation Brittle Days".

1995	Flowermix (Hidden Art) Deleted	Cass	Angeldust Faith in You All I See Witching Ovaries Heal The Madness Babyship Blue Sample

Another cassette only mail order item. This was briefly available before being withdrawn and enhanced for CD (see next item). The cassette is unique in that it features a mix unavailable elsewhere as well as an instrumental mix of "Babyship Blue" which later appeared on the *Heaven Taste* CD.

| 10.1995 | Flowermix (Hidden Art Hi-Art2) | CD | Angeldust
Faith in You
All I See
Natural Neck
Heal The Madness
You Grow More Beautiful (version)
Sample
Why The Noise
Born Simple |
|---|---|---|---|

This CD features reconstructions and re-workings of songs from *Flowermouth* by No Man and some of their friends.

| 5.1996 | Housewives Hooked On Heroin (Third Stone STNECD026) | CD | Housewives Hooked on Heroin
Hit The Ceiling
Housewives Hooked on Methadone (Scanner Remix)
Urban Disco
Where I'm Calling From |
|---|---|---|---|
| 9.1996 | Wild Opera (Third Stone STONECD027) | CD | Radiant City
Pretty Genius
Infant Phenomenon
Sinister Jazz
Housewives Hooked On Heroin
Libertine Libretto
Taste My Dream
Dry Cleaning Ray
Sheeploop
My Rival Trevor
Time Travel in Texas
My Revenge on Seattle |

4.1997	Dry Cleaning Ray (Third Stone STONE034S)	7"	Dry Cleaning Ray (remix edit) Time Travel in Texas (radio session version) Watching Over Me (radio session version)
5.1997	Dry Cleaning Ray (Third Stone STONE035CD)	CD	Dry Cleaning Ray (remix edit) Sweetside Silver Night Jack the Sax Diet Mothers Urban Disco Punished For Being Born Kightlinger Evelyn (the song of slurs) Sicknote

This CD is a companion release to *Wild Opera* which features three remixes from that album, "Urban Disco" from the *Housewives Hooked On Heroin* single and five new tracks.

This basically brings the brief history of No Man up to date. Steven has also released his Bass Communion album via Third Stone continuing his association with the label for releasing the "unusual" and at the time of writing a new No Man mini album entitled Carolina Skeletons is due for release on 14 September 1998. See Message From A Self Destructing Turnip for a review.

9.1998	Carolina Skeletons (Third Stone STONE037CD)	CD	Carolina Skeleton Something Falls Close Your Eyes Carolina Reprise

In addition to the above No Man have appeared on numerous compilations and magazine "freebies". To collectors these will be of interest and these are listed below:

1991	Indie Top 20 Issue 13	CD	Days In The Tree (Mahler)
1991	Volume 2	CD	Kiss Me Stupid
1992	Island of Circles (Canadian) (A Donovan tribute album)	CD	Turquoise
1993	Brittle Days (Nick Drake Tribute)	CD	Road
4.1993	Outlook Magazine	Cass	Taking It Like A Man (demo)
7.1994	The Mix Magazine	CD	Simple (alternative mix)
7.1994	The Wire Magazine	CD	Angel Gets Caught In The Beauty Trap Soft Shoulders

This CD also has 2 tracks from the Barbieri/Bowness *Flame* Album

1996	Ambient Extractions (USA	CD	Angeldust
1996	Drop 5 (Italy)	CD	Heal The Madness
3.1996	Wire Magazine	CD	Babyship Blue Angeldust

This CD also features tracks by Jakko and Holi which feature Barbieri/Jansen.

1997	Spaceship (Germany)	CD	Angeldust
1997	A Taste of Third Stone Vol. 2	CD	Sweetside Silver Night

In addition to the above the following titles were due to be given a release but so far remain unreleased.

1989	Strip Wild EP	Cass	The River Song Beaten By Love Dreamer In A Dead Language (I) Dull Day (Beneath An Angry Sky)
1989	Death and Dodgson's Dreamchild	LP	

Did this become the cassette release "Speak".

? Shallow Grave (by Andy Smith) Video
This featured a 12 minute ambient piece called "The Hidden Art of Man Ray". The video never appeared commercially but the track will almost certainly be given a release as part of the No Man reissue program.

If we've missed anything then let us know and I'll update in a future issue.

As previously stated, whilst not Porcupine Tree, it is Steven Wilson related and I hope this has been of interest and whetted your appetite to explore No

Man, if you have not already done so.

Queen Quotes Crowley

Well I honestly thought that my Prog Not Prog musings in the last issue would have provoked some response, but guess what, I received only 2 comments on the subject and one of these was from Steven Wilson who felt I had got the nub of the issue and felt he couldn't have put it better himself. High praise indeed, thank you Steven.

In another letter from Steven he discussed the live Karma tape from Chesham (I had sent him a copy) and I quote from this letter as follows:-

Thanks for the copy of the Karma live recording. I had no idea this tape existed.

The track listing is:
1 Check in at the St Berenice Ward
2 A Peace of Earth and Good Swill to All Pigs Part 2
3 Night Whispers

The line up is:
Steven Wilson – Guitar, squeaky vocals
Tom Dusk – Keyboards
Simon Vockings – Keyboards
Mark Gordon – Drums
Andy Aspin – Percussion

The band split up almost immediately after this gig. The first track I had no recollection of at all. It was a new song and this would have been the only time it was ever played in public. I had to go back to some old rehearsal tapes to establish its title! It is also notable since this was the last ever Karma gig and I would date it at around July 1985. The location is actually the Chesham Elgiva Hall (The Underground was in Berkhamstead) and it was supporting a local band called Burnessence. As you can hear there were only about 25 people there.

And that is about all I can tell you, except that it sounds to me like half the band wanted to be Marillion and the other half wanted to write shiny 80's pop music. a horrible thought, but probably very close to the truth.

The other response I had on the subject of Prog was from Phil Harwood who gives great support to V35, his reasonings become ever more clear when you consider his response below:-

I hate categorising music, so the question are PT prog or not, didn't really matter to me. I couldn't care! I'm old enough to have been buying records in the 70's Prog boom period. Back then Prog for me was "Trespass" by Genesis (who, before then had written songs with stories like "White Mountain" or had produced such powerful songs as "The Knife"), who had done such complexity as "In The Court of The Crimson King" by King Crimson, who such psychological alienation as "A Plaque of Lighthouse Keepers" from "Pawn Hearts" by Van Der Graaf Generator, such technical wizardry as "Tarkus" by ELP? I could go on and on.

However at the time I was also buying Bob Dylan, Amon Duul, Hawkwind, USA West Coast like Jefferson Airplane and Starship, British folk like the Strawbs and Mike Cooper, reggae like U Roy and Big Youth, even soul like the marvellous "Hot Buttered Soul" from Isaac Hayes. In short it didn't matter, if it liked it, I bought it. I was not confined by descriptive boundaries.

I recently told someone I'd bought "Uncut" magazine because there was an article about Neil Young at the time of "Tonight's The Night" CD (A CD I had and couldn't understand, and was interested to know how it had come about) and also because there was a freebie CD on the cover of "alternative country" music. my friend cracked up, he hadn't heard the CD, but because I'd said "country" he immediately assumed it was crap. In actual fact it has spent a lot of time in my player, as there is some fine music on it from Hazeldine, the Walkabouts, Handsome Family, Nadine (a group not a girl), Sixteen Horsepower and others which I bet lots of people wouldn't recognise as country. My point is that music should be accepted as music and not categorised.

The only time categorisation helps, is when you're trying to describe it to others. This sometimes helps eg. Space conjures up Hawkwind type music, metal conjures up Sabbath, but Prog? What is it? Is it keyboard drive? Is it unusual time signatures and structures? Is it strange song topics, if so, then what about instrumentals? I don't think it can be described, so let's forget categorisation.

When I first sent off for "Tarquin's", when it was only a bedroom tape, after reading the review in Ptolemaic Terrascope I was nearly put off by it being described as "Progressive pomp", but intrigued by it being described as "psych"! What attracted me was the fact that someone was making music that sounded complex, with little hope of it selling, but who obviously had a sense of humour in crediting the music to an assortment of unlikely people. When I got the cassette I realised that here was something special, and the rest is history.

I think it is a shame that a lot of good music is never heard. Thank goodness for fanzines like Ptolemaic Terrascope, Dark Star (sadly gone) and Bucketful of Brains which introduced me to many fine guitar bands. And tape labels like Acid Tapes and Music and Elsewhere distributing music at cheap rates.

I get more pleasure sending off for something horribly obscure eg. "The Mystical Path of The Number 96" by the Davis Radford Triad (an amazing storm of guitar mayhem) than going to HMV to buy the latest, by Floyd or the Verve. It's not to say I don't like Floyd or the Verve, I do, but I prefer the buzz you get when you hear something amazing and you know that probably only 50 other people have heard it.

I hope I haven't rambled too much but I say forget categorisation, it doesn't matter. If it's good, it doesn't matter.

Thanks Phil for your views and I couldn't agree more.

I am however surprised that no one has any other views on the subject, but perhaps you are too shy to put pen to paper.

As I've said before this mag is for you! It's for you to express your opinions on anything Porcupine Tree related – so please put pen to paper, you never know your opinion or view may open up a whole new avenue of discussion which no one else had previously thought about but may have valid comments upon.

Another disappointment to me is that no one responded on the origins of Porcupine Tree.

No imagination or what?

Come on all you budding writers, lets have your ideas!

Tim Bowness On Flowermouth And Flame (Interview by Tony Herrington)

"No Man was all about bedroom experiment for the first three years" says Tim Bowness, referring to the group which he formed in the mid '80's with multi instrumentalist Steven Wilson. In 1992 the duo signed to One Little Indian, and their two albums for the label, Lovesighs and Loveblows and Lovecries, are full of the kind of sophisticated, highly literate, open ended music that recalls the halcyon days of such popular experimentalists as Japan, Wire and The Associates. Bowness now regards the group as an attempt to link the rigours of the avant garde and the Glamour and drama of the classic pop song. The duo's new album, Flowermouth, is released at the end of June, which will be followed in July by Flame, a collaboration between Bowness and ex-Japan keyboard player Richard Barbieri. (No Man are big on the '90's collaboration aesthetic. Apart from Barbieri, Flowermouth and Flame feature input form Robert Fripp, Ian Carr, Danny Thompson and another ex-Japan refugee, drummer, Steve Jansen, among others. The CD on the cover of this month's issue of The Wire features two tracks apiece from Flowermouth and Flame. We asked Tim Bowness to talk us through the thinking and practice that lie behind the four songs. Here then is your guide to the oblique contours and strange topography of No Man's land. (Interview by Tony Herrington)

Angel Gets Caught In The Beauty Trap
Imagine a traditional singer songwriter ballad arranged by a Steve Reichian minimalist composer, that was the idea that influenced this song. It's a notion of fusing opposites, a combination of musical extremes. Originally we had a three minute improvisation that Steven worked up into a 90 minute orchestration, or however long it is now (10 minutes actually). We wanted to give the song time to develop rather than go for that epic Prog rock thing.

It was one of our first experiments in using a large orchestration, and large scale organisation; bringing in outside people like Ian Carr, Mel Collins and Robert Fripp. We'd always wanted to use different instrumental textures and voices – mostly because we'd always like records like Sketches of Spain or even mid-80's (David) Sylvian albums that would use lots of players from jazz and classical backgrounds.

We brought in these people because we admired their work, Ian Carr, is obviously a great jazz musician and writer and those first two Nucleus albums (Elastic Rock and We'll Talk About I Later), they were a wonderful British response to what Miles Davis was doing at the time on In A Silent

Way and Jack Johnson, Mel Collins – he's a ubiquitous session man, very talented, incredibly musical. He responds immediately, which is a rare talent. And 90 per cent of what he gives you is useable. There's not a lot of excess.

We'd been fans of Fripp for years. Along with The Velvets, Roxy Music, Television, King Crimson were one of the great multimedia bands. I went to see the Discipline tour years ago and it was a kind of revelation, so intense; jazz spontaneity, rock energy, completely breaking the sound barrier. And he was very inspiring to work with. We recorded him in Steven's bedroom and it was like the best Frippertronics concert ever, in your own house. We invented these obvious strategies for him to work in. so, say we wanted him to do some hoary old rock 'n' roll playing, we'd have these photographs of Buddy Holly and we'd cross-fertilise them with pictures of Fripp. He was witty, astute, intelligent; he didn't dent his legend one bit.

Soft Shoulders
This track was inspired by a Suzanne Vega album called 99.9 Fahrenheit Degrees. It was produced by Mitchell Froom. He's famous for producing people like Elvis Costello and Richard Thompson, and he produced the last American Music Club album. He's probably the only radical producer of the 90s who's doing something fresh but also commercially coherent.

When we heard the Vega album it was a revelation, particularly the blend of emotional songwriting and sonic innovation on tracks like "Blood Makes Noise". That's also a quality that the Bjork album had. Again it's a combination of extremes of experiment and expression. It's what No Man are also trying to do. It's like a bridge between the avant garde and the sheer glamour of pure pop, which you can also hear in The Velvets, Roxy Music, Bowie, Japan. It's something of a buried history. A dream for us would be to hear a player like David Torn working with The Pet Shop Boys, who are a wonderful pop group but it would be great to hear them breaking the edges of their structure. But people don't think in those terms any more. People are either far out or far in the middle ground doesn't really exist. It's still there in film and literature – look at Hal Hartley or Spike Lee or The Piano; there are some brilliant films that are cross-cultural, that are high and low art, fun and serious at the same time, that are massively commercial and also massively ambitious. You don't see it so much in music. but that kind of bridging album, between pop and experiment, which was once the norm, that was one of the reasons that got me into music, records like Bowie's Low, Roxy's For Your Pleasure, Japan's Tin Drum – there are very few of those kind of records around today' the Bjork album, obviously, Vega's 99.9, Jan Siberry, Stina Nordenstam. These are the radical conservatives, the creative mainstream, and these are the people who really shape music.

In the late '80's when we were looking around for a rhythm section to work with, we thought, "Who are the best?" In Japan, Mick Karn and Steve Jansen must have been one of the most original rhythm sections around, and Richard Barbieri is probably the only post Eno keyboard player of note, aside from maybe The Aphex Twin. He took Eno quite literally, using sounds as opposed to musical notes, fused it with Stockhausen and produced something extraordinary.

We did a tour with Jansen, Barbieri and Karn, and Richard and I used to talk about albums that inspired us, which included Remain in Light, the first Velvet's album and Low, but the albums that really mattered to us were a lot of those pure singer-songwriter records, Joni Mitchell's Hejira, Robert Wyatt's Rock Bottom, Lou Reed's Berlin. Our Top Pens were virtually identical. And the elements of Japan I always liked were songs like "Ghosts" and "Night Porter", those kind of Ambient Torch songs. They'd never really done an entire album of those type of songs, and neither had anyone else, maybe Julee Cruise or Stina Nordenstam, so Flame was an attempt to do that. it's more balanced in terms of mood than Flowermouth, which is maybe more eclectic.

Torch Dance
"Torch Dance" and "Brightest Blue" were the last two songs we wrote. I think we got paranoid that on the other songs we'd been so true to our original intentions that there wasn't the diversity that we needed. "Torch Dance" was originally inspired by The Aphex Twin's "Analogue Bubblebath". While I love The Aphex Twin, I still prefer Fripp and Eno's No Pussyfooting, because it has all the same textural, technological and loop possibilities as The Aphex Twin, but it also has a very singular, engaging voice over the top, which is Fripp. So Richard did his homage to "Bubblebath", then we brought in Michael Bearpark, who's a very interesting textural guitarist, to play over the top of it, to hopefully give the song more resonance and depth.

Brightest Blue
This is another song that fits the No Man blueprint, in that it's a fairly simple love song, combined with something sonically interesting from Richard and some jazz folk interpretative playing from Danny Thompson. Hopefully it echoes all those late 60s Nick Drake and John Martyn albums. Those people wrote great love songs which were made more interesting by

the presence of players like Danny Thompson or John Stevens; that 60s UK jazz fraternity. You could imagine a tour coming out of those kind of records, where Ian Carr would be supported by Keith Tippett, supported by Nick Drake, supported by Van Der Graaf Generator. You can hear those kind of possibilities in those records. So "Brightest Blue" is influenced by that attitude embodied by Drake, Martyn, Peter Hammell and Keven Coyne, all these brilliant musicians who have been completely written out of the plot. *(Reproduced from The Wire July 1994)*

Issue 10

Published February 1999
32 Page anniversary issue

Contents:
Intro to issue 10
The latest news
Full Colour Centre spread
Retroactive Ploy (Interview with Steven Wilson from the archives of Organ Magazine)
a full review of Stupid Dream
a short story inspired by the Tree
Readers letters - more on the "prog" issue
Porcupine Tree - personal reminisces by Andy Davis

How I Came To The Tree By Andy Davis

If you ask me, Billy Curie has a lot to answer for. If it weren't for the Ultravox post punk outpourings, I would never have reached the dizzy heights of Porcupine Tree greatness. Before you get bored and move onto the next article, let me explain.

Having been an avid admirer of the aforementioned band, imagine my glee at the news that 'Ultravox' were performing at a local venue. Much to the bemusement of my spouse, I rushed down to the Coal Exchange (as is it's name), and purchased 2 of their finest tickets for the gig that night. I guess that the fact that the tickets were numbered 8 & 9 should have alerted me to something odd occurring. But I made my own excuses to my partner for the band, you know lack of publicity, no promotion of the new album, etc, etc, anyway there was a support act, they might be good.

Predictably the evening eventually arrived, and we set off, with my singing along to various electronic tunes of the appropriate era, an eager anticipation growing. As the foyer beckoned us in for my compulsory T-shirt purchase, I was surprised to find no stall for 'Ultravox' but instead, a well laid out one for 'No Man'. 'Strange name for a band' I thought, "Great name for a band" Ruth said. On the table was a rather fetching T-shirt with what looked like two women kissing, a few "Sweetheart Raw" CDs, posters and 'No Man Speak' leaflets.

Beer in hand we shuffled off into the main hall, I felt such shame at the turn out, I counted a whole 17 people, whilst trying to stifle an hysterical girlfriend, we eventually sat about 20ft away directly in front of the stage. Some chap came on and announced "Thanks for coming" (yeah right) "Please welcome No Man", and on came the band. With a guitar was this hippy with very, very long hair, what looked like a chap with a perm on vocals, a violinist, bass and drummer. These guys started to play in what looked like an impossibly small space on stage, but boy did they play. We were both blown away by the music. No I don't think you fully understand, WE WERE BLOWN AWAY by the music, this guy on guitar was obviously a hidden genius. He was giving it some serious welly on guitar and effects, the chap singing had great lyrics and great expression, and the rest of the band were so tight, it was an awesome, pumping, foot tapping experience of a show, considering all the music was on a first listen basis, I was sent to a musical heaven that I had forgotten existed.

At the end of their set I got to the foyer, got the T-shirt, the CD, the leaflet, these guys deserved to be the biggest thing ever. I wanted to speak to the band, but they'd legged it in some pretty sharp fashion in a rather flash people mover. On further examination the CD gave up the names of the performers, including Barbieri, Jansen & Karn no less. 'What a find!' I proclaimed. I then took upon myself to get everything that was available by these guys, which culminated in the purchase of 'Lovecries and Lovesights: An Entertainment' (Which when now played, is like the surprising return of a welcome old friend). However this was not all there was to be found.

About a year later in an issue of 'No Man Speak', I noted a reference to a solo project of Steven's under the banner of the even more bizarrely named Porcupine Tree. Having a few extra quid's in my pocket, and with the logic, that if Steve has a sideline it can't be all bad, (A fatal flaw in logic, considering all the Pink Floyd solo albums of years gone by). I sent off for 'Up The Downstair' and 'The Sky Moves Sideways', and a week later they were waiting for me at my office one Saturday in autumn, and whilst not looking forward to my weekends work, I thought at least I'll have something to listen to.

Well I guess you've been there, you know the rest, from the opening cacophony of 'What you are listening to...' to the ghostly serenade finishing 'Phase 2'. All 113 minutes 30 seconds were replayed all weekend, without the thought or need of any other sounds emanating from the office music system. The weekend went like a dream, and I was undeniably hooked. Since then my passion for Tree has gone from strength to strength, (a minor highlight being both sets of neighbours complaining about the volume of the track "Signify", but I guess you've been there too).

So thanks for reading along with my introduction to the band that saved my musical being, I hope you've enjoyed it.

Oh and before you ask, it was a great night ruined, Ultravox were worse than crap and we left in disgust during the third song.

The Conversion Of St. Paul By Andy Davis

Following my conversion to all things Tree, I gave tapes of recordings left, right, centre, above and below to various friends, to anyone whom I considered might be possible devotees. And I'm afraid to say there wasn't much of a response, as much as I pushed them they just kept coming back, I guess I could have tried punching them, but hey, they were my friends.

So when the Tree announced they were playing the 'Clwb Ifor Bach' on Monday the 27th October, and with myself having returned to a new bachelor mode, I knew it was going to be a struggle to find a suitable companion for the gig. The task was to find someone with an appreciation for the finer things in music; (Mr Modest Welshman speaks "Just like me").

So eventually it came down to a good friend of mine called Paul. Over the years we'd shared the old Led Zeppelin moment, the mutual rocking of "Highway to Hell", plus many many more, so there was a good chance of some response from the young artist (Paul the artiest would like to note however that he is an actual, and not a p**s).

As we got into the 'Clwb' the support act was just finishing, and we applauded politely. Mineral water in hand, (oh, how the times have changed) we awaited the arrival of the Tree.

I now whisk you back over a year, and refer you to my notes as taken on the night:

'PT came on at 10:15pm finished at 11:45pm and were very professional, and in the tight confinement of Clwb Ifor Bach the evening was just right. The rhythm section was the tightest I think I've ever witnessed, with what seemed to be love and appreciation from Colin Edwin for the beats being put down by Chris Maitland. Barbieri seemed distant, but I suppose he's done it all before, but he still laid some great atmospherics down. Steve Wilson is one superb guitarist, and when he goes for it, he does it with a vengeance, at times the way the Fruit Salad Stage lighting was, he looked like some weird alien or even a version of Michael Moorcock's Corum or Elric, wild. All the way through the gig, a small fella danced/ moved about 3 feet in front of Steve, but they didn't seem to mind to all the songs. Steve joked that this next song (The Moon Touches Your Shoulder) was from their progressive rock album, which got a few of the crowd yelping in joyous approval that prog was still great. Next Steve said that the next track (Dislocated Day) was from their jazz funk album, (not so much yelping then). There was a version of 'Moonloop' that was brilliant, harder than the album or the American "Stars Die" single, but exceptional. If there is a tape of this show I'm in. so with all the old stuff and about 40 minutes of excellent new material being played, it was all in all, a rather hip hop tip top evening, especially as they played 'Voyage 34' in the encore."

When we got outside Paul seemed shell shocked, he said "It's changed my life, I can't listen to anything else again (it was great to be proved right).

He couldn't believe the variety in sounds and styles. He couldn't believe he was so impressed. Steve was the boy as far as he was concerned, also being a 'Japan' fan he was so pleased to be close to a former hero.

It was then decided that we would travel to The Union Chapel in Islington, London for the last night of British tour, but that's a different story.

Queen Quotes Crowley

Amazing what a little cajoling will do! Thanks for all your letters on the Prog Not Prog issue. A selection of letters follows on the subject and apologies to those whose letters did not make it.

I think **Andy Davis** summed it up in his letter
…Unfortunately apathy rules…I have always had the temptation to give you a written account of my Tree experiences for Voyage 35 but I guess like many others, it is just easier to read someone else's experience.

Firstly from Frank Willoughby:
Are Porcupine Tree a progressive band? Absolutely.

As the music/production/skill improves on each band release, my only hope is that the lengthy tracks will remain and not disappear (like a lot of other "progressive" bands) into pleasant (?) ditties of the five minute variety. Too many bands have sold out to commercially ie. personal wealth, stardom and egotism; please not Porcupine Tree. Maybe this is purely a selfish point of view but I know what I like music wise – music that gets you involved.

Are Porcupine Tree Progressive? In the absence of any other suitable label I would reluctantly have to say yes writes Dave Thompson. I am only

---

Martin Gallagher writes "I agree with your viewpoints. I used to listen to bands like Yes, Pink Floyd, Genesis, etc but would not buy any of their music today simply because I find it uninspiring, familiarised and lacking in new ideas, but with Porcupine Tree the music is fresh, inspired and progressive in the sense that each new release has a different musical approach whilst eclipsing previous work.

Sure there are the obvious Floyd references but this has more to do with some of Steven's guitar playing than anything else. I don't find the music retrospective like so many of today's bands who basically lack the talent and invention to create their own sound.

For me the Tree are the only band that excite me nowadays.

reluctant to say yes because I feel that putting a label on a band or artiste can sometimes give the wrong impression of what the music may be like. Unlike some terms Progressive describes a pretty wide field and can mean quite different things to different people. I tend to rely on trying to define a bands music by comparing them to bands the person I am speaking to would know. Whilst in theory this is better than using a label it isn't adequate to describe a band like Porcupine Tree. The obvious answer is to let people listen to the music and make up their own minds.

> As to the name Porcupine Tree – well the Porc-u-pine is that same as Spuds-u-like, innit? Tree-mendous – **Simon Mills**

And penultimately, on the Prog issue **Ken Lowe** writes:

This is of course a big question. Paul Stump takes an entire book (The Music's All That Matters) trying to define the genre and settles on a current position of "A diffuse collection of music characterised by high degrees of instrumental and compositional complexity. Commonplace rock trappings – beat and melody – were withheld in favour of executive musical expertise as a criterion of absolute value…cultural / social relevance was sought through cross-pollination from other music such as folk, classical and jazz" (*phew! – Steve*)

So by that definition, are Porcupine Tree progressive? Er…sort of. My own stab at a definition would be "Ambitious music with a definite rock background, though unafraid to borrow ideas from folk, classic and jazz. Common features are technical expertise, unusual time signatures and a fluid approach to instrumentation".

It must also be said that prog is largely created and enjoyed by white middle class males (?) and is therefore not exactly the music of the oppressed – hence the critical backlash in these guilt-ridden PC times.

My vote therefore – guilty as charged, and hey I didn't mention drugs once!

> Re your request on Voyage 35, I think it represents very good value for the price. It has good quality articles and features about Porcupine Tree projects, and also provides up to date news and information about the [...] up the good work. **Andrew Miles**

David Page writes: Your excellent fanzine is an important link between the band and fans, particularly as the music press generally seems to ignore bands such as Porcupine Tree (with rare exceptions in Mojo and Record Collector). It must be difficult finding enough material for each issue particularly when you have limited info available eg when the bands' abroad, on tour or inactive.

I for one would be quite happy if you included information on other bands who play similar music to Porcupine Tree – I'm sure there must be a lot more groups out there waiting to be discovered. I have found that many friends I have introduced to the Albums have been staggered that they are not more widely known.

Keep up the good work.

My thanks to Andrew and David and all who responded on what you wish to see inside the covers of Voyage 35. I do try to include news of other groups but it is at the more popular end of the market (ie Hawkwind / Floyd) but have tried to introduce you to Nine Invisibles and Electric Orange. As you will have seen this issue I have included reviews from Andy Ashton in what I hope will be a readers review section.

I have also said before that this magazine is for the fans and preferably written by fans (other than myself).

To this end I will reiterate that anyone who supplies artwork, an article or photographs, poems or an original story, which I use (but not letters or reviews which are printed unfortunately) will receive a copy of that issue free by way of a thank you.
So please let me know if you have any ideas – Thanks, Steve

My thanks to the following (in no particular order) who also responded to the various issues raised in my letter / flyer:
Steve Bowden, Chuck Johnson, Georg Kolmar, Simon Thomas, Dennis Gough (Who cares! Class will tell in the end), Peter Clemons.

> Thanks for the tip-off on the No Man Radio Sessions CD-R. You beat their own service in announcing this. (*Pleased to be of help – Steve*).
>
> A couple of points on the No Man feature / discography. You don't mention that when Loveblows and Lovecries come out, initial copies (can't remember how many) came with a second CD of the Lovesighs mini album. Also Carolina Skeletons was very much sold to shops as a mini album and I couldn't get it for less than £7. Even via mail order from the band it was £5 plus postage. Not I feel a CD single price.

And finally from Aled O Jones on Prog: if in doubt remember these simple guidelines, Porcupine Tree and Hawkwind are great – Genesis and Yes are crap. Couldn't be simpler could it?

Only joking!

Issue 11

Published August 1999
Contents:
Intro
latest news
part one of a US interview with Steven,
Reviews of Stupid Dream
Review of the Spring Tour 1999
Letters

Feedback on the No Man special in issue 9:-

Tim Bowness
Just a brief note to thank you for sending me the Voyage 35 No Man special. I was quite amazed by the detail of the discopgraphy, it reminded me of projects even I'd forgotten about. Thanks also for the mention of Darkroom. As well as working on two forthcoming No Man albums – 'Lighthouse' and a contemporary re-evaluation of 'Speak' – Steven's just finished 'Bass Communion II' and I've recently completed a solo album in collaboration with Cambridge based band, Samuel Smiles (including Mike Bearpark on guitar). Although the album mostly operates in the melancholy singer-songwriter territory of Nick Drake, Mark Eitzel, David Sylvian etc…, it also features a new version of the radio session take of 'Watching Over Me' and cover versions of King Crimson's 'Two Hands' and Peter Hammill's 'Ophelia'. The album is called 'World of Bright Futures' and in many ways is a logical continuation of the more understated elements of 'Flame' (eg 'Brightest Blue').

In all probability, both 'Bass Communion II' and 'World of Bright Futures' will be released on Hidden Art via Resurgence sometime in Spring. (3.2.99)

They both have been and Chris and Ali Everest are in raptures over "World of Bright Futures" (although Yvonne is reminded of Boots or Debenhams by the title) by Samuel Smiles. It comes packaged with a free live CD for the first 1000 copies and is well worth getting. A number of tracks will be familiar to those who caught Tim at Colchester and Brighton and although I prefer Tim's vocal live I like this one and so does Yvonne. It's "dark" in places and melancholy, but strangely uplifting at the same time. I can't adequately describe this but if you like No Man you'll enjoy this. And for all those who asked after the No Man special where to begin my recommendation would be with the Radio Sessions CD available by mail order as it gives a flavour of the band over a period of time. Of the commercial releases try Flowermouth.

Retroactive Ploy
Fabrication – a note from Steven and Aural Innovations Interview
At this point I had intended to include an interview which Kevin had translated from a Greek magazine. Fortunately I showed this to Steven and he at first put some of the comments down to mis-translation. However the

further Steven read the more he realised that large chunks of the interview were fabricated. "It's unfortunate that with my world-wide interview tally for Stupid Dream now approaching 200" writes Steven "you should come across this one!"

Kindly, Steven passed me the following interview which first appeared in Aural Innovations, a US Spacerock magazine which he describes as being more accurate and certainly more interesting. So please read on.

Jerry Kranitz (JK): Signify was something of a transitional album being the first full blown band album and you've moved into more song oriented territory. Stupid Dream moves even further into song and lyrical territory. Was this part of a desire on your part to communicate with words just as much as music?

Steven (SW): It's a number of things. It's never as simple as that. The music has always changed. Every album Porcupine Tree has made has been very distinct from those that preceded it. The reasons for that, firstly, is a desire not to repeat myself as a songwriter. Secondly, as a fan of music I am always listening to different things. And whatever I am listening to at any particular time tends to inform my work. And in two and a half years between Stupid Dream and Signify a lot has changed in my listening taste and what I consider to be the kind of material I want to work on. Also, the third element would be increased confidence in myself as a singer and a lyricist, which is something that's come with time. Because I have never really considered myself to be a singer. Its something that was kind of thrust onto me by default because it was a solo project. So I was the guitar player, the bass player, and I had to be all these things. And one of the other things I had to be was a singer and a lyricist. And although that was not something that came naturally to me I think as times goes on I got better and better at it. So there's three different reasons there. The second reason is probably the most significant in the sense that what I was listening to at the time when I was writing this album was a lot more vocally orientated. I would say the major influence on that would be my interest in Brian Wilson and the Beach Boys. I was listening to a lot of stuff like Pet Sounds and all that kind of harmony singing. Also stuff like Todd Rundgren, Crosby Stills Nash and Young, anything with really good ensemble singing. I was particularly into that stuff when I was writing this album. And I kind of got interested in the idea of the pop song as a kind of experimental symphony if you like. I know that sounds pretentious, but that's kind of what I always that Brian Wilson was doing on stuff like Pet Sounds, what the Beatles were doing on albums like Revolver and Sergeant Pepper. You know creating these extraordinary kind of experimental pop symphonies almost. I think it's a great myth but the most experimental music has come from the progressive field and the most experimental music tends to be quite extended pieces. I think the opposite is true I think the extraordinary pieces of pop music still are things like Tomorrow Never Knows from Revolver which is two and a half minutes long. God only knows from Pet Sounds which is two and a half minutes long…they for me represent the pinnacle of popular music and so there was a kind of shift in my thinking away from long abstract instrumentally oriented pieces to pieces that would hopefully have a much more timeless quality to them and would have a good song.

JK: You have really expanded the instrumentation as well. You have got the sax and flute on Don't Hate Me and the spacey jazzy flute on Tinto Brass. Is this something you have always wanted to explore?

SW: Again there's two different answers to this question. The first answer has to do with budgets and financial considerations. This is the first time where we have had a real budget to do an album Signify was recorded for a total of £2,000 which is a pretty pathetic budget. We had a lot more money for this, we spent about £15,000 on this album, which is still pretty small when you compare it to the budgets some bands have. We can do a lot more with money than we used to be able to and one of the things we could do was we could bring in outside musicians, we hired the orchestra. Its something I've always wanted to do but never been able to afford to do. The second answer is again to do with this increased interest in people like Brian Wilson. Brian Wilson was always using 18, 19, 20 musicians in some of his sessions to create this symphonic sound. That will continue. There's lots of other instrumentation I am keen to explore on the next album.

Keith Henderson (KH): It seems that Stupid Dream is a bit of a new direction being a bit dreamier and more richly textured. Some people also say it's a bit more commercial sounding. Now do you feel that the band is heading in a particular direction, or do you think for the next album it might be completely off into a new territory?

SW: Its very difficult for me to say because when I am working on an album I am not necessarily conscience that there has been a change in direction. For me its just where ever my heads at that particular day. And its only really after the albums completed and people hear it and say "well you've really changed direction" and I'll say "have we". I guess we have and I'm glad we have, but I don't particularly feel in a way that this is any more a change in direction than say Signify was from Sky Moves Sideways. For me the change in direction from the instrumentally oriented material to the song material came with Sky to Signify, not with Signify to Stupid Dream. I can see the routes of some of the material on Stupid Dream certainly in Signify. Pieces like Every Home is Wired and Waiting Phase 1 is obviously a move to more song orientated material on that album. So I see Stupid Dream as a continuation of that. the next album is already about two thirds written and there's still a lot of song stuff on there. There is even more use of layered harmonies and layered vocals but there are also some longer pieces this time as well I have written about 3 pieces which are about 10 minutes long. I don't know which pieces are going to end up on the next album. Obviously you are aware that the continuity is very important on all the Porcupine Tree albums. The sequencing, the continuity, and the way the tracks link together is always very important as well, and in some ways it's a mistake to think of a Porcupine Tree album as lots of separate tracks because for me the way they all fit together is very important. I am never a great fan of people coming up to me and saying I bought this album the other day but I have reprogrammed it so I listen to the tracks in a different order because I think it sounds better. I wouldn't like the idea that people would do that with a Porcupine Tree album because I put a lot of thought into the continuity and the way the album flows is very important. So in answer to your question it will be different again. The song based direction will still be quite prevalent I think but I think on the next piece it probably will be even more experimental in terms of the instrumentation and probably some longer pieces this time.

KH: You chose to record at Dave Anderson's Foel Studios in the back country of Wales. What did you think you could accomplish there that you couldn't at home in No Mans Land?

SW: Well first, I can't record drums at my place because its too small. Secondly, again for the reason that it is too small its impossible for us all to set up as a group in my studio and work on the arrangements and the songs as a group. And for the first time we wanted to actually do that. Signify was slightly odd in the way it was recorded in the sense that although it is a band album, because we were never able to actually all be in the same room at the same time, because of physical limitations, with the exception of one track, Intermediate Jesus, which was done outside I tended to demo the tracks to a fairly high level and they would just replace the parts that I had played on synthesisers with the real thing. So there wasn't a great deal of input from the other guys. But what I wanted this time was to make sure there was the opportunity for the other guys to really contribute ideas, to the arrangements and to the overall feel and sound of the album, which they did. To do that we had to go somewhere where we could all literally set up in a room and thrash out the tracks. So we went to Foel Studios...

partly also because it is very remote. I think when you are a band and you are working on material the idea of remote locations is quite appealing because the distractions are reduced to an absolute minimum.

KH: You have had Theo Travis come in who had worked with Gong just recently to play sax and flute specifically on Don't Hate Me and Tinto Brass. Accordingly the jam part on Don't Hate Me even has a Gong like feel to it right down to what seems like you playing glissando guitar. Was that an intentional move and what other artists have you found that you honour, if that's the intent?

SW: It wasn't intentional. Theo obviously has only just played with Gong. He didn't even know Gong until fairly recently. So the fact that Theo is on it is chronologically misleading. Secondly, I have used glissando guitar many times before. I think what tended to give it even more of a Gong feel is the baseline which kind of...it does rather sound like Gong...and then the sax and the flute went on at the end as well...all of those things were never intended when the glissando guitar was originally played. In answer to your question, I don't specifically set out to pastiche, or honour, or however you want to put it, plagiarise, or give tribute to anything in particular. Its like I said at the beginning of the interview, I have a massive, massive, massive musical taste. I like so many different types of things and they all go into the melting pot if you like that produces the music of Porcupine Tree and yes some things do tend to kind of poke through occasionally rather more overtly than other times.

JK: Was forming a band as simple as needing a vehicle to perform live or did you want things to go that way in terms of a more co-operative effort as well?

SW: I think I probably did. Obviously the practical concern of being able to play the music live was the instigating factor. But I think subconsciously I also felt that I'd taken the solo years as far as I'd wanted to because I never enjoyed working with drum machines. That's the first thing. In some styles of music they have their own kind of sound and they're very important. In the kind of music I was making they were a substitute and there's no getting around that. They were a substitute for real drums. On the Sky Moves Sideways, I had a couple of tracks where I actually bring Chris and Colin in for the first time. Stars Die and Moonloop. They were a turning point for me because I realised from that those two tracks for me were the best from the whole sessions. I realised from that point on I never wanted to go back to having to use drum machines, but also I think I've always kind of been in love with the idea of, you know the "rock band", because bands have a kind of glamour and appeal and a romance about them the solo projects just don't have. You know, the way the bands can kind of just go out on the road together and spend time together and the personalities just kind of gel...or they don't, and there's friction, and there are good times and there are bad times, but somehow this creates a real kind of special romance about the music, and I think we're just beginning to get that now with Stupid Dream. I think there's a real kind of band sound, all the personalities come through in the music and we all really have a lot of respect for each other as musicians, and I've always wanted that. The only reason that Porcupine Tree started as a solo project was there was nobody else I knew that wanted to make that kind of music. and so it was kind of like a project that I had to start as a solo project but I guess that I always hoped that one day it would become a band.

1999 Spring Tour
All praise the...Tree

The 1999 spring UK tour kicked off as the last one had finished – in a church. And what a great evening was had by all who attended.

Colchester Arts Centre April 1999
I had spoken to Kozmik Ken the previous week to find out what time the gig was due to start and was totally unprepared for Tim Bowness supporting. His 20 minute set was a great prelude to the Tree and a bonus as far as I was concerned. His set comprised *Watching Over Me, Dreaming of Babylon, Something of You, Come To Me and Never Love Control*. The set was too short but time constraints at the venue already meant a shorter set was to be played by Porcupine Tree so it was understandable and the set was short.

However I was able in the interval to have a brief chat with Tim and I started off by thanking him for his letter and comments on issue 9. Tim confirmed that he had been booked to appear for three months and when he arrived there was no mention of his appearing. He therefore decided to start off with Watching Over Me as anyone who knew No Man would recognise this. During his set Tim mentioned that some songs were from a Radio 2 session and I asked what this was about. "By default we got invited onto Radio 2's Arts Live and we did Norwich Arts Centre and played to a small audience. By default though we actually played to millions – our largest ever audience. We have CD quality recordings from this". Let's hope they release it!

Thanks for your time Tim.

I'll leave the review of Porcupine Tree to Pete Millar from Norwich but first the set list:

Evenless, Piano Lessons, Waiting, Up The Downstair, Don't Hate Me, Signify, Pure Narcotic, A Smart Kid, Voyage 34, Tinto Brass, The Sky Moves Sideways (1), Dislocated Day, Radioactive Toy.

Colchester Arts Centre is an old church and made a wonderfully atmospheric setting for what was the first night of the UK tour. It was great to chat to people I hadn't seen for some time before the gig. I also chatted to a couple of guys who had come all the way from Cincinnati! 9:30pm and the Tree take to the stage to the strains of Even Less, the same length as the album version, the powerful chords reverberating around the church. The spoken numbers at the end of the track are also displayed behind the band. Anyone know what this is all about? Without a pause it's straight into Piano Lessons, any reservations that I might have had about this track are completely washed away. The upbeat feel of the track had people dancing, naturally Alexis was giving it her all!

Steven explains that he is not feeling too great and that he has a terrible cough but manages to struggle on. The girl in front of me was less than sympathetic and just shouted at them to get on with it (somewhat rude me thinks!).

A surprise now hits me as Up The Downstair launches at full pelt, followed by a new track Don't Hate Me, again sounding much better live than on the album (though you could say that about any of their tracks!). Then we are snapped out of our chilled state as Signify blasts our senses. I'm sure this track is getting harder, faster, rawer and it's greater!

Steven announces that it's time for a couple of acoustic based numbers, what he describes as the Val Doonican part of the show. First up is Pure Narcotic swiftly followed by potentially the best track on Stupid Dream, Smart Kid. I feel that Steven has really excelled himself with the incredible songwriting skills displayed on this track. He changes over to electric guitar for the solo at the end. I'm hoping that this track will never end but inevitably it comes crushingly too soon.

Then for the second surprise of the evening. Voyage 34 complete with a group of girls in the audience doing what seemed to be a choreographed dance. Great fun! V34 segued seamlessly into Tinto Brass, I think I may have perforated one of my eardrums!!

Next up, a track that Steven recently (and controversially) said he found too ploddy, Sky Moves Sideways. It's all too brief and the band bid farewell. After much chanting and foot stomping Chris and Colin make their way back to the stage and begin Dislocated Day. How does Colin make those incredible sounds? Richard and Steven join them on stage and go into a rip-roaring version complete with the band stopping. Steven was waiting for Colin to begin the final phase of Dislocated Day and Colin vice versa. Colin playfully refused to instigate the final onslaught and defiantly finished his cigarette. The audience found this highly amusing and so it was left to Steven to start the final phase!

The time now 10:55 pm and they have to finish by 11pm so they bow out with a truncated version of Radioactive toy. It's over. We managed to have a chat with Richard and Steve afterwards (Steven was getting stuck into a bottle of cough mixture, I don't think the dry ice had helped him much this evening!). He told me that he had already written the new Porcupine Tree album and was hoping to get into the studio in June/July to record it. Speaking to Richard he said he had found that people talking during the gig had annoyed him, I must agree, I can't see the point of paying good money to see a band and then just talking all the time. Kozmik Ken reliably informed me that the video for Piano Lessons should be available on the next CD single (possibly Stranger by the Minute). Looking forward to the next tour already!

The Foundry Birmingham 9 April 1999 – Philip Odin, W Midlands
Just a note to say that I've just seen the Tree on a couple of their latest UK dates. Birmingham which was impressive and then in London which again was excellent – I've enclosed photocopies of both tickets for your collection (Thank you – Steve)

The Birmingham gig at The Foundry which is basically one large room with a stage at one end and centre pillar about 20ft from it – so you need to be in front of it for the best vantage point, which after the T-shirt purchase is where I stood – at about 9pm the ambient drone faded and Tree took the stage and for the next 2 hours were spellbinding the audience becoming more mobile as the tempo rose, the new material being unveiled and warmly received. The two stand out newies being Piano Lessons which Steve informed us of being released early due to them getting onto Virgins listening port, and Don't Hate Me. Of the older material Voyage 34 and Radioactive Toy were of course stunning. For the first encore we were treated to an acoustic version of 9 Cats courtesy of a great fan providing the lyrics for Steve which he says is why they hadn't done it for a while since he couldn't remember them and of course after Radioactive Toy it was home time and with the purchase of the Stars Die tape headed for the station and home, but with the memories of an excellent night.

Pavilion Theatre Brighton 10 April 1999 – Phil Morris, Hereford
I know, I know, I should be in Bristol tonight. Various reasons mean that I'm not, so instead I've put Stupid Dream on the CD player and thought I'd write to you. I did get to the Brighton show and enjoyed that immensely. I'm not sure if it was the only one, but we had the added bonus of a support slot from Tim Bowness (I know that he wasn't at Sheffield). Only a few songs, mainly from his forthcoming solo project, but we did get (a radical re-working of) Watching Over Me and Brightest Blue from Flame. No guest spot from Messrs Wilson or Barbieri, unfortunately, which really would have added to the event, but it was this fact which made me wonder whether his appearance was not a one-off. Steven commented during the show that he hoped not too many people were bothered by the lack of variety in the set from the previous two dates.

However, what was played did not match the written set list exactly, so I wonder whether he did make any changes. I was disappointed that – according to the set list – Slave Called Shiver was dropped, although we did get an 'unpublicised' encore of the acoustic Nine Cats.

I was surprised by some of the tracks included from the new album, thinking beforehand that they would either prove difficult to recreate live or wouldn't work as live numbers. However everything chosen warranted its presence. I don't know whether he was joking, but he threatened not to do Don't Hate Me, saying that he had difficulty reaching some of the notes. This also surprised me and certainly there was no evidence of him having any such difficulties. I would have been devastated not to have heard this as it is one of my favourite tracks on Stupid Dream.

The change to the printed Even Less Lyrics ("but I'm a martyr to even less") was interesting as was some of the choice of some of the back catalogue material.

Given his comments about Sky Moves Sideways recently, I was surprised by an inclusion from there. And still getting Voyage 34 was similarly unexpected. I would have preferred more from the new album, but following on from my comments above, maybe this was as much as was felt could be played.

Southampton University 24 April 2999 – Steve Smith IOW
I'd felt a bit disappointed about missing the chance of seeing them at Southampton, but a chance conversation with my wife resulted in her agreeing to go with me. This from a Stevie Wonder, Elton John, George Michael fan. She didn't know what she was in for. Still to soften the blow we had four hours of shopping in the City and a much more pleasurable pastime to her, than to myself, followed by a taxi ride to the University. Even the taxi driver wasn't sure where to go but found the right area to deposit us, as evidenced by one small poster on a window by the entrance.

After a quick pint in the bar, which turned out to be a more leisurely drink when the support act came on and produced some pretty horrific sounds that didn't even warrant investigation. We'd been told the Tree would be on stage at 9:45 whatever and as it was gone 9:15 before the support act started we doubted this. With the return taxi booked for 11:10 to make it to the last ferry across to our detached part of England, there were fears that we wouldn't get to see much of the main act. The bar sojourn was long enough to get into conversation with a true Tree fan who had earlier been to see them at Brighton and the previous night had seen them at Bristol. He wasn't aware of the existence of Voyage 35 fanzine, but hopefully this has been put right now. Whilst talking it was quiet on stage when a few minutes later the distant sounds of Bass Communion style music started up. This is it says Allen, the intro to the main event. We dashed into the main hall to get to the front and waited with anticipation.

On they came and within minutes of the opening of Tinto Brass, off went my wife to the side, saying it was too loud for her. After the opening a few comments came from Steven about certain members of the audience spotted wearing Marillion T-shirts and the questions of "how many of you have seen us before" which brought raised hands from probably 90% of the audience. Steven was disappointed that there weren't more new faces, but it shows the popularity of the band when the loyal fans follow them around. Into the quieter song of Piano Lessons and Waiting, before more new songs, with the whole group displaying their expertise. Up the Downstair was greeted with great enthusiasm, which was even better on The Sky Moves Sideways and Voyage 34. Stop Swimming was played for what was apparently the first time in Britain. Voyage 34 was the last of the main set and as it was now 11:10 it was a dash for the taxi, so the encore was missed where apparently an acoustic Stranger By the Minute was played instead of Nine Cats (as the lyrics had gone missing) followed by Dislocated Day and Radioactive Toy.

What an experience. "The best live band in the World" was seen printed on one poster and who would doubt it on this showing. With ringing ears it was impossible to hold a conversation until the following morning, but what a joy it was to put Stupid Dream on the CD player then, bringing back flashes of the previous evening. It was played through three times before I was satisfied that I'd heard enough. From being judged a pretty ordinary release initially it's now the most played CD. My wife had actually stayed throughout, albeit on the sidelines and admitted she might have liked it a bit more if she'd actually heard some of the music before going, but it was certainly too loud for her.

Bloomsbury Theatre, London 10 May 1999 – Dave Sheen
Arrived at Bloomsbury Theatre rather later than intended and having little time to browse at the merchandise stand or introduce myself to Steve Freight I hurriedly bought the IEM and Pick & Mix CD's before taking my seat a few minutes before the band ambled on stage at 8:45, Steven barefooted but still looming over Colin Edwin. No doubt the lack of footwear facilitates a more nimble and delicate feel on the effects pedals. A fairly predictable but no less welcome start to the proceedings was the bluesy intro and storming riff of Even Less followed by a punchy Piano Lessons. A change of tempo for Waiting (short version) before another stormer in the form of Up The Downstair.

Steven's performance was the most assured I've seen from him in the five shows I've been fortunate enough to see and he punctuated the show with several references to London audiences'' subdued reactions. Chris Maitland performed in his usual effervescent manner – I've never seen a drummer smile and look so happy on stage. The sound was pretty acceptable with the drums well to the fore as usual and for the first time in my experience the band played loud enough to drown out those who for some strange reason go to gigs for a chat. The lack of volume has been my only criticism of previous gigs.

Pure narcotic and Slave Called Shiver sandwiched another slab of riffing in the shape of Signify and by now the audience were warming to the band in earnest. A solid and precise bassline provided the thrust for a fine Voyage 34, Colin uniquely attired in an Eastern-influence shirt and matching headgear. Throughout he smiled to himself as if quietly amused by the goings-on around him – just watch out for those white-coated men!

Steven then announced that we would hear two more new songs before being treated to 'loads of the old slop'. Sky Moves Sideways completed the main set before Steven returned solo with stool and acoustic guitar for Nine Cats. Commenting that it was 'pathetic that after ten years he still couldn't remember the words, he produced the lyrics on a scrap of paper.

Joined by the rest of the band we heard Dislocated Day before the inevitable but unfortunately shortened version of Radioactive Toy, leaving us like all great bands – wanting more but satisfied with a fine performance of well over one and a half hours.

This was the most complete and satisfying show I've seen in several years with Steven's vocals much stronger than before. I for one can't wait for the next tour of hopefully bigger and better venues as world domination approaches for this inventive band.

A Final Note From Tim Bowness And Steven Wilson (As At 19 July 1999)
No Man 'Speak' is also currently available on CD. It's released by Materiali Sonori an Italian company with a good reputation who have previously released albums by artists as diverse as Vini Reilly, Evan Parker, John Zorn and Brian Eno. If you don't already know, it's material recorded between 1987-89 that we've transferred from the old tapes to the studio and then remixed. I've totally re-recorded the original vocals and Steve has re-recorded two of the tracks because of technical flaws ('Curtain Dream' and 'Night Sky, Sweet Earth').

It differs from the original in that two tracks have been added ('Pink Moon' and 'River song') and two taken off (Desert Heart and Forest Almost Burning). Despite 90% of it being very old indeed, it's a strangely satisfying release that we both consider to be amongst our best.

As regards the next album proper, it now looks very likely that it's going to be distributed by Porcupine Tree's new label Snapper/K-Scope. The good news being that it should get better distribution and promotion than we've had since leaving OLI five years ago, the bad news being that it won't be released until February 2000 at the earliest.

Also, the fund-raising compilation 'The Sky Goes All The Way Home' is available on general release. The album (raising cash for a Special Needs school in Derby) features exclusive contributions from Peter Hammill (particularly excellent), Kevin Coyne, Biosphere, Robert Fripp, John Wetton, The Enid, Roy Harper, Rick Wakeman, In The Nursery, Cipher (featuring Theo Travis) and Gordon Giltrap amongst many others.

The No Man piece is an exclusive remodelling of 'Close Your Eyes' with additional samples and a Theo Travis flute solo. It's on Voiceprint via Pinnacle and is available through the same Freephone numbers I gave out for the Smiles and Bass Communion albums.

There'll be a Hidden Art launch gig on September 16th at the 12 Bar Club. Myself and Theo Travis/Cipher will definitely be playing and hopefully Steven will be giving his debut Bass Communion performance. Steven's availability is entirely dependent upon the increasingly busy P.Tree schedule, but it would be an excellent bill if he can make it. If it's of interest to any of your readers, I'm also playing at the Norwich Arts Centre on October 11th (supporting Roy Harper) and the Cambridge Folk Club on December 3rd.

Many thanks for the info Tim, I'm sure it will be of interest.

And from Steven who I asked about the new album:

There is about 80 mins of new stuff so far, but we are still writing. There are some new songs but I doubt that the album will be as song orientated as Stupid Dream – been there done that etc. there are some quite long pieces (eg. Russia on Ice is 15 mins long, Hatesong is 10 mins), which instrumentally stretch out a lot more than the material on Stupid Dream. Of course we have no desire to repeat ourselves, so it's difficult to say exactly how it will end up. Sad that some people always want more of the same, but there you go...

12th June 1999 – Divan Due Monde, Paris – Chris Everest

Porcupine Tree – a band of some moment – a big crushed velvet posing pouch of a band – all the dance ambient prog-rockiness you can keep in your head and still juggle in a dusty sunbeam. They make huge glowing arcs of progressive rock decoded from the early psychedelic experience – taking hostages all the way from there on in. Somehow this all makes perfect sense. Complex songs of pain and pleasure that weave in and out of the shadow producing some of the most hauntingly beautiful melodies that you'll ever catch in passing. This could be as original and inspired a band that we're likely to hear as we stumble into the new Millennium.

The venue, the Divan Due Monde, is a big throbbing, two tiered mass of people. It sits, squeezed in between the live sex shows and topless bars of Paris' red light district – music and sex holding hands in the dark.

This seems a lifetime from the Old Trout and Upstairs at the Garage. Tonight seems close to an almost forgotten evening in Canterbury when the band shook the Penny Theatre's frail balcony and scorched paint from its flaking walls. It seems now from that night on they never looked back.

Tonight Steven announces that they're weary (it's the end of a long tour) – no evidence here of this. There appears to be no lessening of that magic as they thunder through 'Even Less'. What of the set? The songs from 'Stupid Dream' are here – already a brightly shone masterpiece – the dark and brooding 'Signify' collection and the insane and dreamlike 'Sky Moves Sideways' all having new life beaten into them by that special experience of live performance – and live this band are powerful.

You can tell this isn't England – the French crowd are instantly up for it – they roar, yell and stamp with gallic enthusiasm and try to dismantle the place after every song. The band continue to fuse heat and light with power all evening and as an encore something special, not played often live – 'Stupid Dreams' classic song 'Stop Swimming' *taking sound and fury and making it blush. No longer a singular indulgence this band. They are now an awesome and complete unit – shooting stars caught in the spotlight, centre stage. An evening of music about as good as it gets.

*(Perhaps one of the best No Man/PT crossover songs. No Man, that blue lipped, thin waisted dominatrix, stiletto heels and the slap of whip against leather. The Tree, her decadent sibling forever locked behind the looking glass, adrift and bitten).

Thanks Chris – don't know what you were on but can I have some please. Also I know there was a rather heavy session after the gig with a certain female fawning over a certain band member (no, I am not naming names but if the female concerned wishes to write an after gig commentary well...)

Seriously though I'm pleased so many of you have given me your views this issue. Without these I would not be able to issue this mag. Please therefore keep them coming, if not the next issue may take some time.

Issue 12

Published January 2000
Contents:
Intro to issue 12
Part 2 of US Interview with Steven
Gig Reviews from Autumn 1999 tour
the usual reviews section
your letters

This issue features colour cover and photo spread from the Scala gig.

Record Collector said
...there's a good amount of info on those out of their Tree. An Aural Innovations interview with Steven Wilson covers the various side projects including Fish-y tales, and there are numerous reports on the '99 tour, not least the storming Scala bow. a few pieces of news and that's yer "we're not prog" neo-prog lot!

Welcome to Issue 12

Hi all and welcome to issue 12. A Happy New Year to you all.

Well, it appears that issue 11 courted a bit of controversy, totally unintentionally, and to anyone who thought I had let a bit of "personal" comment through in my editorial control, I apologise. I would like to point out that Steven does receive a proof copy before I print and has the opportunity to comment on any aspect of the magazine. Indeed he did request, as you know, that I pull the interview I had originally intended including for the sake of accuracy. For more on this subject please see Queen Quotes Crowley, beginning on page 13.

I expect I will get some comment from those of you who use PT-Trans. While this is probably a good vehicle for exchanging views I was very disappointed at the level of personal abuse which was going on at anyone who did not share their views. Everyone is entitled to their opinion but those of you who thought I had lost my editorial control in the last issue should see some of the comments on there. PT-Trans is not the only site where this happens though, but if you sign up for a service I feel disappointed if 95% of what I get is unrelated to the original subject (i.e. Porcupine Tree)

Retroactive Ploy The Aural innovations Interview part 2

Last issue I printed part one of an interview with Steven from Aural Innovations. Here is part 2 as promised:

Jerry Kranitz (JK): In terms of Porcupine Tree, IEM, No Man... how have these different projects been vehicles for expressing all your musical interests?

Steven Wilson (SW): I don't even think in those terms. The way I work is I just... I make music, and I make music without thinking necessarily to begin with whether it's Porcupine Tree, Bass Communion or IEM. I mean sometimes I know I'm writing for Porcupine Tree, but very often I get tracks which don't necessarily fit into a project. Then what happens is they go into my archive and then later on I'll do something else which seems to go with that other track, and suddenly I know I've got a project. It's not necessarily something that's been premeditated, I mean, that's certainly the way it happened with IEM, and certainly with Bass Communion. It's a need, musically, to express certain things I want to express, and so in answer to your question, it's very important for me to have all these different avenues because I've always found it surprising that there aren't a lot of other musicians like me who have all these projects. I've never quite understood why that should be because for me it seems almost unhealthy to be using all your creativity on one project with the same people all the time in the same style all the time. Although Porcupine Tree does grow, and it does develop and change, there are lots of other styles of music that I love to explore and love to experiment with. I don't understand why it's not the norm for musicians in bands to have side projects where they do completely different things.

JK: Is it just a way for you where something is a little different so maybe it fits into No Man, or formed IEM because the existing bands don't necessarily fit what you were working on at the time?

SW: Yeah, IEM was something I started...I was very into Krautrock at the time like Can , Neu, Faust, Amon Düül and Ash Ra Temple and all that stuff, and I just started doing tracks in that vein because I loved it and I wanted to do it. Before I knew it I had an album, so there it goes, there's another project. Bang. Same with Bass Communion. I was doing a lot of ambient stuff and textural stuff and some very long pieces. The first thing I did for Bass Communion was this 25 minute piece using loops Robert Fripp had given me of his soundscapes. There's no way I could have put out a Porcupine Tree album, you know it would have been half the album. So it just naturally became another project, and there will be more I can assure you.

Keith Henderson (KH): So money aside, which one is the most fun for you to work with musically speaking? I assume all of them.

SW: You've answered your own question. It's not fun for me to do the same thing for too long. It gets frustrating. For example, now Porcupine Tree have been on the road since the end of March and I haven't been able to work on any other music other than what we play every night. And I'm looking forward to giving Porcupine Tree a rest for a couple of months and working on some other stuff. It would be very unhealthy for us now I think just having come off the road to go back into the studio as a group. We need a break from each other. It's not like we all hate each other or anything. We get on fine. But, I just think it would be healthy now for people to go off and do some other things for a few weeks. And then we come back and there's a freshness and there's a newness about it. And that's the way it works. They're all fun if they're happening at the right time. I think a lot of the reasons bands break up is because of that very reason.

Musical differences, personal frustrations, and the fact they're all cooped up together for twelve months of the year. Every year.

KH: How do you operate in the studio? Do you sometimes get impatient or irritable when you're on the clock?

SW: Well we're never on the clock you see. Well, actually that's not true we were on the clock when we went to Foel Studios, but we booked a long session and we took it very relaxed. Because most of the work is done at NoMans... I mean Foel Studios was like a month. The rest of the ten months of work was done at NoMansLand. And there is no clock. Originally we told the record company we'd have it out and finished by June. We didn't finish it until November. Because there was no rush. Because I'm a perfectionist, and the other guys are perfectionists. It's not gonna be delivered to the record company until we're happy with it. We can afford to do that because we record at our own pace on our own budget in our own studio. And I can't imagine doing it any other way. The great advantage is if I want to spend two weeks working on a track and then after two weeks of having worked on it to turn around to the other guys and say I don't think this track's working let's throw it out... you can do that when you're in your own studio.

JK: You produced the previous Fish album. Any other production work you've done or other projects like that?

SW: I've done a couple of small projects but they've all been at my own studio so the same thing applies. The Fish thing was slightly different. It was his studio so again there wasn't the pressure there would have been if it had been at a commercial facility. But, having said that, he was pressured all the time to get the damn thing finished. So that album was kind of not finished quite to my satisfaction. But I'm very happy with the album.

KH: One thing I've noticed about your music, and which I really like, your compositions are seemingly pared down to only the really essential elements. In other words, you resist over composing the music and boring the audience with pointless complexity. Do you find yourself sometimes cutting out lyrics and passages that you've written or do you start with the less is more approach right from the get go?

SW: No. Well, sometimes. Both to be honest. Sometimes I want to keep the arrangements very sparse. In the case of "Even Less", it's a classic case in point. That track originally was seventeen minutes long and was recorded as a seventeen minute long track, and it had everything on it. Just ridiculous amounts of overdubs on that track. This is another thing about being able to get things right in the studio by taking the time. It's almost a case of finding the right way to put the jigsaw puzzle together. Which elements are essential, which elements are superfluous. And that was something that happened in the mixing. A lot of stuff was left out in the mixing. The thing about Porcupine Tree music is... you've hit on something there... Porcupine Tree music is very very simple. There's nothing complex about it at all. The complexity is in the production. The complexity is in the way the albums are constructed. All of the work goes into creating the texture and the sound, and making it sound right. There's nothing complicated about the music at all. And that's really why I have to take issue when people describe us as progressive rock. I don't think we are a progressive rock band. I think we're just a rock band. I think what leads people to give it that kind of progressive tag is the way the songs are produced. That epic quality you referred to. "Even Less" is just a very simple pop song really.

JK: Are you satisfied with the way things have been going on this tour, audience responses and such.

SW: Yeah, definitely. It's been quite stressful. I'm just kind of getting used to how things work over here. We've had a lot of problems with equipment. A lot of technical problems. Y'know, we learn by mistakes. Next time we'll know what to expect more in terms of that. But the shows themselves and the audiences have been fantastic. We've had extraordinary good turnouts. Only a couple of quiet nights. It's a mixture of people that have just discovered us on Stupid Dream, but also obviously had a lot of fans who have been waiting for us to come and play for years and years and years, and they're shouting out tracks from the first two or three albums, which is nice too. And also the fact we've come over here has galvanised a lot of media attention. Loads of radio play. "Piano Lessons" has been playlisted on lots of channels. So the whole process of our coming over here has been useful not just in terms of playing, but in terms of us being here. Radio and media seem to take us more seriously. Which is how we were told it would work. If you want to get airplay in America you've got to come over here, and talk to these people. And that's the way it's worked and it's been fantastic. We're already looking at coming back in the Fall to do a longer tour. Maybe that might be too optimistic, but certainly if not late this year, early next year.

JK: When you came to America had you been touring continually...

SW: Yeah, we started in late March in Europe. We did a bit of Italy,

Greece, we did shows in the UK, Poland, Holland, Belgium, then here, and we're going to France, just for one show actually after we finish here. So it's really been a case of touring as much as we can to support the record.

JK: Have you gotten a feel for any level of airplay you've been getting over here on the radio?

SW: It's very difficult to me to assess because I don't really understand how the American media... [everyone laughs]. But I've certainly done a lot of radio interviews here and we've been playlisted on some very big stations. I don't know whether it's a drop in the ocean or whether it's actually going to amount to anything or not. Certainly we've noticed in the U.S. the record is everywhere.

KH: You've gone through three U.S. labels in the last couple of years. Do you think this deal with Snapper is the answer to long term stability?

SW: Where we were at the time we signed with Snapper they were absolutely the right label. And I hope they will continue to be the right label. It's difficult to say. Compared to the Sony's and the Warner Bros. of this world they're still a small company. But they are much much bigger than the company we were with. And they're the right company for us to be with at this time to take us to the next level. And I hope that they will grow with us. Certainly with Delerium we reached a point where we were too successful for the label. Because the problem was that we needed, with this album Stupid Dream, a lot of money spent up front. We needed to make a video, we needed to release three singles from the album. All the bullshit, and all the games you have to play... I mean I don't like the fact that you have to do all that but the reality is you do have to do that if you want to get to people. And there's no way Delerium could possibly have bankrolled that so we had to move.

KH: So what does it take now to survive as a professional musician in the 90's?

SW: Well we all have to do different things. We don't really make much money from Porcupine Tree. All of the money we make we put back in. For example, Chris and Colin, the rhythm section, both teach their respective instruments. I do a lot of music for TV in the UK. I do music for adverts and stuff which pays very well and means I can do what the hell I like the rest of the year. Richard Barbieri, the keyboard player, has other projects, and he has his own label with his colleagues in his other project. So I think you kind of have to diversify what you do and occasionally you have to do stuff for money so that you can do the stuff you believe in without having to water it down. It would have been so easy for Porcupine Tree to have... actually some people have accused us of doing it anyway... to have sold out, and gone for whatever the kind of fashion was. It probably would have been very easy for us to try and dumb our music down a bit. But because we make our living from doing other things we can afford to be really bloody minded when it comes to doing the Porcupine Tree stuff. We keep it very pure. And the only consideration is what we want to do artistically. Which is a luxury, I know. But it's a luxury bought by virtue of doing... occasionally... things that we would probably rather not be doing, but they don't take up much time and they mean that we're financially secure. So it's not an issue.

JK: I didn't know you were doing television work. Have you done any film work at all?

SW: I haven't done films, no. I've done songs for TV shows. I've done a lot of adverts and stuff. And before you ask I'm not about to tell you which ones. [everyone laughs]

JK: Just out of curiosity is that a pay the bills thing or are there certain challenges and rewards in that as well?

SW: Some of them are good. The majority are horrible. But occasionally I've done some really nice... in fact, the guy that's just directed the video for "Piano Lessons" was a guy that I did a lot of ads for. He makes a lot of commercials in England. And the stuff I was doing with him would always be really really good fun. And I always thought they were great films and great ads. So he was someone I kind of wanted. I knew that I wanted him to do the video. So there are certain directors and people I've met which have been very useful... even moving over into the part of my life that has more integrity. I've brought some of these people with me. Cause these guys have integrity too. A lot of these guys are in the same position as us. They'd love to be making features, y'know. But again, they do adverts so they can pay the bills and then work on their screenplay the rest of the year.

JK: It sounds like there's a networking benefit for you there as well.

SW: There is. I mean in every field you kind of meet people who really at the end of the day... they may be really well paid people, but what they really would love to do is something they would do for next to nothing if they had the opportunity. So we've had some great people work with us that usually wouldn't work for anywhere near the money that they're getting paid by us, but they do it because they're into the music.

KH: The cover art to Stupid Dream is a picture of a CD manufacturing plant. Is that any representation of the commercial nature of music...

SW: Well kind of. One of the themes that runs through the album is all to do with what I've been talking about and the fact that you... to be able to pursue a pure artistic vision... to be able to do that without having to compromise yourself at all is very hard. And it's very easy to become very cynical working in the music business because there's a lot of people that control a lot of the music industry that are complete idiots, and have no interest in music and no idea about music at all. And you come up against these kind of people all the time. And I found that when I was writing the music for this album a lot of the songs were about me and my relationship with the music industry and how I felt about where I was going in the music business and all that. Things like "Stop Swimming"... maybe it's time to stop swimming... and this kind of whole impulse to just give up and go with the flow can be very strong sometimes. I mean I've never given into it. I never will. But sometimes it can make you very depressed. Y'know, you're doing this very amazing... I think really important work, and it's still selling comparatively tiny amounts compared to what I could do in an afternoon if I wanted to. And there's also this whole thing about how when you're writing music... when you're being artistic... there's this kind of purity to what you do. So you try to avoid any considerations to do with being commercial, oh is this the kind of thing the record company can release as a single. I don't care. I don't even want to think about that. But the moment you finish the album you suddenly have to go from being an artist to a businessman. And it's a really tough transition to make. They're two opposite extremes. This whole kind of idea that you're supposed to be this artist but you have to do all this other bullshit stuff. Like sitting down with the record company to discuss how we're gonna market this album. And at that point your record becomes a product. And I just had this image of these CD's just coming off this conveyor belt. And obviously it's at complete odds with the music. But I wanted to have this kind of contradictory feel to the colour.

KH: It's also kind of blue and ice cold looking...

SW: It's very icy. It's a very kind of ironic comment on Porcupine Tree because Porcupine Tree obviously are a band that for our fans, and for us, we're a band that have incredible integrity and they know that we would never sell out... although a very small minority think we have sold out. The bottom line is, the people that get into Porcupine Tree know that we're exactly not the kind of band that ever consider our music in terms of product and shifting units. So I thought it would kind of be fun to put an image on the album which is a comment on that. What could be a more stupid dream than wanting to make music and sell it. Having said that, I kind of enjoy all the bullshit that goes along with making records, but I would never want to mix the two. I've been in situations, not with Porcupine Tree but with No Man, where record companies have said can you write something we can get played on the radio'? And I said no, we can't. We just write what we write.

KH: Having seen the band play live twice now the one thing that has stuck out as being different between the textural material on the album and going to see the band live is your drummer Chris Maitland really cranks up the energy. I was wondering if there was going to be an attempt to bring that out on the studio albums?

SW: Obviously when you go to see the band live people do their own thing. Chris is a very very very busy drummer. He's like Keith Moon. He doesn't like to settle into grooves. I find it really exciting to play with him on stage but I don't particularly like that style in the studio. I prefer a more controlled... which he can do too. He can do anything. But live... he just goes mad. I'm certainly not a technically proficient musician at all. I'm a very sloppy guitar player. For Richard Barbieri it's all about the sound. It's not about the technique at all. I kind of prefer that. Colin, the same. It's very kind of solid. What he plays is very simple but very effective. Chris is like the opposite. It's as technical and as complex as it can be. Which for me is more kind of progressive. But it's great fun to play with him live. I think he's one of the best drummers in the world. But when I get him in the studio, because I'm producer I tend to...

KH: You reign him in a bit.

SW: Yeah. A little bit.

JK: Even though you have moved into being a full band is Porcupine Tree still ultimately a vehicle for Steven Wilson's vision?

SW: To a degree. But... ok, I write the songs. And I'm still the director of the overall sound if you like and the ideology of Porcupine Tree. But to use that kind of film analogy, a director obviously has lots of other very important people which are very responsible for the film as well. The performances of the actors, the cinema photographer, all of those things are equally important and can have just as much of an impact on the look and the feel of the film as well. Porcupine Tree's kind of that way as well. I can tell you that Stupid Dream if it was a solo record would not sound anything like it does. All of the parts that those guys play are their own parts. I write the songs, I play them the chords, I write the melody and I write the words. But the drum parts, the keyboard sounds are all Richard Barbieri... so there's a very very strong band. But I believe, and I know the guys agree with me on this, I don't think it's possible for a band to not have a leader. I don't think it's possible for a band to be a true collective. Even if there was I don't think it would last very long. Because if you don't have someone who basically is in control I think very soon it becomes watered down and there's too much give and take. If you've got a group where everybody is given their own space I think you tend to get something that's very compromised. With me, because it's my vision, and I know at the end of the day the kind of record I want to make, I've got this sound in my head and I want to get it out... there's no compromise. If somebody does something that doesn't fit into that I'll say, no I don't like that. They might like it. Chris might play a drum part and he thinks it's great. I'll say, no I don't want that Chris. Because ultimately he will find something else that's just as much him, but that also fits into... do you see what I mean? They can all do things which would sound great on their own projects, but maybe not quite right for the way I hear the Porcupine Tree. And we've got to the stage now where they're almost aware of that even before I have to say it. They know what will fit and what won't.

[And we went on to enjoy a great performance by the band. Thanks to Steven for spending time with us and thanks to Veronique for helping to arrange our chat. I've kept my eyes open and both Stupid Dream and Signify seem readily available in U.S. records stores. For earlier releases, contact Delerium Records at PO Box 1288; Gerrards Cross; Bucks; SL9 9YB; England.]

Aural Innovations is a quarterly magazine and can be ordered by sending $3 (U.S./Canada) and $4 (Everywhere Else) to:

Jerry Kranitz
1364 W. 7th Ave #B
Columbus, Ohio 43212 U.S.A.

Queen Quotes Crowley

Did you make it to the Scala on Monday? Begins **Peter Clemons** letter.

The band played an incredibly good set in far better surroundings than the rather sterile Bloomsbury (the only thing in common being the expensive crap beer!). Considering it was the last date of a hectic looking tour I thought they performed brilliantly, playing something for everybody, throwing in new music for good measure. Russia On Ice in particular whetted the appetite.

Back to the magazine. I was slightly saddened by one of the Stupid Dream revues (although I'm sure there was no intent). An opinion as to whether or not you like an album or artist etc. is a right we all have. After all, thankfully, we are not all the same. I do, however, get dissapointed when those opinions get down to a personal level, as I was when I read the words "whinging pratt". *(It was actually whining pratt—Steve).* Steven Wilson is not going to please all of us all of the time and he can hardly be blamed for us not enjoying a particular tune or album. Personally, never having written a song in anger in my entire life, I do not feel qualified to pass judgement on an individual or group who has. Please, opinions yes, personal criticism no.

I have received several similar comments to the above and as stated in the introduction to this issue I apologise for any offence given. I honestly believe and still do, that Andreas was using this in a descriptive sense, the same as if we were to describe a piece of music as progressive, soul, dance etc. We all know what the music will sound like. The same goes I believed for the description Andreas used for Steven's voice on this particular song. Although I disagree, it was Andreas's view, and so I left it in. I do try to be fair and do exercise care over some comments I receive. I do not like this magazine to embrace the view that the band are THE great thing and can do no wrong, as other band's fanzines and web sites would have us believe, and so when I get a negative comment that can be fairly balanced I will put this person's view forward. We are all, as Peter says entitled to our opinion. I wrote to **Andreas Stuwe** expressing these views and he writes:

It's true, I haven't called Steven a "whining pratt", it's just his voice which sounds whining, especially on "Stupid dream" where it is multi-layered.

For those interested in Andreas's view of Stupid Dream following the last issue he continues:

I remember I sent you a letter complaining about Stupid Dream. I still think it's not good and I still can't stand "Pure Narcotic" and "Don't hate me". But "Even Less", "This is no rehearsal" and "Tinto Brass" are great tracks, though I prefer the live versions. I saw PT live in Utrecht on 7.5., and it's the same as with Stupid Dream - there were brilliant moments there but also during some songs I was on the verge of leaving the venue! Anyway, I'll try them once more on 6.11. in Zaandam, the last gig on the continent.

And I hope they'll do some worthwhile new tracks.

He also sent me a short review of this gig which he posted to PT-Trans and was attacked for. Surely the last thing one should do when we have free speech. It's like I said previously, some people are so intense when it comes to a band they really like that they are not balanced in their views. I have included Andreas's short review elsewhere in this issue and am sure you agree his views are as valid as anyone else's.

Onto last issues "pulled" interview. Kevin Windall, who translated the review and Interview has written to me thus:

It was nice to see my translated review in print but I was more than a little shocked by Steven's comment that parts of the interview were fabricated. At first I thought it might have been a problem with my translation, however looking back I remembered that it had been very straightforward to do, much easier than the Stupid Dream review.

I spoke to Kanellos Tertzis, the author of the review and he said that he wasn't that surprised. He had been scheduled to do the interview instead of the other journalist, Kostas, as he knows a lot more about the band and had interviewed them before. However he was unable to do so and Kostas, who hardly knows the band , was sent instead. Kanellos reckons there was probably a lot of "journalistic licence" in the article.

So, sorry about that—I really had no idea about the fabrication and please pass on these sentiments to Steven W. *(Done as you can see Kevin. - Steve).*

And now from David Keable a new convert who contacted me by e-mail at *voyage35@hotmail.com*

Thanks for the info. I would like to buy a complete set of those issues still available, so please hold onto a copy of those issues in short supply.

Regarding articles for the fanzine I have done a few things for the Uriah Heep Appreciation Society (UHAS) but that's a band I've followed closely since seeing them in Chelmsford around 1969 before they were even called Uriah Heep.

Unfortunately my knowledge of the Tree is lacking hence my need of your back issues. I did buy 'The Sky Moves Sideways' when it came out, but then lost touch of them until seeing 'Stupid Dream' in the Our Price £7 rack a couple of months ago. What a masterpiece that album is - I just can't stop playing it.

Since then have acquired most of their previous albums, and am now looking for any singles, and material by spin-off bands. I am currently using an article in Record Collector from Nov 96 as my source of information. The recent gig at the Scala was my first introduction to them playing live and they just knocked me out. Unfortunately I could not make the Colchester gig earlier in the year due to business commitments.

Anyhow once I get into the band more I may get some inspiration for articles, but don't hold the front page just yet.

Welcome on board David. Hope you enjoyed the back issues and will find the time and inspiration to write for the mag in the future. Steve

Gig reviews—Autumn 1999

Firstly from Andreas Stuwe, the review that the PT-Trans subscribers did not like.

Here is the setlist of PTree in Zaandam/NL, De Kade:
1. Russia on Ice - quite nice lengthy new track
2. Waiting - usual version
3. Don't hate me - But I hate this!
4. 4 chords that made a million - Nice and rocking
5. Pure narcotic - Superfluous
6. Where we would be - Hopefully not on the next album!
7. A smart kid - 3rd song in a row with semi-acoustic guitar
8. Even Less - Not the full version, but much better than the album version
9. Piano lessons - a bit more drive and some great guitar, but it still doesn't grip me
10. Tinto Brass - By far the best track this evening, and miles ahead of the studio version
11. Slave called shiver - Again superfluous
12. Up the downstair - They put nothing new to this old track, sadly
13. Dislocated day - 1st encore
14. Voyage 34 - 2nd encore
Total playing time: 100 min
Overall not a bad gig, but too many tracks off Stupid Dream. A few more older songs in the set would have been better. And why is this tour called "Stranger by the minute - tour" when this song isn't played (not that I

missed this)

A personal opinion which did not deserve a vitriolic attack. I think the use of one word descriptions does not reflect a person's true feelings. For example the use of Superfluous, could, and probably did raise hackles of people who really like these songs. In fact the 2 tracks mentioned are amongst fans favourites on the last album, and are to my mind experimental as far as the band is concerned. I still believe Stupid Dream to be a natural "progression" (if you will pardon that word) of Porcupine Tree's sound and Philosophy.

Let's hope this is the end of this type of discussion. If you feel anything is rubbish then why not just say that you do not like it, after all that is what you really mean. This would lead to a discussion on the relative merits of that particular piece of music (or indeed artist) and you never know you may well come to appreciate it then, or at least re-evaluate it (or them). I subscribed to PT-Trans for a while myself and whilst I did not post any comments, I was myself dismayed at the unwarranted attacks on people who did not share their views. I await the mailman with interest for having expressed my views!

The Scala, Kings Cross, London 8.11.1999 (by Steve Freight)

I wasn't sure where to include this in this issue, but where better than before my review of the Scala gig. My thanks to Jonny at Snapper for providing this:

Tip Sheet 18th November 1999
Gordon Loncaster - XFM Radio UK

The Porcupine Tree at the Scala was a superb gig last week. Steven Wilson is one of the greatest guitarists of our generation. Eventually this will be recognised and he'll pick up the same accolade for writing. A rare, rare proposition which will mean their gigs won't be filled with session musicians. Within two or three years he'll be the darling of the inkies in the UK. As they leave the gratuitous atonal scales and smarty pants prog rock on the horizon and create the song based masterpieces that we've seen on Stupid Dream. We're going to be forced to join in later. Why? Why? I'll tell you why. As a country we're totally shit at acknowledging true talent. We're so far up our arse with trendy samples, anodyne spray polished R & B and terminally street cred baggy e-head dance grooves that we've

become hilariously snobbish about people who can actually write, play and perform really well. The yanks take it on face value and I love them for it. Meanwhile, we shun "real bands".

The review:
As you can see by the photo's in the centre spread I was there.

What an evening! The two sets the band did on the night totalled 132 minutes of pure unadulterated excitement and variety.

The first I knew of the band splitting the performance was when I arrived and talking to various people "in the know". The first half would contain "the Fans Favourites" the second half designed as a showcase as various radio producers had been invited along. I believe Mark Radcliffe was also in the crowd and he continues to plug the band where he can. He shortlisted Stranger by the Minute as a song of the week, but unfortunately was seen off in the phone vote. Thanks for trying though Mark, we'll get there one day.

Opening with a stunning Tinto Brass, the band moved onto a new epic Russia on Ice which Steven introduced a being a long one. If this translates well in the studio it will be awesome. My favourite from the last album follows, Don' Hate Me and without breath the strains of "we invite you, wherever you are to put your feet up and relax" and Stevens guitar explodes from the speakers full pelt for what was possibly one of the best renditions of this I have heard.

We then get to the point in the evening for the first of the evenings acoustic sets. Steven is obviously much more comfortable now with his vocals to do these sets and Baby Dream in Cellophane is the first song he does. Then to my surprise, and I suspect the entire audience he introduces Fadeaway, which has only previously been performed live once before, and judging by the reaction this should be included in more sets in the future. Stripped bare of the studio effects it is still hauntingly beautiful.

We then have the second new song of the evening. Leaving it to our imagination who this is about, he introduces a song which really rocks (in an "indie" style) called Four Chords That Made A Million.

We have by this time had 43 minutes of the band onstage, "by a strange co-incidence" says Steven "43 is 34 backwards". And indeed we are presented with Brian's rocky journey again (poor boy). Perhaps he needs as I explained in issue one to move onto Voyage 35 and have a good read!

"Half Time" shouts Steven as they leave the stage and it's time for us to draw breath.

During the interval I catch up with a few people including Didier Withoos (nice to see you again - perhaps I'll see you on your home-ground one day) whose web site - Linton Samuel Dawson you should visit, and Pete and Sam Millar from Norfolk, Sam who has brought her parents along. Her Father I found out later thought the band great, but her mother whose taste is for Cliff Richard (and there is nothing wrong with Cliff (in the early days), who along with the Beatles got me interested in music) was not so keen.

The second half is really a showcase for all, not just radio producers and begins with Evenless. This song just gets better live the more I hear it. I do mourn the passing of the fifteen minute version sometimes (and those different lyrics) but you don't have time to draw breath before Chris is hitting those sticks, (Rolf (Sun Arise) Harris style?), and we are into Piano Lessons. Waiting follows, and I don't know about you, but Steven seems to have added an extra quality to the solo in this. The guitar sound "tingly" now (hard to describe) and better for it. Part 2 of the evenings acoustic set follows with Pure Narcotic. One I was not keen on originally but now adore. Following this, in similar vein is Where We Would Be, the third new song of the evening, and one which to me is not an instant hit but may well grow as Pure Narcotic has.

A Smart Kid follows and this is tremendous. I love this one and Stevens playing at the end is inspired. He really is one of the great guitar players of the decade (ever?). Steven's screaming vocals bring Slave Called Shiver to life and we are then entertained with the "Charade that is Up The Downstair". Why Charade, well Steven has been playing the audience along since some one shouted for Radioactive Toy and he says we (the band) have to go through the charade of leaving the stage for us to cheer them back for encores before we get to this. After Up the Downstair the band leave the stage for us to shout ourselves hoarse before Steven returns for another stab at an acoustic song . This time it's Stranger by the Minute. He introduces this as being poor form in releasing a single and not playing it live. I totally agree but have to ask the obvious question **What about Stars Die then?** Hopefully Steven will tackle this as he did Fadeaway earlier in the evening - Please!

Colin and Chris then do battle before the band launch into Dislocated Day, with Steven and Colin seeing who will weaken first to take up the second phase.

Another charade of an encore cry and with the last notes of Steven's final solo of the evening, Radioactive Toy finishes and the band leaves to tumultuous applause.

To my mind this is the best I have seen from the band live to date. They are so tight and know each other inside out now, and being this comfortable it shows. Chris and Colin keep the rhythm holding together and I am sure I saw Colin smile at least twice during this performance (only kidding Colin, I don't want to spoil your reputation - he did smile afterwards though), Richard seems as relaxed as ever and really gets some incredible sound's out of his keyboard, as does Steven out of his Guitar. Just how he does it I do not know but it's all pure genius, 4 parts who collectively go to make up the most exciting band there currently is around.

After the gig there is time to snatch a few words with Richard, Steven and Colin, who were pleased to learn that the split set had gone down well with the people I had spoken to at least, but not so keen to learn that some of the radio producers had not showed, ultimately defeating the object of the evening. Still I for one really appreciated the time and effort the band had obviously put in and felt the 2 part concert added something to the evening.

I suppose because they ended up playing for longer than if they had had a support band or played the "traditional" set. There is something to be said for being able to tailor the gig this way, and indeed have seen the Moody Blues use it to their advantage as well.

I mentioned the Unusual Fruit demo tape Colin sent me which I reviewed last issue and asked if this would be made available even for fans. Unfortunately at present there are no plans to make it available, but the good news is that the music from it will form the basis of Colin's new venture. More news on this when I get it. Judging by the demo tape should be good.

Thanks for taking time out lads to talk - greatly appreciated.

Issue 13

Published May 2000

Contents:
This issue features an extensive Interview with Steven Wilson and takes up the majority of the issue.
Also featured are Reviews of
Lightbulb Sun
4 Chords
Voyage 34 CD
Yellow Hedgrow Dreamscape Vinyl edition
a communication from Tim Bowness on No-Man and Samuel Smiles projects.

A Letter from Tim Bowness

Kicking off this issue is Tim Bowness with some details of the forthcoming No-Man album plus other releases of interest.

Steve,

I've just been given issues 11 and 12 of Voyage 35 by Steven, thanks for sending them and thanks for the mentions.

As we have done on numerous other occasions in the last couple of years, we think we've completed the new No-Man album. It's a 9 track, 51 minute album and is as yet untitled (we're considering several options including 'Lighthouse', 'Slow It All Down' and 'Returning Jesus). It's probably the most unforced work we've done. It's far more intimate than the previous two releases, "Wild Opera" and "Dry Cleaning Ray" and yet in certain respects (the sophistication of production and arrangements/the additional musicians) it echoes aspects of 'Flowermouth', though mostly, I'd say there's little comparison. It contains some of the most complex and some of the most basic music we've ever produced. Due to Steve Jansen drumming on two thirds of the material and Colin Edwin's bass presence on four tracks, the album probably has more of a band feel than any other No-Man release.

The album will feature 'Carolina Skeletons' and contains performances by Ian Carr, Steve Jansen, Colin Edwin, David Kosten (Faultline) and singer-songwriter Ben Christophers amongst others.

I think No-Man go through phases of distinctively reflecting the current musical climate ('Lovesighs' and 'Loveblows And Lovecries'/'Wild Opera' and 'Dry Cleaning Ray') and phases of retreating into ourselves and trying to produce something we consider timeless and meaningful ('Carolina Skeletons and 'Flowermouth'). The new album definitely fits into the latter category.

Tim Bowness/Samuel Smiles are releasing a live album on Hidden Art. Called 'How We Used To Live', it's fairly evenly split between new and old songs/album and non-album material. As the sleeve notes say: 'How We Used To Live' is a direct to CD recording of a performance by Tim Bowness and Samuel Smiles on the evening of December 3rd 1999. What you get is what actually happened, with, as the gatefold sleeves of all 1970's live doubles will untruthfully tell you, 'no overdubs'. In our case, for once we're not lying.

Maybe it was hubris, maybe it was a barely suppressed admiration for Neil Diamond's 'Love At The Greek' and 'Kiss Alive II', but we felt the time was right for another, less celebrated, entry into the rogues gallery of the live album.

After hearing it back for the first time, we hastily scrawled into our respective notebooks, 'some magic, some fluffs'. Hopefully that's enough.'

Simultaneously there should be the release of a Hidden Art sampler featuring unreleased tracks from No-Man, Smiles and Colin's new project Ex Wise Heads. The Ex Wise Heads album is also going to be released on Hidden Art at around the same time (June 2000?).

There's a brand new and rather excellent No-Man fan site at http://come.to/no-man. *(I've had a look and it is worth a visit)*

Anil Prasad's excellent Innerviews ezine (http://www.innerviews.org) will celebrate it's new look by publishing a recent interview with myself and Steven

P.S. Yvonne was right, by the way. the title of 'World Of Bright Futures' actually came from a trip I made to Debenhams' Croydon branch sometime in the mid-90's. I've still got the badge to prove it.

Thank you Tim for your e-mail, and for taking time out to pass on the information.

Interview with Steven Wilson

Hi Steven and thanks again for taking time out of your no doubt busy schedule to answer some questions. As you are aware I asked for questions prior to the knowledge that Lightbulb Sun was to be released. Some questions therefore may appear ancient by comparison with other interviews you are doing to promote the new album, but are still relevant, I feel, in the realm of fandom. I have included some questions based on the new album at the end to bring this interview up to date.

Before we start 2 questions which have puzzled me for a while. Firstly where do the samples from Voyage 34 come from, and on what format was this (TV documentary or recorded)?

They come from LSD propaganda vinyl albums that were issued in the late 60's – some were pro-LSD (the one's made by Timothy Leary) and others against (including the one that features the transparently contrived 34th bum trip of 'Brian'). The cover to V34 is a pastiche of the cover to a Timothy Leary album called LSD which some of the samples are taken from. These albums are very rare in original vinyl pressings, but I believe some have been reissued on CD – mainly the Leary ones.

Can you give us any info on its availability past or present?

The 4 phases were originally issued in Nov 92 (1+2 CD and vinyl) and Now 93 (3+4 vinyl only) as long play singles and were deleted shortly afterwards. A slightly remixed version of Phase One appeared on a CD given away free with a Japanese cyber-lifestyle magazine (no really!) and later was included on Delerium's Pick n Mix sampler CD. A remixed edit (without the voice samples) was included on a compilation CD called 'The Phenomenology of Ambient' released on Crammed Discs in 1994.

The new CD compiles the original versions all 4 of phases in new, sonically improved mixes.

And what was the significance and the numbers at the end of Even Less?

The counting is taken from a recording of a shortwave numbers station. It is understood that these stations are used by intelligence agencies to transmit coded messages to overseas operatives, although no government agency has ever acknowledged the existence of these stations or what their actual purpose might be (taken from the FQA page on my website).

Now for some readers questions:-

Andy Ashton asks:

Given that your music with PT, No Man and various solo projects is very structured and obviously has a lot of care and attention put into it, do you ever get the urge to simply plug the guitar in and create an album of rifts and solos (or whatever) without worrying too much about the production/ atmospherics side?

Yes – this for me would be the IEM material which by my standards is quite rough, ready and indulgent. Most of the tracks are recorded in 2-3 hours at most, but I still try to make sure the production quality is high. None of the tracks are composed in the traditional sense – I just set up rhythm tracks and blow over the top. I've recently completed the second IEM album which is even more indulgent than the first and has lots of speech cut ups and audio verite tracks spliced into the music. it's quite inspired by Zappa's Lumpy Gravy in that respect (anyone who has the Escalator to Xmas 12 inch EP will know what to expect).

Why wasn't 'Coma Divine' released on vinyl? Judging from the success of the various limited vinyl releases I would have thought it would have made a great double album with an opportunity for maybe a couple of bonus tracks etc? Andy Ashton

The market for vinyl is fairly small and even smaller if the music is already on CD – the limited editions have all been things not available or long deleted on CD. However, we are discussing doing a double vinyl edition of Coma Divine which would also include the 20 minutes of music on the information service subscriber only Coma Divine 2 CD. This will only happen if we are sure that we could sell enough to make it viable as the cost of doing double vinyl in a gate fold sleeve is high and the profit margin non-existent.

Do you plan your career and where do you see yourself, PT and other projects in say 10 years time? Martin Gallagher/Andy Ashton/Fernando DiDonato

No and I've no idea. I'd like to work with other musicians and more as a producer in the future as one thing that does get boring is working on my own so much of the time.

What are your thoughts on 'Stupid Dream' and how easy/difficult was it to write in comparison with other PT releases? Martin Gallagher

At the time I felt it was the strongest thing we had done. In retrospect I think the sound was generally too smooth and some of the quirks and psychedelic aspects of the band were lost. The new album for me is a much better combination of songwriting and experiment. Stupid Dream I think will be seen as a transitional album. I'll probably get in trouble with the rest of the band for saying that because they think I have a tendency to dismiss all of our previous records within 6 months of making them and will fully expect me to do the same with Lightbulb Sun!

As regards the writing – it's always easy and it's always difficult.

How do you feel Lightbulb Sun has progressed and differs from Stupid Dream? Steve Freight

Better in every respect. The major improvement for me is in the production which is not as 'shiny' as Stupid Dream. The sounds are much more organic and less treated and you will particularly notice this on the vocals which – as befits the lyrics – are much more up front and raw.

Now that you have moved to a new label, will you be required to release so many albums within a given time period or have you been able to retain full artistic control over what is required from you? Martin Gallagher

There is no time frame stipulated in the deal with Snapper – albums will be recorded as and when the material is ready and deemed good enough. There's no question of Snapper having any say in the content of the albums.

Are there any plans for a video release? Martin Gallagher

No

Do you think the band will ever record a full concept album, or are you opposed to the idea? Simon Mills

I doubt it. In my opinion the 'concept' albums that do work tend to be simply a group of songs that share a theme (eg. Hawkwind's Space Ritual, Nine Inch Nails, The Fragile or Dark Side of the Moon). The ones that try to tell a story very rarely work for me because the narrative by definition has to be more important in the structure of the album that what would naturally work musically.

What's your full equipment set up? (ie make of guitars, effects, pedals, amps, etc) Simon Mills

I play an ESP Stratocaster guitar. This goes through a wah-wah pedal, volume pedal, Rat distortion, Boss distortion, compressor, Alesis Quadraverb and TC2290 digital delay. My amplifier of choice is a VOX AC30.

Do you plan to issue further material by 'Bass Communion?" Simon Thomas

Almost certainly. I don't plan any of my projects too far in advance in the same way that I didn't plan Bass Communion to happen in the first place. I just found myself working on a different kind of music which did not fit into any of the existing projects so I invented a new one. But of course once a project has been instigated it will always be there for me should I want to make another album in that style.

Have you any new projects in the pipeline and if so can you give us an idea of what to expect? Simon Thomas

I have just completed the second IEM album which will be out later this year. Also there is still work to do on various reissues/compilations by both PT and No Man. I don't have any new projects of my own, but I am producing 2 albums for other artists this year.

There are many definitions of 'producer'. Can you tell me how you worked with Fish on the 'Sunsets' album and do you have any plans to produce for him again or any other artists? Leendert Flier/Jeremy Buchan

For me a producer is someone who comes up with ideas that affect the overall sound and direction of an album – it's not necessarily someone who has any technical involvement at all. On Fish's album I also wrote and played on many of the songs. In that instance I was involved in every major decision – how the songs were structured, how the musicians would play on them, how the sounds would be 'treated', the running order, etc…

I have 2 production jobs lined up this year – one with a Norwegian singer Anja Garbarek and one with a black metal group Opeth. I'm particularly excited about the latter as I've been wanting to do a seriously HEAVY album for a while now.

Did 'Periscope Studios' exist and if so, where? Jerry Furneaux

This was part of the entirely fictional history of Porcupine Tree from the booklets accompanying the first 2 cassette releases, so the answer is no. sorry if that disappoints you!

Why don't you play Middlesborough (not the football team, though you'd probably win) or somewhere close? Graham Canwell

(Middlesborough can be changed for many 'out of the way' areas according to questions received. I seem to recall a similar question in a previous issue from Norwich. Do you feel there would be benefit in playing different areas, or is it just not cost effective for the exposure you will receive? – Steve)

Unfortunately we don't and can't choose where we play. We have to play at the venues that show interest in having the band and are therefore prepared to promote the dates properly and pay us a fee which at least goes some way to covering the losses we incur every time we play. Some promoters still don't know who we are since their knowledge of what is worth booking comes from the NME and Melody Maker. On the other hand if there is a venue that does want the band but they are in a place 'out of the way' or near another show we sometimes turn it down because with the possible exception of London WE ALWAYS LOSE MONEY WHEN WE PLAY IN THE UK! We have to concentrate on shows that cover the most ground in as economical way as possible.

Do you find it easy to keep finding the inspiration to write new songs etc, if not is there anything you usually do to try and stimulate ideas. Steve Bowden/Mike Newall/Andrew Miles

I always expect the inspiration to dry up, but so far (touch wood) it never has. Sometimes I can go for 3 months and not produce a single decent song, but then life starts happening to me, inspiration strikes and 4 or 5 songs will come in a relatively short space of time.

Can you describe if your way of composing and recording is primarily a skill of making new original songs or is it (also) a process of translating your emotions/feelings into melodies? Leendert Flyer

Well, both. Even when I am not conscious of channelling my feelings into the music, they are of course still there, whether I want them to be or not. I hope this gives all the music I'm involved in a recognisable personality.

Were your hopes in sale terms realised for 'Stupid Dream' and will you be hoping that Lightbulb Sun will reach the Top 40 Album Charts or doesn't it worry you? Steve Freight/Steve Bowden

I shouldn't care if we get in the charts or not from an artistic point of view, but it seems to matter a lot to the rest of the industry and that is why it is also important to me. If Lightbulb Sun does reach the album top 40 we will find we have offers of gigs, festivals, TV etc that we previously did not. It is an unfortunate thing that most people in the music industry are too fickle/stupid to actually decide they like something until they see that lots of other people like it first. It's the major tragedy of trying to be an artist with integrity.

What is a day in the life of Porcupine Tree like (working day). Fernando Didonato

That's really impossible to answer as every one is different.

How do you see the band progressing in the future, are you prepared to sell out (so to speak) to become commercially acceptable. Jeremy Buchan

God no. musically we've never been prepared to make any compromises – I know some people consider the more song orientated direction to be due to record company pressure or market forces but that's not the case. As regards methods of promoting the music to a wider audience, we have no problem with doing things like videos and making use of other marketing tools.

Did you get the idea for fictitious band members names from XTCs 'Dukes of Stratosphere' incarnation? Pete Millar

Yes – well spotted. And the first ever PT song I recorded Jupiter Island was heavily indebted to the Duke's Bike Ride to the Moon!

Was there any significance in the words 'cream cakes, 'pate' and 'cream cheese' as heard backwards on Queen Quotes Crowley or was it just your shopping list? Pete Millar

Ah – is that what the words are? I suspect that Malcolm Stocks (for it is he) was just coming up with the most ludicrous words he could think of so that people couldn't read any significance in to them! Perhaps he failed on that count.

Do you ever feel that you, or your various projects / works would benefit if you concentrated purely on one of them? Gordon Elcock

No – quite the reverse. Inspiration soon dries up if I am working always on the same project. Coming back fresh after working on something else does wonders for the vibrancy of the material.

Do you think that you have a recognisable musical identity although you express yourself in various styles of music (PT, No Man, SW, IEM)? Leendert Flyer

It's difficult for me to say because a lot of my personality probably comes through without me intending it to. I think that Bass Communion (ambient music) for example has nothing in common with Porcupine Tree (a rock band), but other people tell me that they hear strong similarities. So you tell me!

*Are you still producing music and incidental music for Sky and Adverts?
Leendert Flyer*

Not telling.

If so do you ever use any of these musical ideas in any of your projects. If so can you give an example? Steve Freight

Yes – but again not telling. It would only spoil it for you!

Onto the new album and related topics (questions by Steve Freight)

I've been privileged to hear the music on the new album and find it quite an eclectic mixture (you've seen my review). What music were you listening to at the time and do you feel that it had an influence on the end product?

Certainly it will have had an influence on the sound of the new album, as much as what was happening in my life at the time. I can't be specific because when I hear the album I just hear Porcupine Tree, but I was listening a lot to Nine Inch Nails 'The Fragile' when we were recording. And I remember going home and writing 'Russia on Ice' after going to see a Red House Painters concert.

Many of the songs seem to have a theme of loss of one sort or another/ broken relationships, and the lyrics seem very emotional. Was this deliberate and were they based on personal experiences. Am I right to read this into the lyrics?

Firstly if they are from personal experience then what is in the songs is as much as I can or am prepared to express at the moment. Secondly, don't assume that everything written in the first person must be autobiographical.

Was this album more of a group contribution than past albums or are the songs very much your creations, and recorded as you demand them?

The songs are my creations but some of them have evolved a lot in the studio with the contributions from the other members (and also with the addition of the string arrangements). As a rule I would say that the more tightly arranged songs (such as Lightbulb Sun, How Is Your Life Today? And 4 Chords...) are very close to my demos and the more extended instrumentally based pieces (such as Hatesong, Russia on Ice and Last Chance to Evacuate Planet Earth...) have strong group contributions and changed a lot in the studio.

Did you have any guests on this album, and if so in what capacities?

Dave Gregory (formerly of XTC) has written and arranged strings for 3 tracks. These parts were performed by 6 musicians on cellos, violas and violins.

On Stupid Dream, Even Less changed enormously, especially the lyrics. Was there a deliberate reason for changing the lyrics from the 'religious' lyrics featured on tour. Did you ever record a studio version with the alternative lyrics?

Yes – a demo was recorded with the original lyrics, but after playing the song live I felt they were too 'preachy' and overblown so I rewrote them. I'd already explored anti organised religion themes on Signify anyway.

Were other lyrics changed from their original form on that and the latest album? If so is it a question of getting the music down and filling in with incomplete lyrics to see how the song 'sounds'?

That's exactly it. When inspiration strikes I use whatever words fit musically sometimes without too much consideration for content. Afterwards it is sometimes necessary to rewrite completely (for example the demo of Piano Lessons used nonsense words) and sometimes not at all – for example Feel So Low was a stream of consciousness lyric that came fairly automatically and had a raw emotional power that would have been watered down the more I tried to refine them.

You seem to be moving towards including a number of acoustic numbers in the Live set and indeed on record (something I enjoy by the way). Is this something you are comfortable with, as I understood originally you did not enjoy performing in this way.

Originally I never intended to be a singer and the early albums and live performances featured much less singing than they do now. This is really a consequence of increased confidence in my abilities as a singer – I'll never be a particularly good singer technically but I think I have realised that I can deliver a song with some emotion even in a stripped down acoustic format. It's also fair to say that the songs are better now and can stand up on their own without the full production.

Will we see a complete set of Steven Wilson Acoustics issued from the various store (there are live tapes of these around and they sound very good) and radio appearances you have done (perhaps as a Transmission gift?)

It's possible. I played my first solo acoustic show in Holland recently and enjoyed it. It would be nice to write some songs especially for the format and combine it with some PT favourites and cover versions for a live or studio recording.

How do you feel when you read negative comments on the Albums and Live performances? Do you take these as personal comments, or criticism which will enable you to go on and produce new material, with these comments in mind?

I don't read reviews as a rule and the criticisms I get from fans tend to say more about that person than it does about the music. For example some people who think we are a 'progressive rock' band have been very critical about the song direction. Of course I don't take it seriously when one of these people tells me Stupid Dream or the new album is 'crap'. What they mean is that the direction does not appeal to them. So I would be foolish to listen to anyone else's opinions but my own or the rest of the band. Better to create an audience, not cater for one.

Are you happier now that you are playing larger venues and getting the audiences (especially in the UK) who appreciate the music, and are not just out for the evening down the local venue?

Of course – I hope that we have paid our dues now, in England at least.

I thoroughly enjoyed the split set you performed at the Scala last year. I know the initial reasons for doing so was to promote the band to interested parties, but did you enjoy the format and will you repeat it?

Yes we did and yes I think we will.

How do you compare the working arrangements you have with the rest of the band and your collaborations with Tim Bowness on the No Man albums. What procedures do you go through with each and whilst you have said you 'lead' Porcupine Tree, are you and Tim equals or does one of you 'lead'?
No – definitely in No Man it is an equal partnership. It seems to work that way. Interestingly although the sound has changed radically over the albums we have made as No Man we always seem to be totally in sync as regards when and in which direction we should be moving.

How did the Muslimgauze collaboration come about and were you happy with the results?

I was a fan and contacted Bryn myself. Originally I only sent him some CDs of my own work for his interest, but after about 3 days I received about 2 hours of remixes and reconstructions of the material! As it was not possible for me to make use of all of his mixes I suggested to Bryn that we use them as the starting point for a collaboration. I am very happy with the work we did together. On the forthcoming second and final part of the collaboration, you can actually hear that one of the pieces started life as a Muslimgauze remix of PTs Moonloop.

Do you like remix works based on your originals? I often feel remixes (in general) are so far removed from the original there is nothing left and can often be totally new creations.

I like the principle of remixes and reconstructions but like anything they can be very varied in quality. For example I love what Astralasia did with PTs Voyage 34 but what Scanner did with No Man's Housewives Hooked on Heroin was not so good. Sometimes remix albums can destroy whatever was special about a track in the first place, sometimes enhance it and sometimes improve on it!

Would you ever consider letting remixers loose on various songs to compile a Porcupine Tree/No Man or IEM remix album?

There are a few artists I would love to hear rework Porcupine Tree (Nine Inch Nails and Front Line Assembly for example) so maybe one day there will be a remix album. Of course No Man have already done a remix album and may well do another. I can't image combining mixes of more than one of my projects onto one album though.

Will the Band be undertaking a full scale tour this year or keeping appearances to low key one offs?

There will be a lot of touring throughout the year.

Did you record many new songs for this album which were not ultimately part of the final product? If so will you be keeping these back for the next album or will all be released as additional tracks on singles?

There are 4 or 5 other tracks which will appear across the various formats of the next 2 singles. Some of these are songs that didn't quite make it, others are studio improvisations in the style of the Metanoia album.

How many singles are planned for this album?

Three – probably Shesmovedon and The Rest Will Flow, though not necessarily in that order.

Can you give us some idea of what the Delerium Years CD will feature which has not been previously released or is it too soon to say?

I'm still discussing the format with Delerium so don't hold me to this but at the moment the plan is to do a double CD and a triple vinyl edition. The CD will include 3 or 4 tracks from each of the first 4 studio albums, any non album single tracks including B sides, plus 3 previously unreleased tracks. There will also be a hitherto unheard 8 minute version of Synesthesia.

The triple vinyl will be the same except it will substitute alternate versions of the tracks wherever they are available. For example it will include the Pick and Mix version of V34, the short radio edit of Radioactive Toy (with a different guitar solo) and the work in progress mix of Fadeaway. Most importantly one side of the vinyl will feature a completely different longer take of The Sky Moves Sideways Phase One which has totally different lyrics and much music not included in the album version. I worked on this piece during the best part of a year and it went through many versions before I arrived at the finished one. To pre-empt anybody who may complain that this is not on the CD; the set is supposed to represent the best of PT from the Delerium Years. I do not consider this version to be as good as the album version, but as the vinyl edition is intended more for the collector rather than the casual buyer it seems appropriate to make it available on this format.

When Metanoia is released on CD will you include some more of the studio jams as bonus tracks?

Maybe the track 'Insignificance' from the cassette of the same name, since this comes for the same source. Otherwise no.

And lastly can you explain the reason for the missing 6 minutes from Voyage 34 (Phase 4)?

Listen to the original version and the new version one after the other and tell me if you can honestly hear what has been edited out. I think you will find it very difficult, the reason being that the new version has not omitted any of the content, just compressed into a more compact form. As the original 12 inch was meant more for use in ambient clubs it could go on a bit without so much concern for making it so interesting to listen to. For the CD I have just tightened it up a bit as it did go on a bit.

(I think I have to agree here but there will be purists out there who will have wanted the full thing. It does however keep the 12" remix single a collectable item).

Many thanks Steven for your insights into the topics covered and I'm sure the readers will agree an interesting interview; and good luck with the Album.

MONUMENTS BURN INTO MOMENTS - By LEE WAINMAN 97c.

Issue 14

Published June 2001 (please note that this issue was only available for orders received before 31 December 2001)

Contents:
This issue features an Interview with Steven Wilson, first conducted for the Marillion E-Zine and reproduced with permission
Also featured are Press Reviews and Reactions to
Lightbulb Sun
4 Chords
Voyage 34 CD
Yellow Hedgrow Dreamscape Vinyl edition
A communication from Steven Wilson
Review of the Athens Gigs April 2001
The usual round-up of news on all things Tree
The passing of Linton Samuel Dawson

Linton Samuel Dawson / Voyage 35 - Publications to Remember?

They say all good things come to an end and this is particularly so with the demise of Didier Withoos's very informative website.

Didier had put his soul into producing the site and filled it with so much information that it was an impossibility to keep up with.

With the advent of www.porcupinetree.com, the official website, Didier did not feel his services were wanted by the public anymore and would only be a duplication of information. From the e-mails I have seen this would not have been the case but I understand Didier's point of view and I am in very much a similar situation with the publication of Voyage 35.

With Voyage 35 being the first Fan publication anywhere in the world dedicated to Porcupine Tree and Linton Samuel Dawson the second of any type (and the first website) we both have faced difficulties. Didier has given me some thoughts which will be published later but I would like to say a few words on this publication first if you will bear with me.

Voyage 35 – The End?

When I started this magazine it was with the intention that I would collate and publish fan's view on any aspect of the band that you wanted to air (libels aside). This seemed to work well initially but contributions soon dried up except for a hard core of fans. It seems to me that people are quite happy hearing other views but not necessarily contributing ideas.

Having said this, the readership of Voyage 35 has also tailed off despite the huge increase in the Bands popularity. This also coincided with the rise of a number of other fan based websites. I feel that a large number of fans now get their information from the web and, as more instantaneous that getting a Fanzine are not now so interested in paper based publications.

In view of this I feel that despite being the first publication, and therefore having a place in Porcupine Tree's history, this could be the last issue I publish unless there is a change in the fanbase or more articles forthcoming from you, the fans.

I appreciate that there are a number of you out there who do not have access to the internet and rely on Voyage 35 for information, but the numbers have been dropping issue by issue and it is now becoming increasingly difficult to cover the cost of producing. It is also very time consuming, and although satisfying to see a finished publication, I do not now feel there is an appreciation of the magazine at large.

I have not yet taken the final decision to call a halt, but YOUR reaction to this could either save or force the closure of Voyage 35. I leave the decision to your own individual conscience.

Apologies for the rant but I hope you appreciate the sentiments I am trying to convey.

Steve

A Message from Didier

The first time I saw Porcupine Tree was at Planet Pul Festival in The Netherlands.

It was raining like hell that day so I stayed at the Echoes (Pink Floyd) booth where we sold CD's and magazines. When PT gave acte de precence I came out of my shelter because this was the first (and only) band wich was worth to get a wetsuit for. I went to the stage and after 45 minutes I went back to the booth, totally drenched.

Delirium had a booth opposite the Echoes booth so on the way back I visited Ivor and bought most of the stuff except for YHD cause I didn't have more money with me.

When we got home I wrote to Delerium to order YHD, Psychedelic psauna and a lot more.

I really liked the band and well, when I like something I want to know more about it. The result of that was that I had a reasonable pile of clippings, reviews and such.

In March 1996 I got connected to the internet and after a few months of 'surfing the WWW' I thought it would be a nice idea to publish all the things I knew/collected of the band on the internet. Not only to share it with other people who liked Porcupine Tree but also to promote the band and bring fans news of them. After all there was almost no mention of PT on the web. Ivor helped me a lot with that and providing the news was the main course for me.

So LSD saw the light of dawn at August 8, 1996, which I did in my vacation. This was just the start. After those couple of pages and making it known to the rest of the world I got a lot of support from all over the world and that the nice thing about internet...when I say all over the world I really mean all over the world. People were looking for more info AND when they had something which was not to be found at the LSD site they would send it to me.

When I took LSD offline at August 5th 2000 it used up 30 MB of server space, which is quite a lot and the info was very in-depth and was hard to find according to a lot of people who sent me a mail after LSD got off-line. The reason of the closure of LSD is that porcupinetree.com came online. It's the official site of the band, which provides the fans with the latest news.

So LSD became obsolete and I didn't want LSD to become an archive.

Didier's Final Web Message
Hey all,

When I started LSD it was my intention to keep people informed about the band and bring you the latest news but now that http://www.porcupinetree.com is online (which looks great, btw) I feel LSD has become obsolete.

In other words...LSD has gone off-line.
Best wishes
Didier

A Communication From Steven Wilson
I had the opportunity to send Steven an advanced copy of issue 14 and he gave me some up to date information, and responded to some of my comments as follows:-

The forthcoming live double CD has no title yet but will contain the following tracks: CD One – Even Less / Slave Called Shiver / Shesmovedon / Up the Downstair / Lightbulb Sun / Last Chance to Evacute Planet Earth Before It Is Recycled / Russia On Ice. CD Two – Pure Narcotic / Where We Would Be / Hatesong / Tinto Brass / Voyage 34 / Stop Swimming / Signify.
Most of the album was recorded during a live broadcast for Polish Radio III

in Warsaw on April 6th, but there is also some music from the band's London concert on May 11th. All of the music has been remixed from the 24 and 32 track multi track tapes recorded at these concerts. Expected release date is September. It will only be available directly from the band via mail order or gigs.

There are no plans to issue any of the tracks that were earmarked for the Stars Die vinyl. In addition the CD version keeps being delayed as we're just been too busy working on new material and the live album to get this ready for production (it's the artwork allowing things down). Inevitably we are more interested in the future than we are in the past, but we are aware that a lot of people are looking forward to this release, so we will try and pull our fingers out for a release as soon as possible.

The 4th and final Transmission release is going to be the complete 40 minute Moonloop improvisation – that should be going out in the next month to anyone that has re-subscribed (no more subscriptions are being accepted now). Transmission has also been a victim in the massive growth in the band's profile on the internet, so we decided to fold it now – people have come to realise that they can get much more up to date info from the www. However, we will continue to make available free music to the fanbase via occasional MP3 downloads from the www.porcupinetree.com website.

I must confess I didn't read the reviews of the gigs as opinions are opinions and I very rarely agree with them, even when they are positive! But here's my answers to a couple of the questions you raised in your editorial:-

Why is Recordings not filled to capacity with other tracks?
I'm only interested in making good cohesive albums, not throwing tracks together regardless of their quality or context. I think of Recordings as a companion album to Lightbulb Sun and Stupid Dream and if you forget the fact that some tracks have already been available to the people who picked up the singles (don't forget they are a minority as some of the singles were limited to 1000 copies) I think it works well as an album – it was never intended to be a completists mop up exercise. Some tracks are best left as rarities on singles for those who wish to seek them out.

Why the version of Disappear from Lightbulb Sun sessions and not the demo?
I was not aware that a previous demo take was in circulation and I still

don't know which one it is – the track has been demoed about 6 times since 1997 in many different ways, so much so that one possible idea for a Transmission release was "The Evolution of Disappear", containing only versions of that track! Suffice it to say that the only version we liked enough to issue was the relatively short gentle version on Recordings.

OK, Steve, best of luck with the future of the zine. I hope V35 survives as you do offer things that websites do not traditionally offer, such as archive interviews and pieces on some of the obscurities. Have you considered making V35 web based and perhaps also taking some of the best material from Didier's site which has not been reproduced elsewhere? (*Yes I did consider but I feel a site needs to be up to date to keep peoples interest and I personally prefer the printed word – Steve*).

Anyway, keep me posted and thanks for all the support V35 has given us so far – long may it continue!

Peace,
Steven Wilson

Thank you Steven for the encouraging words. I would really like to continue Voyage 35 but as stated elsewhere, I find it difficult to keep the 'zine fresh, but if I get the support from you, the readers, well...

Retroactive Ploy
Steven Wilson Interview by Simon Clarke

This interview was sent to me by Simon Clarke (SC). He conducted this with Steven for the Marillion web fanzine in Autumn 1999 (conducted August 1999 (www.marillion.com for details)). My thanks to Simon for providing this to be read by Voyage 35 readers.

SC – you're soon going to start the second leg of the Stupid Dream tour, does it feel like you've made significant progress commercially in the last year with this album and the tour?

SW – significant progress commercially. We've made significant progress. I think we've just about doubled our sales, but it's difficult to answer that question because I mean we don't make records, I know some people think we do, certainly some people I know thought that with Stupid Dream it had been a very conscious effort to make a commercial record, it certainly had not been. We just made another record and we were kind of surprised that people said made another record and we were kind of surprised that people said "My God it's so different to Signify" and I'm sitting there thinking is it? Signify had Waiting on it, you know that's a pop song. We had Every Home is Wired, you know I'm thinking is this so different, but obviously people found it very different. I can't explain why that was the case. But having said that I think it would be naïve and disingenuous of me to say that we weren't aware that Piano Lessons, Stranger by the Minute and Pure Narcotic have a lot of potential commercial radio play whatever you want to call it aspects to them and so yes I was disappointed that Piano Lessons didn't get more radio play and I would be disappointed if Stranger by the Minute doesn't get more radio play, but then having said that I've been in this business long enough to be very cynical about those things anyway. I don't really expect, I hope, but I don't expect. I hope to the extent that I'm disappointed when it doesn't happen. So yes in answer to your question I'm pleased that the commercial profile of the band has continued to grow, but obviously I'm still disappointed that we're still not selling as many records as bands that I would consider to be contemporaneous to us who sell millions. That's always the disappointing thing when you measure yourself against other bands that you consider to be doing similar stuff or certainly appealing to a similar audience and obviously not crossing over.

SC – are there still plans for dates in the US on the upcoming tour?

SW – No

SC – right. I saw that had disappeared from the website

SW – we can't afford it. It was ridiculous. We lost £1000 a day in America and we had really hoped to go back, but when the accounts came through from the last leg it was like a grand a day, we lost £10,000 doing ten shows and we just can't afford to do that twice in one year, but we are going to go back to America probably in the Spring now.

SC – it seemed to me that the feedback via mailing lists and websites and stuff is that the shows went down really well

SW – it was great

SC – and some of the radio stations out there are picking up on Piano Lessons and stuff like that so it looks like you've got the foot in the door

SW – it really helps and we're going to keep going back. You know obviously making money is not the issue, but at the same time, you'll know this from Fish and Marillion have exactly the same discussion with their fans and the fans have it within their own circles, about the expense. It's not a question of we're quite happy to lose the money, but obviously you have to keep it under fairly close rein because I mean if we kept going to America and losing £10,000 a pop the record company would pretty soon say "we can't afford to keep this band on" and drop us and then we would never be able to go back to America ever again.

SC – right so they supplied tour support while you were out there

SW – yeah, they have to underwrite the tours. So they were happy to do that the first time around because as I said we did pick up a lot of radio play. We really got our foot in the door as you say, but they felt that they couldn't justify another tour quite so soon. It will happen, but it's not going to happen in November as we'd hoped.

SC – there are many collectable items in the Porcupine Tree back catalogue, one of which is Yellow Hedgerow Dreamscape which is being re-released on vinyl only. Is this a deliberate attempt to piss people off without turntables?

SW – (chuckles), l oh I like that yeah. No because I think if you look on my website you'll see that it does say after that please note that this will come out on CD eventually. I tell you I always find it slightly disappointing because I think whatever we do to an extent we tend to disappoint someone because for example we did Coma…only on CD and I remember a lot of people that were real vinyl purists said why haven't you done this on vinyl. Well you know obviously every time you do a release whether its on vinyl or CD or whatever it takes a lot of time, even vinyl is a completely different packing concept. You have to master it, it takes time. For whatever reason we never got round to doing a vinyl addition of Coma Divine, although we are going to do one and with Yellow Hedgerow Dreamscape my whole philosophy of that was originally it was supposed to be a limited, I don't particularly like that material, there was a very good reason why it never came out originally and that's that I didn't think it was good enough. However, what started to happen this is going back to '93, '94 was that as Porcupine Tree started to become quite well known the profile, there was obviously a lot of bootlegs, I don't mean CD boots, but home taping and tenth generation copies and I thought well okay let's just do a limited edition on CD of this stuff and we did 2,500 and I thought that was going to be more than enough and the whole thing is if you say to people this is a limited edition at 2,500 copies and I hate this because there's so many bands that do this. They say it's a limited edition and then they just bloody re-issue it and it seems to insulting to the fans to do that who've searched high and low and felt they've got something really special for it only to appear in the shops. And so I was really reluctant to do another issue of this and then there's a company in America called Gaiter Dawn who specialist in very, very high quality vinyl and they gave me some of their pressings and the quality was stunning and I thought well okay we've done a CD of this, I said we would never do another CD, but let's do vinyl edition for the first time and then of course having done the vinyl edition and I'd managed to improve the sound so much and I'd also replaced a track and I thought shit we can't do this, this is going to piss off the fans, so I said okay we'll do a CD, but at the moment we haven't addressed that, but we're going to. The vinyl edition is going to come out first anyway and there will be a CD and it's the same with Metanoia, there will be a CD one day with Metanoia, the only thing I've always said and I still stand by this, there will never be another issue of Spiral Circus.

SC – you're not particularly happy with that or...?

SW – not particularly no

SC – I mean it was only a freebie to start with

SW – exactly, but everything else will get re-issued on different formats eventually. And the other thing as I say about this I've always liked the, I mean I'm a collector myself, I collect certain bands, I like the whole thing about the collectability of certain things, different formats, different tracks on different formats. I mean some people complained that we put a different track o the 7" and the CD single. I mean I would have thought that would be a plus. I'm giving you more music for God's sake! Why are you complaining? I think some people don't realise that there are strict rules you're under with singles. For example you can only have a maximum of 20 minutes on a CD single and 3 tracks. So they said to me why didn't you put the Oceans Have No Memory track on the CD as well. The answer is there were already 3 tracks on the CD, you put 4 tracks on a CD you get disqualified from the charts, ultimately the chains won't stock you, blah, blah, blah. All the sort of bureaucratic bullshit. Maybe people don't realise that.

SC – I think may be people outside of this country don't realise how ridiculous the UK chart rules are

SW – for example I wanted to put the whole 16 minutes of Even Less on the new CD single, but we couldn't do it because the CD single was too long we'd have been disqualified. We don't get in the national charts anyway, but we get in the Indie charts and the Indie chart is still a good forum for us to gain profile and so we'd be shooting ourselves in the foot for a silly thing like that and I know it's frustrating and it's frustrating for us as well. All I can say is b-sides always end up being compiled anyway I mean people must know that.

SC – still on the same subject really I've heard there's a Delerium Years compilation being released soon. Is it a best of?

SW – its something, have you come across, there's a cassette that's come out of Poland called Stars Die, rare and unreleased.

SC – Yeah I saw it on the last tour

SW – it's kind of a mopping up, exactly what I was talking about a minute ago, it's kind of a mopping up of b-sides, obviously Stars Die has never been on a European issue. It's got Stars Die, the b-sides to Waiting, it's got a handful of tracks from the Insignificance as well and the Delerium Years compilation will kind of be a much more comprehensive version of that, so it will mop up any rarities but it will also have, which the cassette doesn't have, a selection of highlights from each album. I don't quite know what form it will take, it'll probably be chronological so there'll be a couple of tracks from each album and then an attendant to each album will be the singles and the rarities that go along with that and also a couple of tracks that have probably never come out before. It'll be a double CD and we'll just try and do a nice package with lots of historical femora as well, you know like tour passes and press releases and abstracts from reviews.

SC – it sounds great

SW – you know the kind of thing

SC – a very fan based king of package

SW – it's a bit like they (Marillion) did with 'Best of Both Worlds'. That kind of thing. Again we haven't really looked at that properly yet, that's in the pipeline. The next thing that's in the pipeline is Voyage 34 which is what we're working on at the moment, the re-issue of that, but once that's done we'll start working in earnest on doing the Delerium years double CD.

SC – I've already seen it on one website advertising it as a November release

SW – what Voyage 34?

SC – no the Delerium years

SW – oh that's severely misguided. It's not going to be this year. It may end up being late next year

SC – right I think that's pretty much all the burning questions so thanks, and very much

SW – it was a pleasure.

Thanks again Simon for allowing this interview to be reproduced.

Porcupine Tree – Athens gigs

Friday 20/4/01

Set List:

1 Even Less
2 Slave Called Shiver
3 Shesmovedon
4 Up the Downstair
5 Lightbulb Sun
6 Last Chance to Evacuate Planet Earth Before it is Recycled
7 Russia on Ice
8 Pure Narcotic
9 Where We Would Be
10 Hatesong
11 Tinto Brass
Encores:
12 Voyage 34
13 Signify

Start: 10:13 Finish: 11:45

With a sense of punctuality not found in the local population, Porcupine Tree enter stage left on the first of two nights here at Rodon music club in downtown Athens (an ex-cinema for anyone interested). The opening slide chords of Even Less herald the beginning of their first gig here in more than two years. "It's been a long time", comments Steven. Most of you will have already had personal experience of most, if not all, of this material live, so I won't bother to give my own personal opinions of individual songs, except to say that I had not heard any of the material for Lightbulb Sun played live before and was very impressed by the way the songs translate to the live arena. This is an album that I had a little difficulty coming to like, despite having played in many times. I don't really know why – the songs are played to a very high standard, the arrangement are excellent and there is an increasing depth to Steve Wilson's lyrical output. I came away from the concert with a much more positive impression. The Lightbulb tracks benefit greatly from the beefier live sound, especially Hatesong and the title track itself, which would not make a particularly appropriate single released in its live form. Last Chance…is, in my opinion, one of the finest tracks on the album and comes over well live, but I still think it should be 5 minutes longer! The only track I am not greatly enamoured of is Where We Would Be. This, I imagine from the very personal lyrics, must be a Steven Wilson favourite, so we can't complain if he likes to play it!

The audience is not too lively (though they are at least respectfully quiet) and there is not much interaction with the band. Overall, an enjoyable concert and good to see them live again after so long, even if it would be nice to hear a two-hour (plus) set!

Saturday 21.4.01 10:14 – 11:48

Set List:

1 Even Less
2 Slave Called shiver
3 Shesmovedon
4 Up The Downstair
5 Lightbulb Sun
6 Last Chance to Evacuate Planet Earth
7 Russia on Ice
8 Stop Swimming
9 Where We Would Be
10 Hatesong
11 Tinto Brass
Encores
12 Voyage 34

13 Radioactive Toy

One of the roadies had told me the previous evening that the band would play the same set, which was a little frustrating. Anyway, the Friday gig had been great, so I settled down to enjoy the replay. True enough, after Slave..., Steven asked if there was anyone in the audience who had been there the previous evening.
Not many people responded. "So you don't mind if we play the same songs!". At least this time we had dry ice and a much more animated audience (sold out at 1,000 people!! The previous night there were 750, so I think we could call it fairly intimate). The band, too, definitely seemed to be enjoying themselves more, for whatever reason. Chris Maitland, never particularly subtle in the way he strikes his drums, was really going for it – Up The Downstair featured an especially great performance from him. I love the way he laughs while he is playing. I think he honestly has a wonderful time. The set moved on...then the really great news, for me at least, as Steven announced they were going to play something different – "something we reserve for really special audiences" – Stop Swimming. I love this track, and this change alone would have made the evening. The inclusion of Radioactive Toy as a second encore instead of Signify (excellent the previous evening, incidentally) was an added bonus. Needless to say, I went away very happy! How they managed to play almost exactly the same length of time even with an altered set is beyond me...

Interesting to note the way Steven prefaced Hatesong on both evenings with a diatribe against glossy, superficial, manufactured pop groups – Whitney Houston and boy bands came under fire, among others. The track is PT's answer to meaningless love songs, and what better way to do it.

So there you have it – two excellent nights (especially the second) at Rodon and now a long wait till the next time!

Wevemovedon – The End?

And so it ended.

With the rise of the internet and the ability to receive information almost in real time, the demand for printed fanzines waned.

Issue 14 was printed on demand and resulted in around 30 copies being requested. Previous issues had peaked at well over 100 copies. Issue 1 had a run of around 200 in all, but not all were sold as I gave a large number out to various radio stations / record shops in the hopes of garnering an interest in the band.

Issue 14 also coincided with my losing interest in the band. As I mentioned previously, Steven Wilson produced many curveballs and produced one too many for me with the band moving in a direction I found less interesting. There were still one or two tracks per album that catered for the original fans of the Bedroom Tapes and early albums. I know some who wrote to me apologising for not buying Voyage35 from me anymore after both Signify and Stupid Dream, but I personally, really enjoyed those 2 albums (although I think the demos of some of Stupid Dream are better).

So there you have it – A potted history of the band as seen through their first printed fanzine. Hope you enjoyed the nostalgic romp through old articles.

Steve Freight 2020.

Robert Newton Calvert: Born 9 March 1945, Died 14 August 1988 after suffering a heart attack. Contributed poetry, lyrics and vocals to legendary space rock band Hawkwind intermittently on five of their most critically acclaimed albums, including Space Ritual (1973), Quark, Strangeness & Charm (1977) and Hawklords (1978). He also recorded a number of solo albums in the mid 1970s. CENTIGRADE 232 was Robert Calvert's first collection of poems.

Hype 'And now, for all you speeding street smarties out there, the one you've all been waiting for, the one that'll pierce your laid back ears, decoke your sinuses, cut clean thru the schlock rock, MOR/crossover, techno flash mind mush. It's the new Number One with a bullet ... with a bullet ... It's Tom, Supernova, Mahler with a pan galactic biggie ...' And the Hype goes on. And on. Hype, an amphetamine hit of a story by Hawkwind collaborator Robert Calvert. Who's been there and made it back again. The debriefing session starts here.

Rick Wakeman is the world's most unusual rock star, a genius who has pushed back the barriers of electronic rock. He has had some of the world's top orchestras perform his music, has owned eight Rolls Royces at one time, and has broken all the rules of composing and horrified his tutors at the Royal College of Music. Yet he has delighted his millions of fans. This frank book, authorised by Wakeman himself, tells the moving tale of his larger than life career.

"So many books, so little time."
Frank Zappa

There are nine Henrys, purported to be the world's first cloned cartoon character. They live in a strange lo fi domestic surrealist world peopled by talking rock buns and elephants on wobbly stilts.

They mooch around in their minimalist universe suffering from an existential crisis with some genetically modified humour thrown in.

Marty Wilde on Terry Dene: "Whatever happened to Terry becomes a great deal more comprehensible as you read of the callous way in which he was treated by people who should have known better many of whom, frankly, will never know better of the sad little shadows of the past who eased themselves into Terry's life, took everything they could get and, when it seemed that all was lost, quietly left him ... Dan Wooding's book tells it all."

Rick Wakeman: "There have always been certain 'careers' that have fascinated the public, newspapers, and the media in general. Such include musicians, actors, sportsmen, police, and not surprisingly, the people who give the police their employment: The criminal. For the man in the street, all these careers have one thing in common: they are seemingly beyond both his reach and, in many cases, understanding and as such, his only association can be through the media of newspapers or television. The police, however, will always require the services of the grass, the squealer, the snitch, (call him what you will), in order to assist in their investigations and arrests; and amazingly, this is the area that seldom gets written about."

"Outside of a dog, a book is man's best friend. Inside of a dog it's too dark to read."
Groucho Marx

Bill Harkleroad joined Captain Beefheart's Magic Band at a time when they were changing from a straight ahead blues band into something completely different. Through the vision of Don Van Vliet (Captain Beefheart) they created a new form of music which many at the time considered atonal and difficult, but which over the years has continued to exert a powerful influence. Beefheart rechristened Harkleroad as Zoot Horn Rollo, and they embarked on recording one of the classic rock albums of all time Trout Mask Replica - a work of unequalled daring and inventiveness.

Politics, paganism and ... Vlad the Impaler. Selected stories from CJ Stone from 2003 to the present. Meet Ivor Coles, a British Tommy killed in action in September 1915, lost, and then found again. Visit Mothers Club in Erdington, the best psychedelic music club in the UK in the '60s. Celebrate Robin Hood's Day and find out what a huckle duckle is. Travel to Stonehenge at the Summer Solstice and carouse with the hippies. Find out what a Ranter is, and why CJ Stone thinks that he's one. Take LSD with Dr Lilly, the psychedelic scientist. Meet a headless soldier or the ghost of Elvis Presley in Gabalfa, Cardiff. Journey to Whitstable, to New York, to Malta and to Transylvania, and to many other places, real and imagined, political and spiritual, transcendent and mundane. As The Independent says, Chris is "The best guide to the underground since Charon ferried dead souls across the Styx."

This is is the first in the highly acclaimed vampire novels of the late Mick Farren. Victor Renquist, a surprisingly urbane and likable leader of a colony of vampires which has existed for centuries in New York is faced with both administrative and emotional problems. And when you are a vampire, administration is not a thing which one takes lightly.

"The person, be it gentleman or lady, who has not pleasure in a good novel, must be intolerably stupid."

Jane Austen

Los Angeles — City of Angels, city of dreams. But sometimes the dreams become nightmares. Having fled New York, Victor Renquist and his small group of Nosferatu are striving to re-establish their colony. They have become a deeper, darker part of the city's nightlife. And Hollywood's glitterati are hot on the scent of a new thrill, one that outshines all others — immortality. But someone, somewhere, is meddling with even darker powers, powers that even the Nosferatu fear. Someone is attempting to summon the entity of ancient evil known as Cthulhu. And Renquist must overcome dissent in his own colony, solve the riddle of the Darklost (a being brought part way along the Nosferatu path and then abandoned) and combat powerful enemies to save the world of humans!

Canadian born Corky Laing is probably best known as the drummer with Mountain. Corky joined the band shortly after Mountain played at the famous Woodstock Festival, although he did receive a gold disc for sales of the soundtrack album after over dubbing drums on Ten Years After's performance. Whilst with Mountain Corky Laing recorded three studio albums with them before the band split. Following the split Corky, along with Mountain guitarist Leslie West, formed a rock three piece with former Cream bassist Jack Bruce. West, Bruce and Laing recorded two studio albums and a live album before West and Laing re-formed Mountain, along with Felix Pappalardi. Since 1974 Corky and Leslie have led Mountain through various line ups and recordings, and continue to record and perform today at numerous concerts across the world. In addition to his work with Mountain, Corky Laing has recorded one solo album and formed the band Cork with former Spin Doctors guitarist Eric Shenkman, and recorded a further two studio albums with the band, which has also featured former Jimi Hendrix bassist Noel Redding. The stories are told in an incredibly frank, engaging and amusing manner, and will appeal also to those people who may not necessarily be fans of

To me there's no difference between Mike Scott and The Waterboys; they both mean the same thing. They mean myself and whoever are my current travelling musical companions" Mike Scott Strange Boat charts the twisting and meandering journey of Mike Scott, describing the literary and spiritual references that inform his songwriting and exploring the multitude of locations and cultures in which The Waterboys have assembled and reflected in their recordings. From his early forays into the music scene in Scotland at the end of the 1970s, to his creation of a 'Big Music' that peaked with the hit single 'The Whole of the Moon' and onto the Irish adventure which spawned the classic Fisherman's Blues, his constantly restless creativity has led him through a myriad of changes. With his revolving cast of troubadours at his side, he's created some of the most era defining records of the 1980s, reeled and jigged across the Celtic heartlands, reinvented himself as an electric rocker in New York, and sought out personal renewal in the spiritual calm of Findhorn's Scottish highland retreat. Mike Scott's life has been a tale of continual musical exploration entwined with an ever evolving spirituality. "An intriguing portrait of a modern musician" (Record Collector).

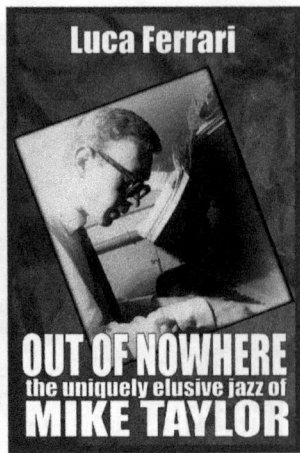

An erudite catalogue of some of the most peculiar records ever made. We have lined up, described and put into context 500 "albums" in the expectation that those of you who can't help yourselves when it comes to finding and collecting music will benefit from these efforts in two ways. Firstly, you'll know you are not alone. Secondly, we hope that some of the work covering the following pages leads you to new discoveries, and makes your life slightly better as a result.

Roy Weard was born in Barking, then a part of Essex, in 1948. He spent most of the mid-sixties through to the mid seventies involved first in folk music and then in the psychedelic hippie scene. He toured with many bands in various capacities from T-Shirt seller to sound engineer, production manager and tour manager. He was involved in several bands of his own, played at many of the iconic free festivals, made three full length albums and two singles, wrote for music magazines, computer magazines and produced copious MySpace blogs. He has lived all over London, spent four years in Hamburg, Germany and finally settled in Brighton where he now resides. He still sings in a rock and roll band, promotes gigs, does a weekly radio show and steadfastly refuses to act his age. This is his story.

Michael Ronald Taylor (1938 - 1969) was a British jazz composer, pianist and co-songwriter for the band Cream.

Mike Taylor drowned in the River Thames near Leigh-on-Sea, Essex in January 1969, following years of heavy drug use (principally hashish and LSD). He had been homeless for three years, and his death was almost entirely unremarked. This is the first biography written about him.

"I have always imagined that Paradise will be a kind of library."
Jorge Luis Borges

The OZ trial was the longest obscenity trial in history. It was also one of the worst reported. With minor exceptions, the Press chose to rewrite what had occurred, presumably to fit in with what seemed to them the acceptable prejudices of the times. Perhaps this was inevitable. The proceedings dragged on for nearly six weeks in the hot summer of 1971 when there were, no doubt, a great many other events more worthy of attention. Against the background of murder in Ulster, for example, the OZ affair probably fades into its proper insignificance. Even so, after the trial, when some newspapers realised that maybe something important had happened, it became more and more apparent that what was essential was for anyone who wished to be able to read what had actually been said. Trial and judgment by a badly informed press became the order of the day. This 40th Anniversary edition includes new material by all three of the original defendants, the prosecuting barrister, one of the OZ schoolkids, and even the daughters of the judge. There are also many illustrations including unseen material from Felix Dennis' own collection…

Merrell Fankhauser has led one of the most diverse and interesting careers in music. He was born in Louisville, Kentucky, and moved to California when he was 13 years old. Merrell went on to become one of the innovators of surf music and psychedelic folk rock. His travels from Hollywood to his 15 year jungle experience on the island of Maui have been documented in numerous music books and magazines in the United States and Europe. Merrell has gained legendary international status throughout the field of rock music; his credits include over 250 songs published and released. He is a multi talented singer/songwriter and unique guitar player whose sound has delighted listeners for over 35 years. This extraordinary book tells a unique story of one of the founding fathers of surf rock, who went on to play in a succession of progressive and psychedelic bands and to meet some of the greatest names in the business, including Captain Beefheart, Randy California, The Beach Boys, Jan and Dean… and there is even a run in with the notorious Manson family.

On September 19, 1985, Frank Zappa testified before the United States Senate Commerce, Technology, and Transportation committee, attacking the Parents Music Resource Center or PMRC, a music organization co founded by Tipper Gore, wife of then senator Al Gore. The PMRC consisted of many wives of politicians, including the wives of five members of the committee, and was founded to address the issue of song lyrics with sexual or satanic content. Zappa saw their activities as on a path towards censorshipand called their proposal for voluntary labelling of records with explicit content "extortion" of the music industry. This is what happened.

> "Good friends, good books, and a sleepy conscience: this is the ideal life."
> Mark Twain

www.ingramcontent.com/pod-product-compliance
Lightning Source LLC
Chambersburg PA
CBHW062155080426
42734CB00010B/1694